THE CALL OF THE AWE

THE CALL OF THE AWE

Rediscovering Christian Profundity in an Interreligious Era

Gene W. Marshall

Writers Club Press
New York Lincoln Shanghai

The Call of the Awe
Rediscovering Christian Profundity in an Interreligious Era

Writers Club Press
an imprint of iUniverse, Inc.

For information address:
iUniverse
2021 Pine Lake Road, Suite 100
Lincoln, NE 68512
www.iuniverse.com

Author Contact Information:
Rt. 3 Box 104-A5
Bonham, TX 75418
books@RealisticLiving.org

Cover Art by Lee Sax
Cover Design by Wayne Marshall
www.marshallarts.com

ISBN: 0-595-26353-4

Printed in the United States of America

To everyone who feels called

to inquire into the depth

of being human.

Contents

Acknowledgments

First of all, I want to express my very warm appreciation to Marsha Buck who has enthusiastically encouraged and assisted with this work for several years. She has made important writing suggestions and spent many long hours editing this manuscript and assisting me in preparing it for publication.

John Howell has also read every word of this manuscript and made hundreds of corrections and suggestions for improvement.

Many other friends have also contributed their suggestions and evaluations. I especially want to thank my fellow workers in The Symposium on Christian Resurgence.

My wife Joyce has not only contributed editing and writing assistance but has also been my companion and often my lead in exploring these dialogues. Her contributions to this book are incalculable.

There have been scores of personal teachers and authors who have contributed wisdom and inspiration for this book. Joseph W. Mathews was probably the first of these persons and without his inspiration I might never have sought out the others. So I want to acknowledge this one remarkable but relatively unknown teacher as a symbol of my thanks for all the other teachers who have inspired me.

Introduction:
The Call of the Awe

While I was doing the breakfast dishes the call came. I left the dishes half done and answered the call. As I sat on the commode, it occurred to me that the call to be religious is somewhat like the call of the bowels. When the call comes, you simply answer it. If you do not answer it, there are consequences. You make a mess in the kitchen.

In the early 1950s I was pursuing a degree in mathematics, on the path for a doctorate, and perhaps becoming a mathematics professor. The call to be religious came to me at that time as a call to be a new kind of Christian. It was also the call to be a more inward looking and a more socially responsible person than was popular at that time. Many factors went into this call. A run-in with hypnotism convinced me that the human mind and consciousness were more mysterious than the linguistic reasoning of mathematics could encompass. The nuclear arms race convinced me that humanity was so off the mark that we were indeed capable of blowing ourselves up. An encounter with the New Testament gospels convinced me that abundant life was to be found not in the externals of life but in a reorientation of our inward attitudes toward whatever was happening to us.

To the astonishment of my friends and the disappointment of my parents, I left my math career and went to seminary to study theology and ethics. This was my first step in answering the call of the Awe. I sometimes wonder what might have happened to my life had I remained on my mathematics track. I am guessing there would have been some kind of mess in that kitchen; for when the call of the Awe comes, it is best to go. Mathematic is a noble profession, and one can be both a mathematician and a Spirit person, but for me at that time continuing in the mathematics path would have been a narrowing of my life and a suppression of awarenesses that needed to be matured and followed.

It was a fortunate time to go to a liberal Christian seminary. The stodgy, sentimental liberalism of the early 20th Century was under assault from the vital explosion in Christian theology that had originated on the European continent and been transported to American shores by the Niebuhr brothers, Paul Tillich, and the many students of Rudolf Bultmann, Dietrich Bonhoeffer, Karl Barth, and Søren Kierkegaard. My seminary in Dallas, Texas–Perkins School of Theology at Southern Methodist University–had four or five such teachers. These men completed the deconstruction of my naive liberalism and gave some lasting shape to my view of a religious calling.

It was decades later before the term "Awe" took root in my thinking. Rudolf Otto's *The Idea of the Holy* was one resource that gave impetus to this word. In this book, Otto suggests that the religious life begins with a shocking encounter with mystery, the *mysterium tremendum*. This dread of the Infinite Presence is the beginning of religious wisdom. Fascination with mystery follows. And Awe becomes real in our lives when we find the courage to live openly in that dread and that fascination.

Joseph Mathews, a very important teacher in my life, helped me to stretch out this elemental understanding of Awe into a full philosophy of religion. Why do we do religion? Religion appears in human life because every human being, even if not fully aware of it, lives in a land of mystery with rushing rivers of freedom, imposing mountains of care, and wild seas of tranquility. This land of mystery penetrates the land of ordinary living at every point. This Infinite Boundless Actuality of Mystery is present in each and every event. Mystery is present in the comings and the goings of each finite being or process.

As Otto suggests, this land of mystery first appears to us as states of dread and fascination; but if we become open to this initially scary direction, other states of Awe follow. These states have been pointed to with words like freedom, care, and tranquility. These words are just pointers; and other words may be needed to indicate the full scope of what they mean: trust, compassion, love, equanimity, peace, rest, still-ness, joy, bliss, deathlessness. All these words point to states of Awe. There are endless states of Awe that fill out our ongoing encounters with and responses to that ever-present land of Mystery.

I am capitalizing the word "Awe" because for me it has become another word for "Holy Spirit." Consider what seeing Spirit as Awe does to our understanding of Christian scriptures. It enables us to read poems like the 139th Psalm in a fresh light.

> Infinite Awesomeness, where shall I escape from your Awe?
> Where can I flee from your Presence?
> If I climb beyond the stars you are there.
> If I make my bed in the land of death, again I find you.
> If I take flight to the frontiers of the morning
> or dwell at the limit of the western sea,
> even there your Awe will meet me,
> and your Awe will hold me fast.
> If I say, "Surely darkness will hide me;
> night will protect me from you,"
> darkness is not dark for you.
> Night is luminous as day;
> to you dark and light are the same.
> (a slight rewording of verses 7-12 in the New English Bible)

Many awarenesses are present in these verses. This Psalmist realizes that human beings are prone to flee from the intensities of being in Awe. We want to get back to some unaware peace and quiet. We are reluctant to volunteer for the Awe-filled life. But this Psalmist is also aware that there is no escape from that Awesome Presence or from the Awe. It is futile to flee. Awe and the Awesome are everywhere.

So what makes religion good or bad? Good religion is an attempt to give human form to living an Awe-filled life. If religion is obedient to whatever Awe is Awe-ing us, it is good religion. And there is bad religion—just as there is bad economics or bad any other human social process. Bad religion assists us to flee from the Awe. Bad religion may comfort people with temporary unawareness. But in the long haul bad religion leads us on a journey into the hell of despair, for there is no escape from the inescapable. Bad religion leads us on a hopeless quest. Bad religion is a refusal to answer the call of the Awe, and this refusal has consequences. Bad religion is, in the end, one huge mess in the kitchen.

*   *   *   *   *   *   *   *   *   *

In the first seven chapters of this book, I will say more completely how I understand "Awe" and how this understanding has enriched my appropriation of Christian heritage. In these chapters I will also develop how I understand religion and the place of religion in human societies. Implied in each of these chapters is the understanding that we live in an interreligious era and that Christianity needs to be interpreted for others and ourselves with this background of interreligious dialogue clearly in our minds.

In the eleven chapters of part two, I will share how the Awe approach to religion has helped me appropriate treasures from several other-than-Christian heritages. These chapters will share some of my adventures in interreligious dialogue. In each of these chapters I will be primarily focused on how these experiences enrich and clarify my own Christian understanding. I will not be attempting to write an inclusive summation of any of these religious traditions. I will not be exploring their vast variety or their perversions. I will not be providing very much of their history or saying much about the challenges these traditions currently face. These chapters will simply share some of the ways that I have been Awed by certain aspects of these various traditions and how these experiences have provoked me to reflect more deeply about being a Christian. Furthermore, I am not attempting to comprehensively compare Christianity with these other religious traditions. Although I will be making some comparisons between some of my understandings of these religions and my understandings of Christianity, these comparisons are meant to clarify an ongoing dialogue rather than close the discussion. In making comparisons, I certainly do not mean to demean other-than-Christian traditions. Finally, I am sure that my understandings of these other religions will not please every member of these traditions.

Also, my understanding of Christianity will differ from the understanding of many Christian-identified persons. For example, I am critical of any form of Christian exclusivity: my commitment to Christian practice does not reject the relevance and wisdom of other religious traditions. I am critical of rigid moralism within all religious traditions. And although I see myself as a contemplative, I am also a scientific-minded person who resists all religious sentimentality. This critical seriousness does not, however, exclude playfulness or a sense of humor. Most good religion, it seems to me, is humorously playful and playfully humorous.

One of my modes of religious play is drawing visual diagrams. If you become weary of reading, you might simply scan through this book and look at the diagrams. When you understand what these diagrams are pointing to, you have grasped a great deal of what I am attempting to share in the writing of this book. Poetry is also important to me as a playful mode of expression. When theological discourse numbs your mind, read the poems and then perhaps return to my more prose statements. I am attempting to express profound Spirit discoveries in terms of everyday experiences. I sincerely believe that Awe or Spirit can be as understandable and everyday and down-to-Earth as bowel movements. And let us not think of that as crass but consider the notion that nothing whatsoever is crass—neither the uncanny emergence of birth nor the inevitable decay of death.

PART ONE:

How Awe Gives Depth to Christian Theology

1.

Encircled by the Awesome, Centered in Awe

One of the assumptions that my seminary education assaulted was the notion that we can talk about God in the same way we talk about a worm or a robin or a cat or a planet or a galaxy. Each of these "things" is part of the universe, a thing alongside other things. If we presume to view God as one more thing alongside other things, we are not using the word "God" to point to the Infinite.

When we take literally the symbols of above and below, heavenly and earthly, supernatural and natural, we are viewing "God" as a thing among things. Furthermore, we need to ask, "Where are we standing to have such a view?" If we are literally viewing a natural and a supernatural realm, then we have to be standing or hanging out in "nowhere land" in order to have such a view. Consider this diagram:

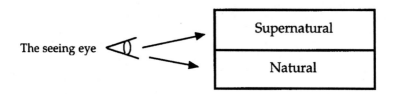

Clearly, "natural-and-supernatural" is not a human experience; it is a picture in our heads. So if we see God as a person-like being in the supernatural part of a two-story universe, we are not talking about a real experience; we are talking about an abstract picture in our heads. This picture is ancient and imaginative, but in what sense is it real? This two-story picture is and always was a metaphor for talking about something we experience. If we take this metaphor literally, we must deal with the absurdity that we, the literal see-ers, are hanging on some invisible hook out there in "nowhere-land."

When I view my actual personal experience, I see that I am living wholly within the crunch of nature and viewing whatever I might mean by "God" from that location. In this era of realistic science and philosophy, I can talk meaningfully about being encircled by the Awesome and centered in Awe, but I cannot talk meaningfully about a literal supernatural realm of being. Furthermore, I need to explain to myself and others that when the religious geniuses of previous eras spoke of a supernatural realm, they were not literalists, as you and I tend to be. During those many centuries previous to our own, religious thinkers were quite comfortable talking metaphorically (or mythologically) about final meanings while at the same time approaching practical everyday matters with realism and logic. Science is a sophisticated development of practical realism and logic. Science has rightly challenged our literal interpretations of our religious myths and metaphors. As a member of modern culture, I have to discover afresh how to talk about God in a manner that is understandable in relation to my own depth experience as well as the depth experience of others. I, like all members of my culture, am a scientific literalist, but I am also a contemplative. By "contemplative" I mean an inquirer into my actual inner experience. I have found that I can learn to look within and describe in an "objective" manner the phenomena of my own inner experience. Science and contemplation are the only two paths to truth that I can honestly honor. And since I don't outwardly view or inwardly experience a supernatural realm, I cannot talk meaningfully about the existence of such a realm.

So, if God is a being in a supernatural realm, I cannot believe in God. Or to put my situation more accurately, in order to believe in such a God, I have to swallow this belief on the authority of some religious body that presumes to know this to be true. Or if I am a Bible-loving Protestant, I might say that I have to swallow this belief on the authority of a scripture presumed to be inspired or literally written by that very supernatural being in whom I cannot believe.

What is theology anyhow? The word "theology" means the study of or the knowledge of "theos" or God. But if the word "God" does not point to a thing among other things, then knowing God is a paradoxical sort of knowing. Theology entails a different sort of knowing than biology, geology, cosmology, or any other "ology."

The word "know" in the ancient Hebrew usage was also used for making a sexual connection as in "Adam knew his wife Eve and she conceived." When the Hebrew heritage applied the word "know" to knowing God, a vivid personal connection was also meant. Hebrew heritage never spoke of knowing God in the sense of comprehending God or of having objective knowledge about God. In ancient Hebrew heritage, the word "God" pointed to that which was forever incomprehensible and uncontrollable. So knowing God never meant comprehending and certainly not controlling. Knowing God was closer to having a sexual union. Knowing God was an experience of personal connection.

So let us open our minds to the paradoxical nature of all speech about knowing God. And let us insist that if knowing God is not a personal experience that is at least as vivid to us as sexual union, then we do not know what we are talking about.

This paradoxical quality of knowing God is not maintained by many, and perhaps most, contemporary Christian thinkers. When, in one of his book titles, the reform Catholic theologian Hans Küng asks, "*Does God Exist?*" he implies that God is an existing actuality in the wider field of existing actualities. This approach avoids the far more basic question, "What actuality are we pointing to with the word 'God'?" The Protestant scholar and theologian Schubert Ogden titled one of his books "*The Reality of God.*" This likewise implies that God is some reality in the wider field of realities. Such thinking can never arrive at what we might mean by a personal experience of God.

Nature and Society

I want to take a small detour into examining what we can know in a personal way. We can know human society and we can know nature. We know that society is made by human beings who are part of nature. We know that society is an overlay upon the wild nature of this planet. Here is a diagram that holds this basic overview.

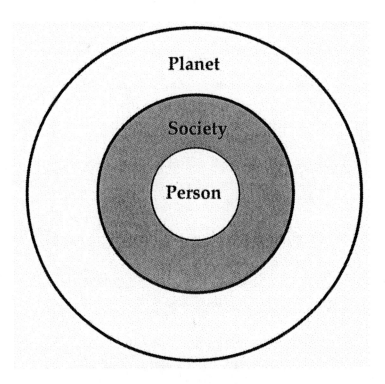

While human society is an essential part of human existence and serves the practical purpose of giving focus and order to our lives, human society is also subject to vast perversions. Human society, like the dark ring in the above diagram, is set down upon the white circle of nature. Inside the ring of society are wild, natural human persons who have created this society and who maintain it. Outside the ring of society is the wild natural planet or cosmos upon which all the functions of society depend for their survival.

The natural person and the natural planet may be viewed as one circle of reality upon which human society is a ring of human-made reality. Human society is the world of the human-made set down upon the world of the naturally born. In one of my favorite poems of

e. e. cummings, this tension between the world of born and the world of made is satirically examined.

> Pity this busy monster,manunkind,
> not. Progress is a comfortable disease:
> your victim (death and life safely beyond)
>
> plays with the bigness of his littleness
> —electrons deify one razorblade
> into a mountainrange;lenses extend
>
> unwish through curving wherewhen till unwish
> returns on its unself.
>   A world of made
> is not a world of born—pity poor flesh
>
> and trees,poor stars and stones,but never this
> fine specimen of hypermagical
>
> ultraomnipotence. We doctors know
>
> a hopeless case if—listen:there's a hell
> of a good universe next door;let's go[1]

But there is no good universe next door; we must make human society on this planet work for us as well as for the frogs and other forms of life. For at least ninety percent of the history of our species, humanity has lived in human-made societies that mimicked the world of born. It

---

[1] cummings, e.e.; *e.e. cummings: a selection of poems* (Harcourt, Brace and World: 1965) page 123

was the dawn of what we call "civilization" that has changed that emphasis to the top-down control over nature and over most humans.

Industrial civilization has strongly emphasized the human-made over the wild natural world. We are addicted to artificiality–to the human-made. We give our children plastic play-toys and protect them from interesting fellow creatures like beetles, crawdads, and grasshoppers. We drive air-conditioned cars to shopping malls on concrete highways and spend less and less time noticing the birds, the animals, the grasses, and the trees that surround and penetrate all our social inventions. We marvel over the so-called "artificial intelligence" of a fancy robot while we neglect to stand in wonder of our own even more remarkable "natural intelligence." Compared to the natural intelligence of a dog or a cat or a human being, our most advanced "artificial intelligence" is not worthy of the name "intelligence."

"Wilderness," "wildness," "wild animals," and "the wild" have become important words for ecological reflection. Nature is wild. It has wild animals, wild plants, wild weather, wild stars, wild galaxies, and wild combinations of all these wildnesses. Even we humans are wild and remain wild no matter how thoroughly we are civilized.

A good society expresses this wildness rather than strives to get rid of it. A good society recognizes that society building is itself a wild process. Society building is wild action done by wild human beings. We often attempt with our human intelligence to tame everything, to civilize everything, to make everything conform to some humanly invented order. But the human brain is itself part of our wild biological being. Thinking is a wild process. There is no way to fully tame or civilize our thinking process.

In their overall quality, industrial societies are like an alien order from some other planet forced down upon this planet's nature and thereby oppressing its optimal operation. Most people in our culture believe that civilization is an improvement upon nature–that nature needs to be tamed in order to be useful to humans–that humans themselves need to be tamed relative to their natural desires, emotions, and natural connections. We mistrust our own natural existence; we suppress our feelings; we don't express what we are really experiencing. We play it safe–that is, we accommodate to our cultural climate even when that cultural climate is killing us. We want to be civilized, rational, normal, well adjusted, and well accepted by other people. We are willing to accommodate with people who see nature as basically alien to humanity. So instead of identifying with nature as our larger body or our larger self, we only use nature to serve whatever greedy purposes or whims occupy our powerful minds. Thus we don't really care if entire ecosystems are disrupted. We don't grieve these travesties. We seem to be saying, "Ecosystems are not me. I am a human being. Ecosystems exist for me. If I don't value them, they have no value; for I and my species are the center of all value." This anthropocentric way of thinking and valuing is as much a cultural malady as sexism and racism and every other form of oppression. Whatever language we use, we need to let some fresh biocentic air into this stuffy anthropocentric house.

God and Nature

Theology, if it is to be relevant today, must enter into this discussion about nature and society. So how does the knowledge of God figure into our knowing society and our knowing nature? Perhaps no theological issue is more important than forging a fresh understanding of the relationship between God and nature. Not doing so places Christians in the role of furthering rather than assisting in the alleviation of the ecological crisis. Much of our culture's alienation from nature is rooted in conservative Christianity's literalistic otherworldly concepts of God, concepts that imply that nature is less than sacred, that nature is even a crass Earth-suit in which our holy souls are unfortunately trapped. Much standard liberal theology also demeans nature. This demeaning is more subtle. In much liberal theology, nature is affirmed insofar as it is useful to rational and virtuous human beings. Liberals also commonly assume that God is a "spirit power" that assists us humans to cope with the difficulties of nature like sickness and death, and to control the benefits of nature for our own human purposes. Such liberal theology expresses little or no tension with the attitudes of arrogant transnational corporations that treat the Earth as a mere resource for our unlimited human use.

A fresh discussion about God can begin by noticing that actual nature is not synonymous with our society's knowledge of nature. Nature remains mysterious as expressed in the now familiar slogan, "The more we know the more we know we don't know." As our knowledge of nature expands, our awareness of the mystery of nature also expands. The naive hope of early philosophers of science that we would one day have a complete theory of nature that explained everything has now become a relic on the shelf of obsolete ideas. Nature participates in the realm of the humanly known like a floating iceberg participates in air. Only the top layer of nature is known, while the vast body of nature is still beneath the water in the dark realm of the unknown.

This dark realm of the unknown and/or the unknowable is an experience we can each have. And this is an Awe-filling experience. It is an experience of the Awesome. It is an illustration of what it means to say that our lives are surrounded by the Awesome and centered in Awe. Here is an expansion of my circular diagram to include the Awe and the Awesome.

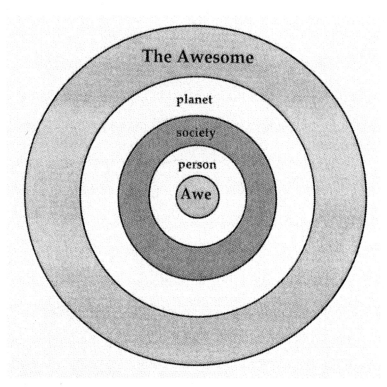

This diagram completes the previous one by picturing how nature is encircled by the Awesome and how our natural person is centered in Awe. Notice that Awe and the Awesome are parts of one large lightly shaded circle. Upon that circle the other rings are sitting. The dark ring of society sits on top of the wide white ring of nature (person/planet). The entire diagram points to this personal experience: we wild natural humans can have wild Awe bubbling up in our inner being when, through the events and processes of nature and society, we encounter the Awesome that encircles all things.

So understood, the Awesome is not a thing of nature or a thing of society. The Awesome is not a thing at all. The Awesome is the NO-THING-NESS out of which all things come and into which all things return. Further, the Awesome is the EVERY-THING-NESS in which all finite things cohere. So now we have a way of talking about God without using the obsolete two-story picture of nature and supernature. God is the Awesome that occasions Awe within us. God is the NO-THING-NESS/EVERY-THING-NESS that we are encountering in the coming into being of things, the existing of things, and the passing out of being of all things. This personally encountered REALITY is the Awesome because it occasions Awe in the humans who are encountering this REALITY.

I am not talking about ideas here. God is not just an idea that makes sense of our experiences. God is an experience that makes no sense at all. It is misleading to associate the word "God" with "purpose," "design," or "final meaning." When this is done, the word "God" is being used to point to a human idea, an idea conceived for the purpose of making rational sense of things. *The actual experience of God does not make sense; it only makes Awe.* Infinite Actuality is not a purpose or a design or a final meaning. Infinite Actuality contradicts every purpose and every design and every so-called final meaning that the human mind can devise.

God is, of course, an idea in the human mind, but this idea is simply a signifier that points to an experience. The idea of God does not make sense of anything that does not already make sense without the idea of God. The idea of God is useless for making sense. The idea of God can, however, point to that MYSTERIOUS ACTUALITY that never makes sense. And more importantly, the idea of God can be used to indicate a personal relationship of trust toward that Infinite Presence that occasions Awe in our lives.

Does this way of using the word "God" illuminate what the biblical writers were pointing to with the word "God"? "Yes," is my one-word answer. Even though these writers used the two-story metaphor of nature and supernature, earth and heaven, down here and up there, they were using this metaphor as a metaphor and not as a literal scientific fact. If we assume that the biblical writers were metaphorical geniuses rather than scientists, then the sentences about God in the Bible can become meaningful to us.

Thinking with the background of understandings just stated, we can make these statements without reservation:

1. Theology is off the mark when it is thought to be the interpretation of rational dogmas dictated or inspired by a humanoid-type being in an adjacent universe.

2. Theology is off the mark when it is thought to be a set of ideas that completes a rational picture of reality.

So I am recommending that we entirely abandon these two types of theology:

1. that God is a literal being in an adjacent universe

2. that God is an idea that makes sense of everything.

And here is another view of theology that needs to be abandoned:

3. that God is a just a cult belief of particular groups.

Theology is off the mark when it is thought to be no more than a way of spelling out the religious and ethical beliefs of a particular historical group of people. Theology is indeed a group process done by a particular group of people; but theology, the theology I am attempting to describe, is not about beliefs. Theology is about giving human expression to that which is beyond beliefs. The question "Do you believe in God?" is a meaningless question in the context of our times. If the word "God" is used to point to that Awesome NO-THING-NESS/EVERY-THING-NESS that encounters us as a vivid Presence in every moment of our lives, then the question of the existence or non-existence of God does not even come up. The meaningful question is how to regard this inescapable ACTUALITY. And this question is actually a choice which each person makes–either: (1) trusting this Presence as operating for our highest good, or (2) remaining suspicious of this Presence, perhaps hating this Presence as our most vivid enemy, perhaps despairing over the inescapable and undefeatable quality of this Presence.

Whether we believe in some religious dogma or ascribe to some theological schema is not critical for our Spirit life. Trusting or not-trusting this Infinite Presence is the only critical issue. It is trust that makes meaningful naming this Awesome Presence "God." "God" in the biblical heritage is a relational word, a devotional word, a word that expresses personal relationship with THAT toward which our deepest commitment is directed. If we do not trust THAT Awesome Presence, then we mistrust THAT Awesome Presence in terms of something else that we do trust: ourselves, our parents, our peers, our Bibles, our doctrines, our churches, our nations, our sciences, or whatever.

This watershed decision between trust and no trust was clarified by both Paul and Luther, but most contemporary Christians (Protestant, Catholic, and Orthodox) have turned trust into belief and then asked us to believe or not believe Lutheran doctrines or Catholic doctrines or Orthodox doctrines or Pauline doctrines or some other doctrines. I am dedicated to the task of assisting both Paul and Luther to rise from the dead and to help me slay these travesties of theological misunderstanding.

So what happens to theological thought on the other side of electing to trust the Infinite Presence? In the context of trust, we enter a life of continually clarifying what it means to live out of that trust. The choice to trust also brings us into community with those who have likewise made the choice to live out of that trust. Together we think about what all this means. This thinking together is called "theology." It is a group effort. It is a finite effort. It is never completed. The religious beliefs and dogmas of the past are nothing more than scraps of poetry that were found to be meaningful in some yesterday of our group life. Theology, then, is a process of thinking that expresses in fresh ways what it means in the now of our lives to live in trust. Of course, we refer to what was meaningful in the yesterdays of our lineage, but today is not yesterday. Theology is a process, a finite process of reflection upon living a trusting relationship with the Infinite Presence. And such theology is done within actual historical, natural, and social surroundings.

Theology and Order

Though it remains forever true that theology does not make sense of life, good Christian theology is concerned with giving some order to the life of trust. Christian theology has been almost mathematical at times. The triune rendering of the experience of God is a case in point. Important theologians, such as Augustine, Thomas Aquinas, and Paul Tillich, have been amazingly systematic in their expression of what it means to live the life of trust. Such systematic theology has great benefits. It sets wider contexts for our ongoing particular reflections. Yet systematic theology can also tempt us to an authoritative thoughtlessness that is precisely the opposite of the energies that inspired these systematic thinkers. Thomas Aquinas is a case in point. He said something relevant on almost every topic that came up in twelfth century Europe. But Thomas did not speak about sexism, racism, or ecological crisis: he cannot be an all-purpose source for relevant speech on the topics that are coming up in the twenty-first century. The tendency among Catholic, Protestant, and Orthodox Christians to find some authority in the past that can provide absolute certainties in the present is a temptation that I hope to resist with my last ounce of breath. Nevertheless, I admire systematic Christian thought, and I want to think somewhat systematically myself in outlining some basic guidelines for good Christian theology in this first century of the third millennium of Christian lineage.

Interreligious Dialogue

When we use the word "God" to point to the Awesome Presence, we have eliminated the need to disparage non-Christian religious heritages. Our dialogue is no longer a dialogue between their beliefs and our beliefs, but a dialogue between their ways of expressing Awe and the Awesome and our ways of expressing Awe and the Awesome. Christians, Jews, and Muslims may call the Awesome by different names: "God" or

"Yahweh" or "Allah." Hindus may call the Awesome "Brahman." Taoists may call the Awesome "THE WAY." Buddhists may call the Awesome "Dharma" which means both THE WAY IT MOVES and teachings about THE WAY IT MOVES. Perhaps every religious heritage has a way of pointing to the Awesome.

What I mean by "Awe" Christians through the ages have been indicating with the word "Spirit" or "the Spirit of God" or "the Spirit of Christ" or "the Holy Spirit." Christians have pictured this Spirit as a mighty wind that blows through our conscious lives and transforms all our finite relationships. This Spirit is not a sweet civilized attitude. It is a wild reality, the wildest part of our wild nature. Spirit is *freedom*, freedom from cultural conditioning, freedom from our personality patterns, freedom from our addictions, freedom from finite clinging, freedom from the laws of morality, even freedom from the lordship of death over our living. Awe or Spirit also manifests as *compassion* for all beings, love for every being that is neighboring our being. Spirit is most of all *trust* of that Infinite Neighbor who provides all our neighbors and takes all our neighbors away. Spirit is also *tranquility, peace, stillness, rest, bliss,* and *joy* in finding the depth and wonder and glory of being human.

Similar words for the human experiences of Awe show up in other-than-Christian religions. When the Hindus speak of "Atman," they are pointing to experiences Christians are pointing to with "Holy Spirit." When Buddhists speak of "enlightenment" or "the state of no-self," they are indicating states of being that Christians include in the life of "Holy Spirit."

"*Encircled by the Awesome and centered in Awe*" is a context of understanding which assists us to see into the depths of every religious heritage. Conservative members of these non-Christian traditions may be as reluctant as conservative Christians to see beyond their private nest of beliefs. But understanding the presence of religion in human life as a finite process for giving form to Infinite Awe is an approach that can transform interreligious dialogue for centuries to come.

Saying the Unsayable

Every religion on earth has stretched and twisted human language to say the unsayable. Religion, if it is good religion, is full of parables, koans, paradoxes, myths, legends, metaphors, icons, and implausible rituals and ceremonies. The modern cry for absolutely correct dogma is a rebellion against the very genius of all good religion.

The diagrams I have drawn in this chapter are also limited, fragile, human creations. Spirit can be diagramed differently than a small circle in the center of our natural person, for Spirit is actually a relationship to the whole. Relationship includes two movements: encounter and response. Encounter means the movement from the Awesome to the occasioning of Awe in the center of our consciousness. Response means the returning movement from our Awed center toward the encircling Awesome. When one is in Awe, it is not like having a small pain or pleasure in our solar plexus. When one is in Awe every relationship with everything is illuminated with the glow of Awe. Awe is like a light that lights up the entire cosmos. Awe is like a wind that blows through the entire inner and outer life. Awe is the Awesome moving from and returning to itself.

In other words, time and movement are not well pictured in my concentric circles. There is no single diagram that can picture Awe and the Awesome fully. Physicists have discovered that the photons of light cannot be pictured in one picture. Physics requires both the wave picture and the particle picture to handle thinking about these minute actualities. So it is with the actuality of Awe and the Awesome. More than one picture is needed. In the chapters that follow, I will be using other diagrams to further expand this vision of living in Awe before the Awesome. But whatever "more" still needs to be said, it remains true that when we participate in the depths of our human authenticity, we are *encircled by the Awesome and centered in Awe.*

2.

Awe as Great Thinks, Great Feels, and Great Resolves

My early devotion to mathematics and science has been both a gift and a problem. On the positive side, these disciplines have given me a love for clear definitions and rational order. These gifts have served me well in thinking through the maze of bad religion. On the other hand, these gifts have encouraged me to think abstractly and to neglect expressing fully the personal experience that makes the abstractions of religion meaningful. Religion is not about abstractions, though abstractions abound in religion. Religion is about the most personal aspects of being a human being.

So I must warn myself and my readers to keep in mind that "Awe" and the "Awesome" are words, abstractions that can generate a nest of cute ideas that do not then communicate the wild wonder I am hoping to point to with these words. This chapter is intended to illustrate Awe more clearly by examining the ways that Awe is manifest in ordinary living and also the ways that Awe is avoided.

Awe, as I am using this word, points to a wide array of actual human experiences. So what is this array of experiences? What characterizes an experience of Awe that sets it off from a mental paradigm shift or from some strong bodily feeling?

Feelings accompany Awe experiences. I like to think of Awe as a Great Feel occurring in the midst of our ordinary feelings. Awe is also accompanied by thought. I like to think of Awe as a Great Think appearing in the midst of our ordinary thinking. And I like to think of Awe as a Great Resolve made in the midst of our ordinary resolving. I want to illustrate in commonly understood personal experiences how Awe is manifest as Great Thinks, Great Feels, and Great Resolves. The following chart holds the various associations I want to bring to this discussion.

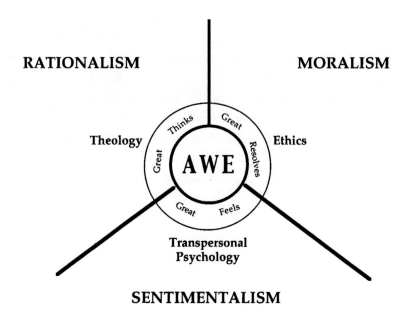

Closely allied with the concept of Great Thinks is *Theology* in the Christian, Jewish, and Moslem heritages. Great Thinks in the Buddhist heritage are usually called Dharma teachings. In all religious heritages we find Great Thinks in the form of religious teachings, stories, scriptures, or traditions that express insights into the Spirit dimension of our lives.

Closely allied with the concept of Great Feels is *Transpersonal Psychology*, if that term means focusing our understanding on the feeling dimension of our states of consciousness when Awe is transpiring in our lives. William James, Rudolf Otto, Ken Wilber, A. H. Almaas and a host of other secular and religious writers might be seen as transpersonal psychologists. We might also call such writers "mystical philosophers." Whatever terms we use, I am talking about honest inquiry that includes examining the feeling states that accompany our experiences of Awe.

Closely allied with the concept of Great Resolves is *Ethics.* Religious ethics might be defined as an exploration into how Awe leads to action and how our most relevant challenges to action inspire Awe within us. Each experience of Awe is a resolve to be in Awe rather than to flee from Awe. When we flee from Awe, we do not actually experience Awe. Experiencing Awe requires the courage to contemplate the Great Thinks and feel the Great Feels, however horrifying or demanding they may be. So our Great Resolves to be in Awe take on very specific ethical forms. To be in Awe means becoming in our actual behavior a person of freedom, compassion, equanimity, courage, creativity, flexibility, boldness, hopefulness, power. These and other such terms typically arise in describing the active qualities of the Awed person or religious saint.

I have also placed on the above chart three great perversions of religion that can be found in all religious traditions: *rationalism, moralism,* and *sentimentalism.*

When we neglect Great Feels and Great Resolves, we reduce our religious expression to mere thinking. Thereby we lose Awe entirely, and our religious expression becomes *rationalism.*

When we neglect Great Thinks and Great Resolves, we reduce our religious expression to mere feeling. Thereby we lose Awe entirely, and our religious expression becomes *sentimentalism.*

When we neglect Great Thinks and Great Feels, we reduce our religious expression to mere moral actions. Thereby we lose Awe entirely, and our religious expression becomes *moralism.*

Great Thinks, Theology, and Rationalism

Nikos Kazantzakis was very helpful to me at a certain point in my life. His poetry clarified for me that religious teachings were not primarily persuasive reasoning. Rather, the effective religious teacher is bombarding his or her listeners (readers) with spins, stories, poems, and provocations that might occasion the inward experience of Awe.

For example, here is Kazantzakis talking about the purpose of life: "Our body is a ship that sails on deep blue waters. What is our goal? To be shipwrecked!…suddenly, in a silent whirlpool, you will sink into the cataract of death, you and the whole world's galleon. Without hope, but with bravery, it is your duty to set your prow calmly toward the abyss."[2]

This poetry is functioning as a Great Think if these words assist you or me to experience the inward awareness that all things do indeed pass away. The stars pass away. The squirrels pass away. You and I pass away. But Kazantzakis' poetry is something more than the mere concept of passing away. His poetry helps us feel the Great Feel component of such an Awe moment and to resolve a Great Resolve to be the courage that embraces the reality indicated by this Great Think.

Here is another example: the Buddha was expressing a Great Think when he taught that the self we each think we are is changing. The ego, the finite self, is part of what is passing away. There is no permanent self, he insisted. Who am I, then? I am not my feelings. I am not my thoughts. I am not my bodily sensations. I am not my social status. I am

[2] Kazantzakis, Nikos; *The Saviors of God* (Simon and Schuster: 1960) page 59

not even a stable self. I can see that I am not the self I once was. I can see that I am not the self I am yet to become. I am not even the self I think I am. Nowhere in my personal being can I find some entity that is enduringly the self I forever am. If I am not some unchanging core self, then who am I? The teachings of the Buddha challenge us to direct our lives toward finding our equanimity in the midst of the passing of all things including the passing of every "me" I might think is the real me. Finding such "enlightenment" means surrender to being a "no-self." Or perhaps we might say that "no self" is the "self" or "being" I really am.

I like the following translation of this saying from the renowned Buddhist teacher Dogen:

To study the self is to know the self.
To know the self is to forget the self.
To forget the self is to be intimate with all things.
Self drops away leaving no trace,
And that no trace goes on endlessly.[3]

This is clearly a Great Think, for it digs below our rational world-views and calls us to an experience of Awe-filled being. When I contemplate Dogen's poem I feel both a sinking feeling and a feeling of extraordinary vastness. Such Great Feels seem to go with this poem's Great Thinks about being "no-self." And I can intuit that flowing from this poem is some Great Resolve to be enlightened about the passing nature of all my understandings of being a self.

Let me also give a biblical example of the Great Think aspect of Awe. Here is a portion of the 90th Psalm: "All our days go by under the shadow of thy wrath; our years die away like a murmur. Seventy years is the span of our life, eighty if our strength holds. The hurrying years are labor and sorrow, so quickly they pass and are forgotten. Who feels the

---

[3] Taken from a speech by Eugene Cash

power of thy anger, who feels thy wrath like those that revere thee? Teach us to count our days, that we may enter the gate of wisdom." [4]

Does this assemblage of poetic words inspire in you a Great Feel (perhaps a somber alertness)? And do you sense in yourself a Great Resolve to actually count your days, to value each day, to see valuing each day as an act of wisdom? If so, then these words of the Psalmist are functioning for you as a Great Think. But if we reduce the Psalmist's poem into some sort of abstract doctrine or theory about something, then there is no Awe for us in these words. For example, this Psalmist is not trying to impress us with the theory that there exists a Supreme Being who has temper tantrums. "Wrath" is a poetic word that expresses the Psalmist's Great Feel about the passing of all things, especially the passing of our individual lives.

This Psalmist is discovering the same wisdom expressed in this Great Think from the book of Proverbs: "The dread of God is instruction in wisdom." (Proverbs 15:33 RSV)

The word "God," used properly, is also a Great Think. In the biblical writings the word "God" points to that Awesome Otherness that is taking away our precious lives as well as sustaining them. Further, the poetic word "God" means a treasured *Reality* that is dependable enough to be worthy of our ultimate devotion. Viewing religious teachings as Great Thinks rather than philosophical or scientific statements allows us to experience the Awe from which our best and most lasting religious teachings have emerged.

Notice that the Psalmist who composed Psalm 90 is not being mournfully glum; he is praying to further embody a Great Resolve toward being tranquil in the midst of the passing of all things. Both the Buddha and this Psalmist are saying something similar, "I have found my Spirit center and hence the passing of all things has lost its sting."

---

[4] Psalm 90: 9-12 The *New English Bible* (Cambridge University Press: 1971)

Whether Awe is experienced as a dreadful oblivion, or as a fascinating fullness, or as a tranquil imperturbability, Awe is manifesting itself in some sort of Great Think, Great Feel, and Great Resolve. Christian theology, properly practiced, is the elaboration of the Great Thinks that hold the Awe experiences of the Christian heritage. So defined, good Christian theology is something very different from finding a rational overview that makes sense of everything. And good Christian theology is very different from merely planting ancient dogmas in the minds of another generation. Placing emphasis upon dogma over experience is an illustration of what I mean by *"rationalism."*

Rationalism in religion means the loss of Great Feels and Great Resolves and the reduction of Great Thinks to Awe-less mental forms. An extreme example of rationalism is believing that Jesus was literally, factually born of a virgin woman, walked on water, and returned from the grave. These common assertions of conservative Christians are a form of anti-intellectual rationalism. Such assertions have been opposed by pro-intellectual, liberal Christians, but many liberal Christians replace conservative rationalism with a rationalism of their own. Liberal Christians are rationalists when they take interest in the historical facts alone and thereby abandon the old poetry and the Awe it was written to express. When liberal Christians do not translate the old poetry into new poems that communicate Awe to people in our times, we are left with nothing more than a liberal type of Awe-less rationalism. Rejecting conservative literalism is a crucial first step, but in and of itself it does not enable us to understand the virgin birth, walking on water, and the resurrection of Jesus as Great Thinks that communicate and enable us to experience states of Awe.

For example, to understand the virgin birth as a Great Think, we need to personally know that your or my or anyone's "conception" into Spirit personhood takes place only when the Infinite "penetrates" our finite, fleshly being and thereby establishes a relationship of parenthood with us. To see "walking on water" as a Great Think, we have to understand what it means for Peter and Mary and Lucy and Bill and you and me to step down from our "safe boats" and walk on the stormy waters of our own actual lives. And to understand the resurrection of Jesus as a Great Think, we have to experience what it means for Paul and Elizabeth and Abigail and George and you and me to be "crucified" with Jesus and be "raised up" with him to newness of life.

Good *theology* cuts through whatever *rationalisms* are clouding the Awe that such Great Thinks were created to express.

Great Feels, Transpersonal Psychology, and Sentimentalism

The expression of feelings has been difficult in our over-rational culture. In our scientific age we have placed great emphasis upon language and reasoning. This has brought many benefits, but it has also rendered many people inept at feeling expression. If, for example, you ask a typical group of American folk how they feel, you will get such answers as "confused." This may be an honest response, but "confused" describes a mental state not a feeling state. So if you ask again, "What does it feel like to be confused?" you might get, "Well, I feel like a person approaching a highway junction not knowing which way to go." That is closer to a feeling expression. So you ask one more time something like, "How does it feel to be in that place?" This time you might get, "Well, I feel scared that I am going to do the wrong thing." That is a feeling expression. The reflection might go even deeper by asking, "Where in your body do you feel that fear?" and then "What is that bodily sensation?"

Feelings can be expressed in language, but feelings are not themselves language expressions. Furthermore, feelings can be expressed in other ways than language. Feelings can be expressed with bodily movements, with facial expressions, or with irrational sounds. Perhaps the most ready expression of feelings are sounds like Ugh, Ouch, Oh, Ah, Ooo, Hmmm, or a laugh.

The feeling content of our Awe experience is likewise a difficult topic in our culture. Take as an example this slight paraphrase of the opening lines of the 23rd Psalm.

The Infinite Presence is like a shepherd to me.
I lack nothing.

What is the feeling expressed here? It is not horror or sobriety or dread. It is somewhere in the vicinity of tranquility or equanimity. It is certainly not giddy or superficial, for as we read the rest of the Psalm we hear that this feeling is taking place even in valleys dark as death and with enemies all around. In these rather grim places it is still true, according to this Psalm, that my head is bathed with anointing honor and my cup is running over. The Psalm ends something like this: "No matter what is transpiring, I shall dwell at home with the Infinite Presence my whole life long." How do we describe such a Great Feel? Perhaps "joyous imperturbability" are words that approach the naming of this Great Feel. In this Psalm, as in other great Psalms, each line is a different way of expressing the same state of Awe. The lines of this Psalm are like a string of Great Thinks, each one designed to express the same state of Awe and thus allow us to experience in our inner beings the same Great Feel.

We are not in Awe if we do not feel the Awe–if we are not appropriating those Great Feels that are already part of each and every Awe experience. This is a significant challenge to many members of Western culture who have overemphasized such attitudes as rational control, playing it safe, politeness, or being "nice." We have to unlearn the suppression of our feelings in order to fully experience and express our Awe.

Some Christian groups have learned the importance of feelings. For example, the Pentecostal forms of Christianity have, to some extent, moderated the rigid rationalisms and moralisms found in other fundamentalist groups. But while Pentecostal Christians have emphasized strong feelings in their religious practice, they have tended to underemphasize rational clarity and ethical seriousness. Thus they tip over into a perversion of religion I am calling "*sentimentalism.*"

Sentimentalism in religion means confusing our strong feelings with true Awe. Revving up our religious enthusiasm can be a very shallow and meaningless experience. If religion is no more than a catharsis, if no ethical and thoughtful implications accompany these feelings, then Awe has been lost as surely as it can be lost in arid rationalism or rigid moralism.

Christian sentimentalism is found in both conservative and liberal churches. Most sentimentalism distinguishes good feelings from bad feelings and then views religious practice as a means of replacing our bad feelings with good feelings. "Good feelings," in this context, mean feelings like affection, contentment, and safety. The bad feelings are fear, anger, distress, anxiety, dread, sobriety, and horror. This view is sentimental because it wishes to close out the grimmer aspects of life and the grimmer aspects of Awe and have only those aspects of life that feel good.

The Christian Scriptures do indicate that perfect love can cast out fear, but this saying need not be interpreted to mean that fear is bad and that pleasant affections must replace fear in order for our lives to be authentic. Rather, a nonsentimental view of the biblical teachings on love and fear might point out that fear is an inevitable part of our finite lives and that being afraid is a good and appropriate way to feel any time danger is near. For perfect love to cast out fear means that our context has moved from the finite scope of our experience to the Infinite scope of our experience. It means that the dread of the Infinite which is the beginning point of all true worship has been gathered up into a state of trust and loyalty toward that same continuingly dreadful Infinite Presence. It is not sentimental to witness how our dreadful trembling becomes gathered up into grateful praise. But it is sentimental to wish to rid our lives of fear and thus have only "good" feelings.

Huge swaths of people in our contemporary culture have a strong appetite for sentimentality. Many books, such as the popular *Chicken Soup for the Soul* series, have been written to appeal to this appetite. Other popular books, like *The Celestine Prophecy,* further illustrate what I mean by sentimentality. Perhaps ninety percent of all popular religion is laced with sentimentality. Even the much-adored volumes entitled *A Course in Miracles* are a sophisticated version of sentimentalism. Such works are entrapping because they contain a certain measure of truth mingled with powerful sentimental escapes from the larger scope of actual living.

Awe experiences can include any feeling whatsoever, and all feelings are good. Dread and horror are good feelings, and may indeed characterize our first conscious encounters with the Infinite. Fascination, love, peace, and joy may characterize other Awe experiences.

Spirit love, viewed in a non-sentimental manner, is different from emotional contentment. Spirit love can manifest as a stern or satirical challenge to illusory living. Spirit love may cause us to be persecuted. It may cause division with members of our own family or with other persons whom we dearly love in an emotional way. In its essence Spirit love is not a feeling but a state of Awe. Spirit love is a strange and wondrous courage to affirm our entire lives including our enemies as well as our friends, our death as well as our birth, our Infinite Tomb as well as our Infinite Source. Spirit love stretches us out of ourselves into an inclusive compassion for all beings. Spirit love presupposes being released from clinging to our finite lives and becoming identified with that deeper being of our "Infinite relatedness." This is the sort of love that can override our elemental dread of death and limitation.

Human beings experience each and every aspect of Infinite relatedness as a state of Awe that is felt in the body. *But Spirit love is more than a feeling.* Spirit love is a quality of our deep being. It is an elemental compassion for our own selves and for all other beings. Spirit love is a glorious possibility and a sobering challenge to expend our entire lives in service to all persons, all societies of humanity, and all communities of nature. Such love is not morbid asceticism or suicidal codependence. Spirit love is a realistic realization that all of us are expending our lives and that we can do this unavoidable expending in a willing, intentional, and joyous manner.

The longing for a feel-good religion is an escape from the Awe and the Awesome. When we flee into sentimentalism we are escaping from the Truth, however good we may feel. Sentimental gooeyness is sin just as surely as arid rationalism or rigid moralism. Sin means estrangement from the Infinite, and no form of estrangement is better than any other. Estrangement is estrangement however pleasant or horrifying it may be. Some may find these thoughts disquieting, but such disquiet may be a Great Feel in some state of Awe. And all Awe is a restoration to the God adored in good Christian theology.

Great Resolves, Ethics, and Moralism

Great Resolves are the third way that Awe is manifest. Great Resolves are part of every Awe experience. If the human consciousness is not choosing to be in Awe, then Awe is not happening. Choosing Awe is part of the Awe experience. But this is a strange sort of choosing. It is more like a surrender than a conquest or an achievement. A Great Resolve is a consent to be what one already is. A Great Resolve does not make you or me something more than what we already are. A Great Resolve is the resolve to be our being as revealed in the Great Think and the Great Feel that comprise some particular experience of Awe.

A Great Resolve does, however, entail newness of life, for through this resolve we are leaving an old life in which escape from Awe was the reigning quality. Each Great Resolve means entering a new life in which Awe is foundational.

So here is one of the most powerful awarenesses I have ever had: Great Resolves are the roots of Christian living and Christian ethics. This beginning point for ethics is different from what we see in much, if not most, Christian ethical thinking. Typically, a Christian theologian will strive to derive Christian ethics from Christian theology. On the above diagram imagine drawing a line directly from theology to ethics. This pictures what Christian thinking often attempts to do. Next picture drawing a line from theology to ethics that passes through AWE in the center of that diagram. This pictures what I am recommending. Ethics is moving out of the Awe center even as theology is moving out of the Awe center. Thus the path from theology to ethics must go through the Awe center. In other words, the Great Thinks of theology clarify the Awe experiences that are the source of the Great Resolves that are the root motivities we express in our Christian ethics.

We have sometimes wondered how people can be motivated to live a Christian life. Here is the answer: the Great Resolves of our Awe experiences are that motivation. If we are indeed in Awe, then our ethical thinking and planning are simply giving form to the Great Resolves that are already in operation in our lives. We do not have to strain to be motivated: we have only to be the Spirit beings we already are. As St. Augustine once put it, "Love God and do what you please." In other words, if you are willing to be in Awe before the Awesome, then you "please" to be in Awe before the Awesome. Christian ethics means creatively giving form to the Awe that you are pleased to be.

Let me illustrate this profound dynamic with that state of Awe which I associate with the "virgin birth." The "virgin birth" is a Great Think closely allied with the Great Think of "second birth." You and I (not just Jesus) are given a second birth (a virgin birth) by the penetration of our beings by the Infinite Presence. In this state of Awe it dawns on me that I am not only the son of my parents and my culture and my past history, but in addition I am the offspring of the Infinite Presence which operates like an ever-loving parent, forgiving me my entire past, and setting before me an open future about which I and I alone must choose without any authorization from my parents or my culture. This is the second birth. This is the virgin birth. Such a rebirth means living in the confidence that I am the one who is beloved by this Infinite Presence.

So if I am in this state of Awe pointed to by the Great Thinks of "virgin birth," or "second birth" what Great Resolves now characterize my being? In order to be in this state of Awe, I have had to choose to be in this state of Awe. In doing so, I establish in my life the Great Resolve to be an outsider–to leave home, my parental home, my cultural home, the home I have made for myself through all my previous choices. I resolve to join a new family, a new society, a new homeland. I opt for son-ship or daughter-ship in the family of the Infinite Presence. I opt for detachment from all my other homes and homelands. I opt to embrace the role of walking the paths of my familiar homes as a stranger, an alien, an outsider who is from elsewhere. I opt to be "from heaven," metaphorically speaking. In other words, I opt to be loyal to the family of those who adore the Infinite Presence. In simpler terms, I opt for *realism* and thus for detachment from all the illusions, half truths, and shallow truths that characterized my previous perspectives on being at home.

Such Great Resolves change everything. Yet everything is still the same. I have the same body. I have the same parents. I may continue to live in the same physical space. I have still been conditioned by the same culture. I have the same past. Yet at this deeper level of living, everything has changed. And the life that I henceforth live will be different, provided that I maintain these Awe-bestowed Great Resolves and do not slide back into my previous state of Aweless wallowing in my shallow attachments to passing things.

Freely and joyously living an Awe-powered Great Resolve is a different experience than straining to apply moral principles to my life situation. The moral principles I have learned from my religious community may be useful tools for designing my free and joyous living, but applying moral principles does not describe the essence of living the

Christian life. The Christian life is a life of Awe-powered Great Resolves. Such a Spirit life affirms the value of moral teachings, but the Christian life exists beyond all morality and in opposition to all moralism.

Every religious heritage has a body of basic moral teachings such as: "Thou shalt not kill" or "Do no harm." Morality is an inescapable part of our lives. These basic moral teachings are useful guidelines for our serious ethical considerations. Moralism comes into play when one or more of these teachings is made absolute for any or all circumstances. The movie "High Noon" dramatizes why even the most basic moral teachings sometimes do not apply. In this Western movie, a sheriff has taken off his guns and settled down with his Quaker and pacifist wife. But on the noon train, four renowned gunslingers whom this sheriff had put in jail are coming to settle the score. The sheriff decides to put on his guns and defend himself and his town from these four men. No one else in the town is willing to help him against these fast guns, so he faces them alone. He finally kills three of them and is about to be killed by the fourth one when a shot rings out hitting the fourth man in the back. The camera then shows us the smoking gun in the hand of the sheriff's pacifist wife. Even to this pacifist woman, "Thou shalt not kill" did not tell her how to behave in this particular situation.

Quite often our life situations require responses that violate our most precious moral principles. Sometimes we do not notice the full extent of life's ambiguities because we have fled for shelter into some cocoon of moral certitude. In such cocoons, we are not letting ourselves be aware of the full ambiguity of our living moments. This is the insidious power of moralism: it offers us a false comfort when painful choices are facing us.

Most of us are clear how corrosive blatant moralism can be. We often cringe when religious groups presume to have certainty about proper modes of dress, hairstyle, or dancing. We may also see moralism in the thinking of those who claim certainty that eating meat is always wrong because it takes an animal's life. Our vegetarian moralism vanishes when we become aware that all living beings live off the death of other lives. It is impossible to be innocent of the killing that must take place in order for any of us to eat and to live. We have lost some of our Awe-filled connection to Reality when we have become certain that humans should only eat plants.

Even when we reject the moralism of others, we may still be trapped in our own subtle moralism. Few of us have fully embraced the shocking truth that in each and every choice we make, we are without an ultimate valid knowledge of good and evil. Morally speaking, we are always choosing between right and right or between wrong and wrong. We never have a state of comforting clarity that we are wholly right or even fully wrong.

Moralism is a flight from real life because it separates us from the full ambiguity of values that are present in each and every situation. As indicated in the Eden myth in the book of Genesis, the knowledge of good and evil is forbidden to the human species. When we eat from the tree of moral certainty, we have committed an illusion. We have entered into the "original separation" from our actual situation—from that situation in which the Infinite Presence walks with us in the garden in the cool of the day. It is our moralism that has forced the Infinite Presence to cast us out of our authentic garden. It is our moralism that condemns us to dwell somewhere to the east of Eden.

If we face up to it, our ethical ignorance can fill us with Awe. Such Awe may be attended by feelings of dread—perhaps horror at the thought of *giving up forever all systems of belief that make it possible to consider ourselves better than other people.* Perhaps we also feel overwhelmed with questions about how to pursue our practical living if our moral principles are not absolutely trustworthy to guide us. Awesome indeed is this challenge to live beyond any and all certain knowledge of good and evil.

When we first consider parting with our moralistic perspectives, the only alternative seems to be license. We fear that giving up our moralism will result in succumbing to the reign of our compulsions, to the sloth of thoughtless actions, to all manner of dissipation and ruin. But the actual experience of living from the place of Awe is neither license nor moralism: it is a Great Resolve to be in the place of Awe that we are actually in. Awe is not license or laziness. Awe is action. Awe is always both a courageous act of freedom as well as an undeserved gift of authenticity. Freedom itself is one of the gifts in every Awe moment. Being in Awe includes the freedom to be our freedom as well as to be in the entire situation in which our freedom is being called for. Being in Awe includes the Awe of choosing to be in Awe. Awe's free act of being our freedom is paradoxically also the courage to be obedient to our actual situation and to the freedom we essentially are in that situation.

Our actual situation fully experienced is a situation in which Awe is present or potentially present. We are never beyond the clutches of Awesome Realty. Every experience of Awe includes the freedom to be in that state of Awe and its Great Resolves. And this Awe-produced freedom is free to choose our specific responses without any restrictions except that one restriction not to eat from the tree of ethical certainty.

I was struck recently by this quotation: "The only sound enough motivation for doing anything is joy. All other motivations, such as guilt, compulsion, obligation, and duty only lead us to dissatisfaction, tension, and resentment. When we are engaged in what truly gives us joy, we lead ourselves inevitably to more and more challenging, powerful work which affects more and more of the world." [5]

What a statement! If by "joy" we mean the joy of Awe-filled living, this quotation takes on great power. Why get out of bed in the morning? Joy. Why do this rather than that? Joy. Why spend hours alone? Joy. Why spend hours with other people? Joy. Why take care of my body? Joy.

---

[5] Nancy Kline and Christopher Spence *At Least a Hundred Principles of Love*, number 72

Why expend my mind and body in constructive work? Joy. Why rest up for another day? Joy.

The joy implied here is not the relief of escaping from life or from death but the glory of full participation in life and in death. Albert Camus was pointing to this joy when he spoke of dying a "happy death."

But a moralistic perspective lacks joy, lacks freedom, lacks Awe, and thus lacks wisdom on the issue of human motivation. Moralism assumes that moral guilt and moral pride (and perhaps also the fear of punishment) are the motivating dynamics for being a good human being. The goodness created by such motivations is a humanly achieved quality that is in fact a separation from our authentic life. The ethics of Awe that I am describing is rooted in a much deeper understanding of human motivation. Being in Awe is choosing to be in the Joyous Awe that is also the motivation to act from this same Awe-filled authenticity.

This perspective enables us to view afresh the meaning of such typical religious teachings as: "Thou shalt not covet," "Love thy neighbor as thyself," "Love thy enemy." These are not moral teachings; they are Great Resolves. They are descriptions of states of Awe. Being in Awe before the Awesome can indeed become manifest as a passion that leads to courage in the face of all intimidating circumstances, to the affirmation of all beings, to an enduring compassion, to an uncompulsive creativity, and to appropriate and happy expenditures of life on behalf of the needs of others and on behalf of the appropriate turning points of the historical drama in which we live. Being in Awe is the goodness that our best moralists are seeking. But moralists err in thinking that we can achieve this goodness rather than receive it as a gift being given free in each and every situation.

The deepest indictment of moralism is that it provides us with an escape from reality, an escape from Awe and the Awesome, an escape from God. In his New Testament letters, the Apostle Paul is conducting one long campaign against reducing the Christian breakthrough to some fresh form of moralism. "Plant your feet firmly therefore within the freedom that Christ has won for us, and do not let yourselves be caught again in the shackles of slavery." (Galatians 5:1, J. B. Phillips Translation) These words refer to such things as dietary practice and requiring Gentile males to be circumcised. But much more is implied. Paul is calling for a relativization of all ethical principles, all rational ethical considerations whatsoever. Paul considers the inherited Mosaic law to be holy and good; but our Christian action, he insists, proceeds from a still deeper rootage–from Spirit, from trust, from love, and from freedom. Obeying the law does not bring freedom; it only makes us arrogant in our moral achievements. According to Paul, the most important role played by the Mosaic law is to awaken us to the various ways we are estranged from the Infinite Presence and from our neighboring beings. This awakenment is a first step in our restoration, but the full realization of restoration requires more. It requires of us a surrender of the ego into the forgiving grace present in each and every Awe experience.

This surrender of ego brings freedom. And once that freedom has come, the most important ethical imperative is to live that freedom and not renounce it in favor of some humanly invented moral principles. Living our freedom includes freely using the law as a guide, but the law is never a certain guide. As Dietrich Bonhoeffer clarified in his book *Ethics*, the responsible person acts in ambiguous situations within which no principle, consideration, or other person can give certainty. The responsible person acts in freedom without support of any law or rational considerations. The responsible action "is performed wholly within the domain of relativity, wholly in the twilight which the historical situation spreads over good and evil; it is performed in the midst of innumerable perspectives in which every given phenomenon appears. It has not to decide simply between right and wrong and between good and evil but between right and right and wrong and wrong. As Aeschylus said, 'right strives with right.' Precisely in this respect responsible action is a free venture; it is not justified by any law; it is performed without any claim to a valid self justification, and therefore also without any claim to an ultimate valid knowledge of good and evil." [6]

This total freedom is paradoxically our obedience to God. The free deed is the good deed because freedom is what is required by each and every concrete situation we face. If we are being our freedom, we are being obedient to that Almighty Awesomeness which we face. If we are being our freedom, we are being obedient to our own deep Spirit actuality, to our Awe-aliveness in the presence of the Awesome.

The Great Resolve to be our Spirit freedom is foundational in Christian ethics. This has been clearly articulated in the writings of Paul, Luther, Bonhoeffer, and many other Christian ethics writers. The free resolve to be our freedom is foundational for any ethics that is rooted in obedience to the encircling Awesomeness which occasions Awe in the center of our being.

* * * * * * * * * * * *

In this chapter I have invited us to contemplate a master picture of Awe, its manifestations, and its Aweless perversions. Awe rescues us from rationalism, sentimentalism, and moralism. Awe manifests as Great Thinks, Great Feels, and Great Resolves that provide the elemental impetus for the formation of our theologies, our transpersonal psychologies, and our ethics. In the chapters that follow I will be pursuing further how good religion, in all of its aspects, is a finite manifestation of the Awe we experience in our encounters with the Infinite Awesomeness that always surrounds us.

---

[6] Bonhoeffer, Dietrich; *Ethics* (The Macmillan Company: 1955) page 249

3.

God and History

In the first two chapters I have described Awe with diagrams that more or less ignore time and history. Space rather than time has been my main metaphor. In this chapter I want to describe Awe in terms of a diagram that depicts time as the key metaphor. In the actuality of our lives, space and time are not separated. We live in a space/time continuum. Similarly, nature and history are not separated. Nature is historical in the sense that nature is an emergent reality. The whole of nature has moved from its big bang beginning through unrepeatable stages of emergence. Nature is going somewhere down the one-way street of time. And human history is not separate from natural history; human history takes place within the flow of time in which all things are included. We might also say that natural history is part of human history, for the story of nature is included within the human story.

In the biblical tradition, God is depicted as an actor in the drama of history–both natural history and human history. The following diagram has been helpful to me in picturing God and history in one diagram.

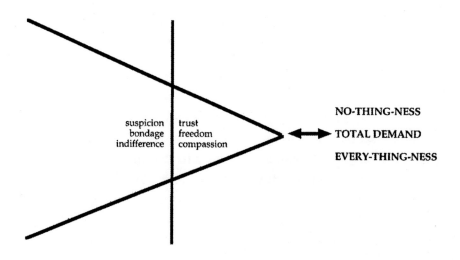

The interior portion of the wedge symbolizes the entirety of humanity. The vertical line indicates the great divide between that portion of humanity that breathes Spirit (Awe as trust, freedom, and compassion) and that portion of humanity that flees from Spirit, flees into suspicion, bondage, and indifference. This great divide cuts through every individual person and through every human group. No person or group is permanently on one side or the other. Decision for movement in one direction or the other must be made in each and every moment of living. Nevertheless, in any one moment part of humanity is moving toward humanity's encounters with NO-THING-NESS/EVERY-THING-NESS and the rest of humanity is not. Within the dynamics of time, NO-THING-NESS/EVERY-THING-NESS blend together into a TOTAL DEMAND calling humanity to freely, honestly, and creatively respond to that AWESOME PRESENCE coming into our "now" as a challenge from the inescapable future.

Trust, freedom, and compassion are three types of Awe that blow through the person or group of persons who are responding positively to the specific encounters with the Awesome Presence that is confronting them.

1. The positive response of *trust* allows the responding person to name this Awesome Presence "God." Using the name "God" for this Awesome Presence expresses a relationship of trust. Using the name "God" is nothing more and nothing less than the statement that the Awesome Presence is trustworthy. And by "trustworthy" I mean that the Awesome Presence is operating for my and humanity's highest good.

Those who trust the Awesome Presence have found that this trust is not an achievement but a gift of the Awesome Presence. Though we humans must do the trusting, trusting is not a human achievement. Trusting is a surrender. Not trusting can be viewed as a human achievement, for it is a human perversion of human authenticity. If we are suspicious, hateful, and despairing we do so as a product of our own fertile imagination. Trusting is our natural or essential state, even though it is rare that human beings manifest trust in a thoroughgoing manner.

The capacity for waywardness is part of our human authenticity, but the waywardness itself is of human origin. Christian theology has frequently indicated that humanity is totally depraved. This should not be interpreted to mean that our essential human nature is depraved. Rather, Awe-filled humanity is our original or essential state, and this state is wholly good with no alloy of evil. In the Genesis myth before the fall of Adam and Eve, we see the Infinite Presence walking and talking with humanity in the garden of innocence. Humanity introduces human depravity into history by seeking to be wise like God rather than trusting God and thereby being the perpetually ignorant finite creatures that we are. Even though the option of trust can be said to be foundational, the option of mistrust can be said to be the general state of existing humanity. All of us have joined Adam and Eve in this movement of mistrust. Once the mistrust choice has been made we have lost our trust and we cannot get it back by our own effort. We must receive trust again as a gift from the Awesome Presence acting in the real processes of history.

2. Not only trust but also *freedom* is the natural or essential state of humanity. The story of humanity is not like an obstacle course on the playing field of good and evil. In explicit rational terms, humanity does not know what is good or evil. Humanity can only know that freedom is good, and that trust is good, and that doing free trusting actions are always good no matter what known rules are violated. In a moment of freely doing the next deed, all past deeds are beside the point. There is no record that must be achieved. Rather, in order for authenticity to be present, every past deed must be surrendered to the God of history. As you may have noticed, the Awesome Determiner of history never gives any deed back to be done over again. Instead, this Awesome God of history can be said to forgive every deed and give us the next deed, challenging us to do that next deed in free and trusting obedience–seizing the opportunity to live the current here and now situation freely. This is what freedom is like: responding creatively to each and every situation, knowing that all rules for responding are human-made. Rules, laws, principles, and all other rational considerations are but finite guides that may or may not apply to our real situation. No human conscience and no sacred scripture contains the rules that must be obeyed in all circumstances. There are no such rules. There is just one overarching demand: *be your freedom.* The demand to be free is the total demand of the Awesome Presence. Only the courageous dare to obey this calling. In fact, courage might be defined as obeying the demand to be our freedom.

Freedom remains one of the most misunderstood aspects of Spirit living. It is not easy to disentangle ourselves from all our ethical confusions and all our arrogant addictions to presumably correct moralities. Freedom scares us. We do not trust in our own freedom or in the God who gives it and demands it.

3. Along with the natural states of trust and freedom goes the natural state of *compassion*. Compassion, like trust and freedom, is the gift of the God who is confronting us in the gift of those realities that require our compassion. Compassion is the Awe state of caring for each and every being in our lives. Compassion is the realization that our own lives are loved by the Awesome and therefore that every other being is likewise loved. We get confused about being compassionate because we think we know in moral terms what loving actions are. Spirit love means surrendering to being the being we are among all the others who are in being with us. This compassion or love is not an achievement. This compassion quite often blows in powerful ways through ordinary and unsuspecting folk who find themselves in situations of crisis and simply choose to deal the best they can with the challenges that face them. After such times, people sometimes say, "My, I don't know what got into me; I have never been a hero before." The deep truth is that no one achieves heroism. Heroism just happens. It is our natural state, a state which we cover over and suppress most of the time. Compassion is just the glory of the Awe-filled life itself operating naturally in real historical moments.

Trust, freedom, and compassion describe our Awe-filled responses to our actual historical encounters with the Awesome No-thing-ness/Every-thing-ness. This Awesome Presence, which is the backdrop of all our real situations, can also be described as the Total Demand. This Demand simply demands that we surrender to living in those real situations rather than fleeing them or fighting them. Our surrender to this Demand manifests as trust, freedom, and compassion.

The biblical heritage uses a personal metaphor for talking about these dynamics. Each person and each society of humans is pictured as being in a personal dialogue with the Infinite, an I-THOU dialogue that is taking place in history. THOU acts creating us and the world in which we exist. We respond. THOU acts again. We respond again. And this dialogue continues until the Infinite THOU has the last word by taking us out of history.

History and the Biblical Witness

The above diagram and discussion is a window into the strong historical emphasis found in both the Hebrew and Christian Scriptures. Every major religious tradition has dealt with the passage of time. Perhaps they created myths of origin. Perhaps they created anticipations of the future. But Judaism and Christianity are atypical in their strong emphasis upon time and history. In order to see the glory of Jewish and Christian heritages, we need to reflect further on the God of time. I want to begin with some basic images taken from the scriptures that Christians call "the Old Testament." Interpreting these writings has been made difficult by two factors: (1) our preoccupation with literal scientific history and (2) our neglect of Awe as a happening in time.

Moses and the Exodus

Central to the ancient Hebrew Scriptures is the event of the Exodus and the stories told about it. The first five books of the Bible are about this event and about the implications of this event for law making and for story telling concerning the origins of all things. In the writings of the biblical prophets, we see these signal luminaries referring again and again to the Exodus as an Awe-event that gives meaning to all other Awe-events.

Potentially, every event is an Awe-event, but some events stand out as Awe-events that shed light on all events. Consider this example. In writing, enacting, or watching a stage play, we can notice that there are "moments" in the course of the drama when we are "dropped" into the depths of our lives. These moments in a play might be called "Awe-moments." They shed light on those parts of the play that led up to these moments and on those parts of the play that follow after them. So it is with human history. There are moments that illuminate the whole story. For those who remembered and revered the Exodus, it was such an event.

Seeing the Awe quality of the Exodus is obscured by our biblical literalism. So often we ask, "What actually happened?" and in our culture we must ask this question. Many biblical conservatives have insisted that what happened is exactly what the Bible says happened. But our liberal biblical scholars tell us that the story of the Exodus grew over the centuries and took on exaggerations that cannot possibly be what actually happened. What both groups often fail to consider is that these exaggerations were never meant to be scientific history but expressions of the Awe that happened in the midst of whatever it was that did happen in the ordinary sense. So what did happen? What would a movie camera and a tape recorder have picked up if it had been there?

At its best, scientific history is about probabilities. We never know exactly what happened in the past, especially when we are talking about events that took place about 3300 years ago. Nevertheless, on the basis of the scientific history I trust, here is my thumbnail sketch about what actually happened in the Exodus. A few thousand slaves of Canaanite descent who were living in Egypt allowed themselves to be led by a charismatic figure whose name probably was Moses. They fled the urban centers on the northern Nile River toward the east. They waded across the sea of reeds toward the desert. The chariots that came after them got bogged down in the mud and gave up the arduous task of pursuing these escapees. Several more astonishing bits of good fortune happened. These fleeing slaves defeated the wild tribes they met in the desert. They found unlikely sources of food. They finally made it to the oasis of Sinai. There, Moses sat them down at the foot of the mountain and interpreted what had happened to them and what they had to do to continue the social innovation that they had begun.

When I try to imagine what Moses actually said to these people, I am thrown out of objective history into some sort of fiction. Nevertheless, I am convinced that the essence of Moses' speech had to do with how the

Awesome had favored them, indeed chosen them for survival against all odds while other groups had failed to escape their slavery. Moses also probably emphasized their freedom in contrast to the slavery they knew in Egypt. Apparently, Moses also realized that slavery was an inward mindset as well as an outward condition. Once you get the people out of Egypt, you still have to get Egypt out of the people. The social cohesion of Egyptian life was based on a hierarchical type of social law that served the aristocracy but oppressed the many. Moses initiated a new view of law, law understood to be derived from loyalty to the Awesome Historical Actor who had favored their escape from slavery. This new law presupposed a freedom and a responsibility on the part of each person that had not been experienced in Egypt. Moses held up two hands. On one of his hands, he itemized the five items that must be followed in order to honor their overarching context of realism, namely trusting the Awesome God of history rather than the other gods they had known. On the other of his hands, Moses itemized the things that this loyal people must do in relation to one another. These were basic things that apply today as well as then: don't kill each other, don't steal from each other, don't mess with another person's sexual partner, don't lie about one another, and don't even covet what another person has. The implication of this tenth item is that each person should be content with the life that the Awesome is giving him or her and not be wasting time longing to be someone else with a different life from the one being given.

Those who listened to Moses' interpretation of their situation were apparently smote with Awe-filled dread. Consider these verses from Exodus 20 as an expression of such Awe-filled responses.

> When all the people saw how it thundered and the lightning flashed, when they heard the trumpet sound and saw the mountain smoking, they trembled and stood at a distance. "Speak on your own," they said to Moses, "and we will listen to you; but if the Awesome speaks to us we will die." Moses answered, "Do not be afraid. The Awesome has appeared to test you, so that the dread of Awesome Reality may

remain with you and discourage you from your unrealistic options."
Still the people stood at a distance, while Moses approached the dark
cloud where the Awesome Presence was hovering.

*(A slight rewording of The New English translation
of Exodus 20:18-21)*

These words of Scripture were probably written years later than that
fateful day when Moses first itemized his ten items. Nevertheless, these
words express a state of Awe that is believable. The prospect of an ongoing commitment or covenant with the Awesome Realism that Moses
articulated called upon the people to make a dreadful and Awe-filling
choice. Were they going to follow Moses in undivided devotion to the
Awesome or were they going to retreat to more familiar modes of living? Probably, some did one, and some did the other. We only know that
some did follow Moses and communicated this context for living to
their children and their children's children on down to us.

The detailed and mostly obsolete laws contained in the books of
Leviticus, Numbers, and Deuteronomy were not all written by Moses as
some conservative traditions maintain. Rather, these books record a
process of law writing that spans many hundreds of years. What is
important about these books is not the rules themselves but the context
for rule writing that is being witnessed to by these vigorous efforts. This
voluminous law writing was an ongoing process in which the issue is
not articulating absolute rights and wrongs but giving additional order
to a society's response to the Awesome as the Awesome is being encountered in each new historical situation. Such law writing is what Moses
did. Such law writing is what his followers did. And such law writing is
what we can still do in the midst of our twenty-first century challenges.
For example, Moses did not need any laws about protecting the natural
planet, but we do. Moses was not being challenged in his hour of history
to do away with all traces of patriarchal prerogatives, but we are. The
rules change from age to age, but the context for rule writing which
Moses initiated lives on.

Isaiah

The prophets express a maturation of the Mosaic impetus. I am still grateful to Bernard Anderson and his book *Understanding the Old Testament* for helping me see the prophets in their historical settings. Others have also helped me with this: Martin Buber, Walter Brueggeman, Marcus Borg, and others. The prophets, I have been privileged to learn, were not magical predictors of the future, nor moralistic preachers, but interpreters of the historical events of their times. Indeed, they were discerners of the Awe, listeners to the Awesome speaking to them in their historical situations. They risked saying to their companions what they heard the Awesome saying knowing that the Awesome is always saying more than any human can discern.

I will first illustrate this historical theology of the prophets with a passage from Isaiah. The historical situation to which Isaiah is speaking is the rise of the Assyrian empire that has already defeated Babylon to the east and is challenging Egypt to the south. Assyria wishes to control the lucrative trade routes that pass through the northern kingdom of Israel and through the outskirts of the southern kingdom of Judah. Isaiah, living in the southern kingdom of Judah, is speaking of the Assyrian conquest of Israel and the threatening conquest of Judah. Speaking for Yahweh, the Awesome Infinite Actor in history, Isaiah pens these words:

> Ah Assyria, the rod of my anger,
> the staff of my fury!
> Against a godless nation I send him
> and against the people of my wrath I command him,
> to take spoil and seize plunder
> and to tread them down like the mire in the streets.

Then speaking of Assyria, Isaiah continues:

> But he does not so intend
> and his mind does not so think.
> But it is in his mind to destroy
> and to cut off nations not a few.

Then speaking as himself Isaiah says:

> When Yahweh has finished all his work
> on Mount Zion and on Jerusalem,
> he will punish the arrogant boasting of the king of Assyria
> and his haughty pride.
> ......
>
> Shall the ax vaunt itself over him who hews with it,
> or the saw magnify itself against him who wields it?
> *(Isaiah 10:5-7, 12, 15 RSV)*

Isaiah sees history as a drama in which the God he worships is actively present in every event. The Assyrian conqueror does not know he is a rod in God's hand, but the Reality that Isaiah calls his God is none other than the Awesome Infinite Reality that is present and operative in every historical event. For Isaiah God is not a magical protector of the interests of Isaiah's nation. Rather, God is the Truth arriving to audit Isaiah's own nation for its shoddy living. Isaiah also clarifies that when he says that God is wielding Assyria, this does not imply a justification of the Assyrian's deeds. In due time, the ax who pretends to be in charge of history will also experience the Ax of that Infinite Reality who is truly in charge of history.

Isaiah is saying something more than the bald fact that all finite realities face the ax of death. He is noting how specific delusions of righteousness and power and security are currently being axed. He is making clear that

he and his people are confronting specific life choices. Isaiah's words are
applicable to our own times, for his basic message is simply this: (1) face
up to Reality and live or (2) flee from Reality and deal with the dire consequences of the erroneous belief that a flight from Reality can succeed.

In our day, hearing Isaiah's words would be like hearing that the God
we worship has used Muslim terrorists to bring down The World Trade
Center towers in order to awaken the United States and other nations
from our delusions of safety and to an awareness of the rage we have
inspired throughout the Muslim world and other places through the cal-
lousness and inappropriateness of our many decades of shoddy dealings.

Amos

Amos addressed the northern kingdom of Israel just before the
Assyrian conquest of that nation. He addressed their delusions of safety
and their delusions of righteousness. He pointed out that their unrighteousness compared with the evil quality of the nations that surround
them in their international scene. If we were to hear an Amos type voice
addressing the people of the United States in our historical situation
today, it might sound something like this:

> Hear the SPEECH of the Infinite Source of all reality and the
> Truth for all humanity.
> For three evils and for four of the terrorist networks of global
> scope, I will not withhold my wrath. For they have taken the lives of
> innocent men, women, and children; bombed embassies and a
> docked ship; and flown commercial airliners into occupied build-
> ings. Therefore, I will turn all the nations of the planet against them.
> I will hound them and chase them until their networks are broken to
> pieces, their training camps are laid waste, and their bank accounts
> emptied. Suicidal terrorism shall become the butt of jokes about
> moronic behavior. This is the SPEECH of the Infinite Silence.
> For three evils and for four of the Taliban, I will not withhold my
> wrath. For they have turned their women into caged animals, their

men into frightened robots, and a religion of peace into a love of war. Therefore, their rule shall be wiped off the face of the earth, their support of terrorism shall be ended, their teachings scorned, and their rigid customs laughed into oblivion. This is the SPEECH of the Infinite Silence.

For three evils and for four of the United States of America, I will not withhold my wrath. For decade after decade they have assisted in the overthrow of legitimate and popularly selected national leaders, replacing them with dictatorial thugs who were willing to do the bidding of greedy corporations. In the pursuit of these ends, they have directly or indirectly caused the deaths of millions of innocent men, women, and children. They have sapped wealth from the poorer nations to engorge their billionaires and indulge their citizens in silly purchases. They have spent billions on costly wars to preserve their oil addiction and their delusions of absolute safety while offering a pittance to assist in the curtailment of an AIDS epidemic in Africa that creates millions of orphans, destabilizes whole nations, and threatens the health of all humanity. They likewise neglect to strongly support the stabilization of the human population, the stabilization of the atmosphere, reversing the depletion of fresh water, ending the improper cutting of forests, reversing the erosion of cropland, saving our last coral reef communities, the preservation of species diversity, and other primal emergencies of our inherited fluorescence of life on this planet. Yes, and this nation has even used moderate and freedom-loving Afghan people to fight the Russians and then abandoned them when their cold war with Russia was over. They trained Afghan terrorists to fight their wars and then abandoned this war-torn and chaotic nation to the worst elements of its population. These dastardly deeds they have done in the pious name of national self-interest, sweeping all consciousness of their own selfishness and grim evil under the rug of patriotic songs and waving flags. They have even presumed to parade themselves as a nation who trusts in God.

Therefore, I will continue to assault this people with grim disasters. I will increase the anger felt against them in hopeless, poverty stricken places. Not only will there be further terrorism, but even the oceans will rise and drown their coastal cities. The weather patterns will change and turn their croplands into deserts. I will push their economy into the worst recession it has ever known. I will bog down their military in futile wars that will make Vietnam look like a picnic. I will expand chaos until they turn and listen to me. This is the SPEECH of the Infinite Silence.

So, U. S. of A., do you indeed long for the end of evil, for the day of justice all across the Earth? What will that day look like for you?

It will be darkness, not light. It will be as when a man runs from a lion and a bear meets him, or turns into a house and leans his hand on the wall and a snake bites him.

For you, the day of justice will indeed be darkness and not light, a day of gloom with no dawn.

I hate, I spurn your prayer days and your flag-waving ceremonies. Spare me the noise of your patriotic songs. I cannot endure another verse of "America the Beautiful."

But let justice roll down like waters,
and righteousness like an ever-flowing stream.

(a paraphrase of part of Amos 1:3-5:24)

Hopefully some of the disasters sited in the above poem will not come to pass, for choices still remain to be made that could evoke a different response from the Reality we face. The words of the prophet need not be accurate predictions of the future. The intent of the prophet is to move listeners to an awareness of the choices that face them.

Hosea

Hosea addresses Israel a few years later than Amos when the Assyrian conquest is further along. The illusory confidence of the nation of Israel has by this time been shaken, its unrighteousness more fully acknowledged, and now feelings of hopelessness and futility have taken over. Hosea does not take back the judgment and doom that Amos has announced, but he addresses the topic of forgiveness and a fresh start for the survivors of the horrific tragedy that is underway. He likens Israel to an unfaithful wife who though deserving complete rejection has been experiencing a period of tough training and is now being offered restoration to full standing as wife in the household of that Almighty Awesome Otherness who rules the course of history. Hosea also likens Israel to a child whom this Awesome God has raised since the days of the Exodus, a child that God loves and will not abandon to complete doom.

Hosea is confronting his listeners with an Awe-filling choice: rather than (1) give up and die out as the people who revere this God, to instead (2) accept the challenge of receiving the gift of forgiveness and begin again to build continuity with the Mosaic breakthrough.

In order to hear Hosea's voice speaking to our situation, we need to discern where we today feel beat down and hopeless and how it is nevertheless true that possibilities still exist. In our recent U.S. history, Martin Luther King Jr. was a voice of hope in relation to an established racism that at the time seemed impossible to break. For those of us who were African American or who identified with the African American oppression in the U.S., King's dream was like a bright light of hope shining in a very dark place. A sermon given by James Bevel, one of King's associates, had a message similar to Hosea's. The title of this sermon and the line repeated again and again throughout this grim but hopeful talk was "Love will find a way."

Jeremiah

Jeremiah lived several generations later than Amos, Hosea, and Isaiah when Babylon had overthrown Assyria and become the world power. Babylon devised a new means of controlling rebel nations. After conquering a rebel nation, Babylon would move a significant portion of its leadership and population into exile in a foreign location. As such conquest and exile are happening to his own nation of Judah, Jeremiah sees these horrific events as the action of the Awesome Infinite Actor. He maintains throughout his tempestuous career that there will be no relief from this dreadful experience of national destruction and exile. He witnesses in his own life and calls his listeners to a new inwardness in their understanding of what it means to be the People of God. He seems to be saying something like this: "We are losing the nation as our outward mode of being the People of God, but we are not losing our calling to be the People of God. Our peoplehood can function in exile anywhere in the world." Through such words, Jeremiah and the prophets who came after him bring the people of Israel into a deeper understanding of what it means to be the People of God. This calling came to mean something more universal than being a model nation among the other nations in the world. "Israel" came to mean those whose hearts are filled with Awe and who trust the Awesome. "Israel" means those who respond to the historical events of their times in trust, freedom, and compassion. Here is an important piece of Jeremiah's writing:

> The time is coming, says the LORD, when I will make a new covenant with Israel and Judah. It will not be like the covenant I made with their forefathers when I took them by the hand and led them out of Egypt. Although they broke my covenant, I was patient with them, says the LORD. But this is the covenant which I will make with Israel after those days, says the LORD; I will set my law within them and write it on their hearts; I will become their God and they shall become my people. No longer need they teach one another to know the LORD; all of them, high and low alike, shall know me, says the LORD, for I will forgive their wrongdoing and remember their sin no more.
>
> *(Jeremiah 31:31-34 The New English Bible)*

Jeremiah was talking about his own immediate future, not about the coming of a Messiah, but it is understandable that Christians saw in this passage an interpretation of what was taking place through Jesus and his emphasis on the inwardness of being the true People of God. Jeremiah's image of a new covenant became a master image for the followers of Jesus. The writings of the New Testament do not speak of replacing the God of Moses with a different God. Rather they speak of a fresh understanding of being in covenant with the same Awesome, dreadful but faithful, God of history that was worshiped by Moses, Amos, Hosea, Isaiah, Jeremiah, Ezekiel, and many other prophets and their followers. I will discuss Jesus more thoroughly in the next chapter, but it is important to keep in mind that Jesus was a faithful Jew for his entire life. *He never intended to start a new religion.* He understood himself to be leading a renewal movement within the tradition of Moses and the prophets. The God whom he called "Papa" was the God of history, the same Awesome Otherness that Moses or you or I meet in everything that is happening to us. Unless we begin with this understanding, we have no hope of understanding Jesus or the New Testament theology that interpreted him.

In terms of religious practices, being a Christian and being a Jew eventually became significantly different; but in Spirit terms, being a true Christian and being a true Jew were then and still are the same basic response. This response is opening ourselves to the Awe being infused within us by the Awesome through the historical events that confront us. And this Awe includes trust, freedom, and compassion for all beings. Being the People of God means being blown by these states of Awe and resolving to be that Awe in obedience to the Awesomeness that inspires the Awe. Being the People of God means living this immediately given Awe of trust, freedom, and compassion on behalf of all the nations of the Earth. The People of God are those who represent humanity in being responsive to the Awesome and thereby leading humanity in this realistic direction.

In the diagram discussed at the beginning of this chapter, the true Jew and the true Christian occupy the space to the right of the great divide, the space that symbolizes responding to the Awesome rather than fleeing from or fighting with the Awesome. Most people (Jewish or Christian or any other practice or lack of religious practice) live in flight from and perhaps hatred of the Awesome. Nevertheless, some people in every group of people who have ever walked the face of the Earth open themselves to the Awesome; and on behalf of the others in their group, lead that part of humanity toward more realistic modes of living. These people who embrace the Awe and respond accordingly on behalf of humanity are the People of God.

This understanding of the People of God means that Lao Tzu, the Buddha, Mohammed, and other religious innovators and their followers can be included in being the People of God if they are indeed open to the Awesome, allow themselves to be filled with Awe, and thus live in their historical situations as the Awed Ones who lead humanity into more realistic modes of living. Such persons may not wish to use the term "People of God" or even the word "God," but good Christian theology can use the term "People of God" to include all these Spirit-filled people. From this time forward in Christian and Jewish theology, being the People of God must no longer indicate being a member of some particular religious group. Being the People of God means being a servant who plays his or her role in a universal dynamic of human history: namely, being an Awed One who is responding to the Awesome and is filled with Awe.

Jesus, as we will examine further in the next chapter, was one of those Awed Ones. He was filled with Awe and was obedient to the Awesome. His trust of the Awesome was expressed in his affectionate term "Abba" or "Papa." His freedom was manifest in his style and his authority. He extended compassion to social outcasts and to all sorts and conditions of humanity to follow him toward being the Awed Ones in history.

4.

Jesus and the Second Third of the God Experience

During my early years in college, I first discovered Jesus as a fascinating figure. I had read several lives of Jesus, and I had taken on the image that Jesus was my example, my model of how I was to live. I had rejected the virgin birth and several other crass miracles, because I felt they prevented Jesus from being my example. How could he be my example if he was born of a virgin and I was not? On Sunday morning I coughed through several parts of the Apostle's Creed.

The part of the New Testament that grasped me most was the Sermon on the Mount and other teachings of Jesus gathered together in the Gospel of Matthew. At that time I was not aware of the extent to which Jesus' teachings had been elaborated by the Gospel writers. I knew nothing of form criticism or of the story of New Testament formation. I was struck by the Jesus I met on the pages of Matthew's Gospel. I was struck by the challenges to profound inwardness that I found there. I was spun into rethinking who I was as an inward being and how I was potentially like Jesus. I was entranced by his mode of living and how it was a calling to me. I can say now that even in these early naive years, I experienced Jesus as an Awed One and myself as Awed by him.

I know now that the historical Jesus is deeply buried beneath the interpretive material of the gospel writers. Jesus (like Moses, Lao Tzu, and most other ancient figures) almost disappears beneath the myths and legends, literary exaggerations, and other interpretations of him. I know now that not a single word spoken by the Jesus figure in the Gospel of John is a quote from Jesus' actual life. The author of this gospel was composing a wildly creative drama of dialogues as a way of making his theological points. I find those dialogues Awesome and I even find Awesome the fact that this author experienced within himself the wild liberty to create such a book.

Mark, Matthew, and Luke were much more conservative handlers of the earliest traditions of the Christ way of being Jewish, but they too were creative theologians whose works cannot be understood as scientific biographies or documentaries. If we want to know Jesus as he was in the flesh and blood of his factual biographical details, we have to work harder than simply reading the stories in the New Testament.

I respect the critical scholarship of Albert Schweitzer, Rudolf Bultmann, and more recently Marcus Borg, John Dominic Crossan, and the other members of the Jesus Seminar. I feel that they have given me what I need to know to glimpse that truly amazing person who initiated all the excitement that flowed from his short life.

But even when critical scholarship has done its best, what do we have? We have the question that Mark puts in the mouth of Jesus, "Who do you say that I am?" Clearly, Jesus had thousands of followers, and they did not all interpret him the same way. The Gospel of Thomas, which did not make it into the New Testament, is a different interpretation of Jesus than the interpretations we find in the writings of Paul, Mark, Matthew, Luke, John, and other New Testament writers. There may be twelve or more different theologies within the New Testament, but all these theologies have a common interest in the cross, in the resurrection, and in giving Jesus the title "Christ." The Gospel of Thomas is interested in none of these interpretations. Thomas, or whoever wrote this book, sees Jesus as a teacher of occult wisdom.

Similarly, there were others, some of whom Paul struggled with in his letters, who viewed Jesus as a significant refreshment of the Mosaic law but who likewise had little interest in the cross, the resurrection, or the Messianic mythologies. Jesus was interpreted in many different ways, and we too must interpret him in some way or another. The simple historical Jesus standing there unvarnished by interpretation is not an answer: he is just a question. Who is this man? What significance is there to me in his life and death? Why did the New Testament writers focus on resurrection and what did they mean by it? Why did they call Jesus the Messiah (or Christ) and what did they mean by doing so? And most enigmatic of all perhaps is this question: why did the evolving church see Jesus, the Christ, as the second face of the experience of God? Why did they insist over and over again that Jesus, the Christ, be understood as wholly human as well as wholly divine?

The Second Face of the One Experience of God

I want to begin by exploring early Christianity's paradoxical vision that the experience of God is both three and one. If we attempt to understand the Trinity as three personal beings sitting alongside one another in a supernatural space, we will be lost in endless confusion. We need to assume that the first creators of Trinitarian mathematics were talking about their own lives. So let us think of their witness as an experience—one experience with three faces. Perhaps then we can begin to glimpse what this ancient discussion was all about.

Let us imagine that we are a group of people with hundreds of relationships to one another and to all the things in the finite world of things. This is symbolized in the following diagram by the lines over the heads of the three stick figures. Next, let us imagine that we are looking outwardly through all these relationships to THE AWESOME–that is, to the No-thing-ness, Every-thing-ness, and Total Demand. Standing in the same experience, let us look inwardly toward the conscious life of our group. In that direction we see THE AWE–that is, we see Trust, Compassion, and Freedom.

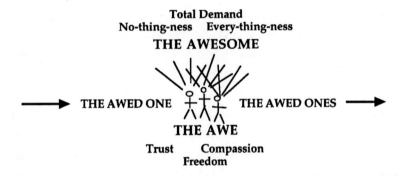

Now let us imagine that Jesus walks up to our group. Jesus is THE AWED ONE who reveres THE AWESOME as papa and is filled with AWE. Let us imagine this AWED ONE awakens AWE in us, thus joining us to him as a community of THE AWED ONES. We now see the Awed One in one another. Let us notice that the Awesome, the Awed Ones and the Awe are three aspects of one experience. There is no Awe without an Awed One who is in Awe. And there is no Awe without the Awesome, which is inspiring that Awe. And "The Awed Ones" means that place in human history where Awe joins a group of human beings with the Infinite Awesome Overallness. The Awed Ones or The Awed One is the second face of this one experience of God. So, here is a viable contemporary vision of the Christian Trinity: the Awesome, the Awed One, and the Awe itself.

Jesus is an example of what an Awed One looks like. He is the whole people of Israel come into a fulfilling moment of Awed living. He is the first fruit of a new Israel living in a clarified covenant with that same Awesome Almightiness celebrated by Moses and the prophets. Jesus, so interpreted, is not merely a singular individual: he is the whole People of God. His death is the death of the People of God. His resurrection is the resurrection of the People of God. His healing effect upon history results from taking his followers through this death of the ancient People of God into this resurrection of a reconstituted People of God. Indeed, the resurrected body of Jesus is none other than that body of people in whom the life quality of Jesus is present in history. And this risen body of Jesus is still walking and talking and eating and rejoicing and suffering and bleeding and dying and continuing to live in human history.

When Paul speaks of being "in Christ" or "in Christ Jesus" he is not talking about being a member in some denomination of Christianity. He is talking about having died with Christ and having been raised up with Christ to newness of life. He is talking about becoming Awed by the Awesome and filled with Awe. He is talking about being one of the Awed Ones. Paul is the first Christian theologian to spell out clearly that Awe is trust, freedom, and compassion. These are Paul's key descriptions of Awe, although he also uses hope, peace, joy, and other descriptive metaphors for the various states of Awe.

Today, Christian theology must be clear that this threefold experience (the Awesome, the Awed Ones, and the Awe itself) is an experience that happens not only to Christians but also to everyone of any background who is Awed by the Awesome and filled with Awe. Anyone participating in this experience can be said to be "in Christ." They may not use that term, but when we who are Christians use the term "in Christ," we need to be clear that we are pointing to a universal dynamic of human history. "In Christ" does not mean in a Christian group. Such usage is bigotry and a denial of the entire meaning of the Spirit breakthrough that took place in connection with Jesus.

Jesus both Human and Divine

So how is Jesus both human and divine? Jesus is human and divine in the same way that anyone who is experiencing the Awesome is both human and divine. Every Awed One is both fully human and fully divine. We who join Jesus in Awe participate with him in a conscious relationship with the Awesome. That relationship is not explainable in terms of finite human processes. One end of the relationship is indeed rooted in human flesh and blood, but the other end of the relationship is rooted in the Infinite. So to be in Awe is to be a relationship that is both finite and Infinite. The Awe relationship is divine because it is a relationship with that Awesome Almightiness that is not a thing among other finite things. And the Awe relationship is human because it is taking place in an ordinary member of our species. Awe or Spirit is not the finite end of this relationship. Nor is Awe or Spirit the Infinite end of this relationship. *Awe or Spirit is the relationship as a whole.*

And what in this context do we mean by "relationship"? Relationship means both encounter and response. Relationship means a dialogue moving in two directions. Awe is finite consciousness being encountered by Infinite Actuality. And Spirit or Awe is also that same Awed finite consciousness responding to Infinite Actuality in a specific place and time. The relationship has been symbolized in the biblical writings as Thou-to-I and I-to-Thou. It is a dialogue that moves back and forth. We are encountered, and we respond. This entire mysterious relationship can be said to blow through our actual finite human lives. This relationship happens to us: it is not of our own making. Yet we fully participate in being this relationship with our entire lives. Spirit or Awe is a whole life experience in which we participate in the wholly human and wholly Infinite at one and the same time.

This underlying experience gives meaning to the human-divine thinking about the Christ figure in ancient Christian theology. The Messianic life, early Christian theology insisted, must not be understood as simply the best of being a finite human being. And on the other hand, the Messianic life must not be understood as some ghostly being who merely appeared to be temporarily dwelling in a human form. The Messianic life, according to early orthodox Christian traditions, must be described as wholly human and wholly divine at one and the same time in one and the same human person. And this applies not only to Jesus but also to all the Awed Ones in any religion and in any place and time.

Jesus and the Christ Title

For early Christians Jesus came to symbolize the full expression of trust, freedom, and compassion. In my words, he was the full expression of being the Awed One—of being what it looks like to be in Awe before the Awesome. This is why some called him "the Christ" or "Messiah." Many people of that day expected the Messiah to be a military leader who would cast off the Roman rule. Others expected the Messiah to be a cosmic superperson who would end all human evil and usher in the age of perfection in all aspects of human life and society. In relation to these expectations Jesus was a flop. He did not set Israel free from Roman rule. He did not end the reign of evil in the general public sphere. Instead, he suffered rejection and death at the hands of the evil powers that remained firmly in control of the general order of human affairs.

Let us contemplate for a moment the possibility that most of us are still waiting for a Messiah who is quite different from the one that Jesus turned out to be. We have all had our expectations that life will be full and complete some day when conditions change. It is a quite general attitude among human beings to expect real living to begin when some problem situation is overcome. When I inherit some money, when I finish school, when I get a job, when I retire from my job, when I get married, when I get a divorce, when I have children, when the children leave home, when I overcome my health problems—then I will begin to truly and fully live my life. Such an attitude is clearly an estrangement from living life in the here and now. Such a "Messianic expectation" is quite the opposite of finding an Awe-filled and thus meaningful life in the actual here and now. In the beginning most of the crowds that followed Jesus, and even his closest disciples, saw him through the lens of Messianic expectations that were an escape from living in the here and now. They wanted out of their here and now situation. Jesus, they thought, was their ticket.

In terms of what most people expected the Messiah to be, Jesus was no-Messiah. To this day people still ask, "What if anything did Jesus actually accomplish?" Perhaps we can hear ourselves say, "Perhaps he said some true things. Perhaps he fought against some bad religion. And he was certainly heroic–getting himself killed for being so brash with the defenders of the status quo. But so what? What did this accomplish?"

In both the first century and today Jesus' Messianic quality has been a deep secret known only to those who have been inwardly delivered from the evil of fleeing from the Awe-filled potentialities of real life. Jesus is Messiah only to those who share his understanding of what human authenticity looks like–namely, being called by the Awesome to the path of Awe-filled living. In the witness of the New Testament writers and the community they represented, Jesus killed their false expectations. When Jesus was crucified these false expectations were crucified as well. Nevertheless, they found this dying with Jesus to be a first step toward being reconciled to trusting in the love of that Infinite Presence which was streaming towards them in the here and now. This no-Messiah became for them a secret Messiah who raps on the doors of cynical hearts and says, "Follow me. Follow me into trust, compassion, and freedom. Follow me into unswerving truthfulness in regard to our actual encounters with Infinite Presence and into unswerving obedience to the callings that issue from these encounters." In John's gospel it is clearly stated that simply answering this call is eternal life. This life is eternal because it knows no threat from external circumstances. This is the life worth living. Every other life is hell, however comfortable it may seem for the time being.

Embracing the Cross

The cross was the hardest pill for Jesus' disciples to swallow. It seemed at first preposterous that the Messianic human was to be rejected and put to death in this most ignominious fashion. If this happened to the Messiah, then all of us who follow in the steps of this Messiah will experience a similar destiny. The disciples were (and we still are) living in a world populated by those who flee the call of the Awe. In such a world, the Awed Ones suffer rejection. Facing up to this grim truth is resisted by all our inclinations to play it safe. But when the disciples had overcome their resistance and surrendered to this Awesome truth, they found the experience of the cross to be profoundly liberating. Such liberty was not popular then, and it is not popular now. The popular mind has constantly perverted the Messiahship of Jesus into some new escape from the experience of the cross.

To affirm the crucified Jesus as the Messiah means dying to our illusions that authentic life is a pleasant picnic in the Garden of Eden. We don't live in the Garden of Eden; we live in history in which the tragedy of inauthenticity is everywhere manifest. So being our authenticity will always entail being a suffering servant rather than a triumphant warrior who cleverly and perhaps violently rids the world of evil.

Such insights as these were seen hundreds of years before Jesus. The anonymous author of the concluding chapters of the scroll of Isaiah also spoke of the People of God as a suffering servant. He said that the people of Israel had endured suffering not only because of their sins but also because of their being the servants of God. The call to be the People of God is a call to be the suffering servant. Generally, we Christians have been more willing to apply this suffering servant role to Jesus than to ourselves. We have skipped over those sayings about taking up our cross and following him. We have skipped over those sayings about how the follower will be treated the same as the master. Christians have generally opted for Jesus doing all the suffering on their behalf and ignoring these somber elements in the calling to follow him. Jesus did indeed suffer and die for us. So did Martin Luther King Jr. and Malcolm X and Gandhi and thousands of others. No healing happens in human history unless someone filled with Awe walks that Awe into the face of the Awe-hating world and Awes that world no matter what the cost. This grim dynamic is itself Awe-filling. Yet with this somber Awe go great liberty and great joy and great courage. Embracing the cross gives us the ability to live and die unvictimized by the fear of suffering and death. And this courage, this liberty, this joy is eternal life, the only life that does not die. Every other life leads to the hell of despair.

This biblical emphasis upon suffering should not be seen as a form of asceticism or as a hatred of pleasure. Nor is it some kind of martyr complex or codependence in which we let other people walk over us like a doormat. Life in the light of the cross is just plain sober realism. And this realism includes the freedom to choose when and for what we are willing to risk rejection, pain, and death. As the brash Jesus of John's gospel says, "No man takes my life from me; I lay it down of my own free will."[7] Unless we can hear the strength and the victory and the freedom in that statement, we do not yet understand what it means to pick up our cross. Picking up our cross is a defeat for our safety-seeking ego, but for our Spirit life picking up our cross is a victory, an aliveness, a power, and an ennoblement that knows no defeat.

And let us also be sober about the alternative of *not* picking up our cross. No one gets out of life alive. Each person chooses what to die for as well as what to live for. Absolute safety is not an option. One can choose to live and die in Awe before the Awesome, bearing all the inten-

---

[7] John 10:18

sity of joy and sorrow that being an Awed One entails. Or one can choose to avoid such a life. But such avoidance will not result in the safety and comfort we might be hoping for. In the final outcome, avoiding the life of Awe is a path that arrives at the destiny of despair. The most common way we avoid picking up the cross of authenticity is simply backing into our graves without ever choosing how to live our lives or die our deaths. Such indecision is also a choice and not a choice that leads to comfort and safety. Picking up our cross may be the narrow path that few travel, but it is a happy path. Other paths may seem easier, but they are not happier. Embracing the cross was equated in the teachings of early Christianity with the joy of being healed, with the honor of being in Christ, with the glory of being an authentic human being in the midst of this world.

The Resurrection as a Historical Event

The resurrection happened in history. This statement is true even though it is also true that every resurrection story in the New Testament is fiction written by the Christian community. As story, the resurrection took about seventy years to happen. But as Awe-event the resurrection may indeed have begun happening about three days after the crucifixion of Jesus.

If we had been there with a movie camera and a tape recorder, we would not have seen anything unusual. No corpse literally got out of its grave. The resurrection was a secret, seen and known only by those to whom the resurrection had happened. The New Testament stories of resurrection are not about something that happened to Jesus. These stories are about something that happened to the followers of Jesus. We do not actually know what happened to Jesus' body. It is possible and even probable that his body, like those of other crucified victims, was cast out on the hillside and eaten by the birds.

To see the empty tomb and the resurrected body of Jesus requires eyes that no movie camera possesses. It requires the eyes of those who have been Awed by the Awesome and thereby filled with Awe.

Here is a story that is not generally thought of as a resurrection story, but I am convinced that this story was written after Jesus' death to interpret what the resurrection happening was all about. *The following is the New English translation of Mark 9:2-10:*

> Six days later, Jesus took Peter, James, and John with him and led them up a high mountain where they were alone; and in their presence he was transfigured; his clothes became dazzling white, with a whiteness no bleacher on earth could equal. They saw Elijah appear, and Moses with him, and there they were, conversing with Jesus. Then Peter spoke: "Rabbi," he said, "how good it is that we are here! Shall we make three shelters, one for you, one for Moses, and one for Elijah?" (For he did not know what to say; they were so terrified.) Then a cloud appeared, casting its shadow over them, and out of the cloud came a voice: "This is my Son, my Beloved; listen to him." And now suddenly, when they looked around, there was nobody to be seen but Jesus alone with themselves.

> On their way down the mountain, he enjoined them not to tell anyone what they had seen until the Son of Man had risen from the dead. They seized upon these words, and discussed among themselves what this "rising from the dead" could mean.

The secrecy of Jesus' significance and the secrecy of his resurrection is a literary device used by the gospel writer Mark. The story just quoted is a good example of this secrecy theme. This story is not about a public event that dramatizes the significance of Jesus to everyone. No, it is a secret event. As literal history, it never happened. It is a story written by those who now know the secret and who also know that a person has to be transformed in order to understand the secret. In the view of the early church, Jesus had been transfigured, but the general population saw nothing. There was nothing for them to see. There never was an historical event in which Jesus' clothes actually became ethereally white and in which a voice was acoustically heard speaking from a cloud. This is fiction. It is, however, religious literature of a great and wondrous sort.

There may be a few historical elements in this fictitious story. It is quite probable that there was a man named Jesus who did have disciples with names like Peter, James, and John. It is also probable that these disciples had "religious experiences" (if not before, certainly after the death of Jesus) that had to do with the relationship of Jesus to Moses and Elijah, and the relationship of Jesus to the God that Moses and Elijah worshiped. Further, it is quite probable that these disciples and the community that they founded became clear (as this passage expresses) that their "religious experience" of Jesus contained a huge paradox. On the one hand, Jesus was dazzling–dazzling with the same dazzle that made Moses and Elijah dazzle. The Awesome Wholeness of Being was filling the eyes and ears of these disciples' inner beings with Awe, and this Awe expressed an overwhelming affirmation of the person Jesus. On the other hand, "when they looked around, there was nobody to be seen but Jesus alone with themselves." There was just Jesus! But in this plain ordinary human being, his awakened followers had encountered the ultimate dazzle. In Jesus they encountered the Awed One who filled them with an Awe that reopened for them the Awe-filling dazzle of Moses and the prophets.

The experience to which this story witnesses is an experience that might take place in your life or in my life. This secret about Jesus can become known to each of us. And seeing this secret is what it means to have a resurrection appearance happen to us.

A strict scientific positivist might argue that no religious experience can be called an historical fact. And it is true that a happening of Awe is a very personal experience that is only plausible to someone who has also had such an experience. So a happening of Awe cannot be verified through objective scientific thinking. In terms of the strict standards of scientific objectivity, any experience of Awe would have to be dismissed as mere "subjectivity," unfit to be honored with the designation of "fact."

But from my or your perspective as an Awe-experiencing person, history can be viewed as a history of Awe experiences. Even as we might write a history of human thought, so we might also write a history of human Awe. And if we did, we would have to allow for the fact that human beings, living before the scientific era, used wildly unscientific poetry for expressing their experiences of Awe. Indeed, we who express our Awe today may also use wildly unscientific poetry to do so. Our task as historians of Awe is to honor the ancestors in our religious lineage by allowing them the right to express their Awe in the ways they chose. Then, we can further honor them and honor ourselves by translating the odd language they used into the language we can use today to talk about the very same Awe-experiences.

Looking at history from this perspective, it is quite plausible to me that the transfiguration of Jesus happened. It is quite plausible to me that the resurrection of Jesus happened. But what actually happened was not some magical event constructed by modern, scientifically minded, biblical literalists. What happened was an Awe-moment in which the historical person Jesus became for some of those who knew him an Awe-event in which the whole scope of Awe and the place of Awe in human living was incredibly transfigured. This happening was not fiction only. It was an historical actuality that changed the course of historical events. But the actuality of the resurrection could only be expressed in religious fiction.

Jesus, the Christ, as Healing Event

Christians have spoken of Jesus Christ as their savior. When we have interpreted "salvation" to mean a literal supernatural soul avoiding a literal supernatural hell and arriving at a literal supernatural heaven, we have lost the wonder of the New Testament meaning of this word. When the word "savior" appears in the New Testament it means "healer." To the New Testament writers "salvation" meant to be healed of a sickness that entered history through the fall of Adam and is still entering history through the temptations of Satan. Adam and Satan are both mythological figures, but these myths were written tell a true story. Humanity does indeed fall away from its authentic essence into estrangement from others, estrangement from our own inner depths, and estrangement from the Awesome Almightiness we have named "God." This fall is not about immoral acts marring our biographical record sheet. "Sin" is about a tragic state of estrangement, bondage, or addiction to less than wholesome attitudes toward everything and everybody. From this tragic condition evil and immoral acts flow, but these acts are only symptoms of the disease called "sin." Acts are not the essence of sin. Sin is a condition of sickness in our Awe-capable lives. Sin is Aweless living, a living that is trapped in rationalism, moralism, sentimentalism, and other such escapes. Salvation meant rescue from these sicknesses.

What, then, is it like to be rescued from sin? And what part does Jesus play in this rescue now? Does emphasizing Jesus as savior mean that only Christians are rescued from sin? Does emphasizing Jesus as savior demean other religions? These are important questions for Christians and non-Christians alike to think through carefully. The following chart notes various aspects of estrangement from being our Spirit essence.

Estrangement	Spirit
Suspicion	Trust
Bondage	Freedom
Indifference	Compassion
Rationalism	Awe
Moralism	Awe
Sentimentalism	Awe
Despair	Hope
Despair	Peace
Despair	Joy
Despair	Bliss
Despair	Tranquility
Despair	Equanimity
Greed	Non-Clinging
Lust	Non-Clinging
Jealousy	Non-Clinging
Envy	Non-Clinging
Gluttony	Non-Clinging
Sloth	Engagement
Rage	Engagement
Pride	Singularity
in Adam	in Christ
in Eve	in Christina

I will comment briefly on the new terms in this chart. "In Christina" is a companion term for "in Eve" indicating that the head of the restored humanity, the model for authenticity is not male only. Perhaps whoever invented the name "Christina" believed that a woman can also be part of the Messianic life. "Non-Clinging" is a term stolen from

Buddhism which I believe is clearer than the terms "Detachment" or "Poverty" commonly used in Christian literature. Non-Clinging, properly understood, does not mean a disparagement of the human body nor of the finite world, but rather a recognition of the passing nature of all finite things and processes. "Engagement" means free obedience to our Awesome encounters in personal life and in the history of humanity. "Singularity" is a secular word for "chastity," for willing one thing–namely being the Awed One, being a Spirit person. The term "Pride" does not mean "self-affirmation" or "self-esteem." These are positive aspects of our compassion for self and others. In the context of Christian theology, the term "Pride" means the insistence on being a self-made self rather than finding authentic life in humble surrender to the "Singularity" of willing one thing–namely, being the Awed One or Spirit Being we already are.

Obviously, all the terms in this chart are material for a thousand chapters of reflection on our actual everyday experiences of Spirit and our escapes and rebellions from being Spirit. Rather than further illustrate these states, I want to focus on this question: "How do we move from the left column of this chart to the right column?" *How does salvation or healing take place?*

The following reflects my experience as well as the witness of contemporary Christian theologians such as Paul Tillich and ancient ones such as Paul, the Apostle. The healing of estrangement from Spirit is never an achievement but always a gift that is given through the action of the Awesome God of history, and this gift is given in the following manner:

(1) awakening our consciousness to specific sicknesses in our current flight or rebellion from Spirit being,

(2) assuring us of our welcome home to the life of health in spite of all our departures, and

(3) providing us the freedom to answer the call to embrace this restoration.

I. Let me illustrate the first of these three dynamics with some New Testament stories. These stories were remembered and told because they were healing stories. These stories may or may not reflect actual events in the life of the historical Jesus, but something like these stories was surely the sort of experience that people had in his presence.

> As the little company made its way along the road, a man said to him, "I'm going to follow you wherever you go." And Jesus replied, "Foxes have earths, birds have nests, but the Son of Man has nowhere that he can call his own."
>
> *(Luke 9:57-58; J. B. Phillips translation)*

Jesus gives this man the opportunity to notice whether or not he is truly wholehearted in his commitment to Spirit living. Jesus announces that following him will not provide the security that Jesus surmises this enthusiastic follower is seeking. Jesus is calling to this man's attention a specific Spirit issue: the need to give up old homes in order to enter the household of the Awed Ones. Whether the man acknowledged his sickness, accepted his welcome home to Spirit living, and followed Jesus we do not know. But if he did, this was salvation–that is, this was movement from the left column to the right column of the above chart.

> But he said to another man, "Follow me." And he replied, "Let me go and bury my father first." But Jesus told him, "Leave the dead to bury their own dead. You must come away and preach the Kingdom of God."
>
> *(Luke 9:59-60; J. B. Phillips translation)*

Jesus sees that this man's sickness is an attachment to family obligations. Salvation for him means turning that loose. Again, we don't know if he did, but salvation for him entailed seeing that issue, accepting his welcome home to Spirit centeredness, and choosing to walk that walk.

Another man said to him, "I am going to follow you, Lord, but first let me bid farewell to my people at home." But Jesus told him, "Anyone who puts his hand to the plow and then looks behind him is useless for the kingdom of God."

(Luke 9:61-62; J. B. Phillips translation)

Jesus calls this man to consider his specific Spirit issue. In this case, the man wants to make everybody he loves feel good about his decision to be a Spirit person. This is a violation of the wholeheartedness required for living the life of Awe. Again, we do not know whether this man received the gift Jesus handed him or not. But if he did, he became aware of his malady, noticed his forgiveness, and enacted a new life in obedience to that fresh awareness.

And while he was still saying this, a woman in the crowd called out and said, "Oh what a blessing for a woman to have brought you into the world and nursed you." But Jesus replied, "Yes, but a far greater blessing to hear the word of God and obey it."

(Luke 11:27-28; J. B. Phillips translation)

In this story Jesus does not deny the truth of what the woman says nor reject her enthusiasm. But he cuts through this woman's images of subservience and challenges her to be a Spirit woman herself and not simply an enabler of someone else. Her sin is not her vision of the greatness of Jesus, but her reluctance to see herself as greatness waiting to be enacted. Again, we do not know if she took this strong hint from Jesus, left behind her old images, received her welcome into the clan of Spirit, and thus did obey her calling to greatness. But if she did, this was salvation.

All four of these short stories emphasize *the first aspect of salvation (or healing)*: being made aware of a currently operating malady of escape or rebellion from Spirit.

II. The second aspect of salvation (or healing) is forgiveness. The parable of the prodigal son is one of the best illustrations in the New Testament of what forgiveness means. Forgiveness is pictured in this story as a welcome home to the Spirit life. I will not quote this well-known story, but if you have forgotten it, you can find it in Luke 15:11-32. What is not always noticed about this story is that it was told to scribes and Pharisees–that is, to a whole group of elder brothers who were offended by the very idea that a wretched slob who had wasted his life in debauchery could be welcomed home, could indeed be celebrated with a feast. Jesus implies with his biting story that the God of Moses and the prophets–the Awesome Otherness who gives us every event of our lives–is not like a record keeper of our immoralities who must enact correct punishments, but like a forgiving parent who rejoices to see each wayward son or daughter return home to the land of Awe.

Forgiveness is a very important theme at the center of the entire New Testament breakthrough. We miss its meaning, however, when we think of forgiveness as a blanket excuse for shoddy living. *Rather, forgiveness is step two in the defeat of our shoddy living; it is step two in our return to the land of Awe.* Accepting forgiveness is a challenge that costs us our pride in seeing ourselves as self-made persons who have achieved righteousness by our own efforts.

Forgiveness makes both our shame over our past and our pride in our past irrelevant. In forgiveness the past is set aside. It is no longer credit or discredit. It is still our past. It may be useful in instructing us how to live or not live our future. But as credit or discredit the past is taken away. In forgiveness the past no longer belongs to us. In truth, the past was always out of our control. The past is done; it is, in that sense, no longer our responsibility. The past is "out there" just as the trees and birds and earth and sky are out there. Forgiveness means a new relationship to our past; it is as if one were to say, "I wasted the first 40 years of my life, and the sky is blue." "I abused my children, and the sky is blue." "I have been a dictatorial tyrant, and the sky is blue." "I have been a milquetoast and allowed people to walk over me, and the sky is blue." Forgiveness allows us to be honest about our lives, including our deepest grief over our past living, and then to transcend that grief and have that past in an objective manner. I own my past with the same objectively that I own the sky.

Furthermore, *accepting forgiveness means accepting our present,* for the events of our past have brought us to this here and now with all its existing limitations and possibilities. In forgiveness, the circumstances in which we live are seen as good, wholesome, our one and only life. Our lives, with all their limitations and flaws, are seen as received or accepted. We are worthy of entering into the land of Awe at this very moment. Nothing in our current lives prevents us from manifesting in our very next acts the qualities of trust, freedom, compassion, and the other Spirit qualities in the right column of the above chart.

It is the deep truth that no one is essentially a person who wastes life, abuses children, or is a tyrant or milquetoast. Such pasts say nothing about who we essentially are. In our next actions we do not have to follow the patterns practiced in the past. So forgiveness is not only a statement about the past and the present: *it is also a statement about the future.* The future is open—that is, freedom is the essence of our existence, not bondage to the patterns we have practiced in the past. Yet bondage to those patterns is real, and that bondage is operative until we are aware of the bondage and notice that this very bondage is forgiven. We can only be free from the bondage of our past patterns when we have become aware of them and have also become aware that we are welcomed home to the land of Awe-filled Reality in spite of the patterns of bondage which have in the past blinded us and hobbled us.

Forgiveness is the dawning in our consciousness of what the New Testament repeatedly calls the "good news" or "gospel." This "news" this "Word of God" can be summarized in the following diagram.

All the pains and pleasures
of living are
good
for our Spirit

All the horrors and glories
of the past are
approved
for objective consideration

All the fears and hopes
for the future are
open possibilities
for our active living

All the weaknesses and
strengths of the self are
accepted
by the Ultimate Authority

This news, this gospel can be communicated in a thousand ways, but it amounts to a simple dawning: namely, that our lives, just as they are, are forgiven. Our lives are welcomed home to the Awe-filled life of human authenticity. One very simple step remains: to trust that this is so.

III. The third aspect of salvation (or healing) is accepting forgiveness. Accepting forgiveness is a decision that each forgiven person must make. This decision is not a wondrous achievement; it is simply a surrender to the way things already are. At the moment of accepting our forgiveness, we are already aware of particular maladies in our willingness to be Spirit. We are already aware that these maladies are forgiven. At the moment of accepting forgiveness, we are also aware that we are in our essential being the freedom to move forward in accepting and acting upon these awarenesses. In Christian tradition, doing this action is called "faith" or "trust." In doing trust we discover that trust is doable and healing.

So let us ask again, *"How does salvation happen?"* It begins to happen through some externally originating event in our lives. Perhaps it happens when our meditation practice cooks up a fresh awareness of the ways we are escaping from living our authentic life. Perhaps it happens when we are reading a book that audits our life in a way that is fresh and clear. Or perhaps we are caught in one of our fleeing tracks by a personal statement delivered to us by a Spirit teacher in our life.

At such moments, salvation can happen provided that dynamics two and three also happen. Dynamic two means that we notice our forgiveness by that Awesome Infinity in whose house we dwell. And dynamic three means that we accept this forgiveness and move into the future it indicates.

What sort of difference does accepting our forgiveness make in our actual living? This next New Testament story illustrates how forgiveness is related to love:

> Then one of the Pharisees asked Jesus to a meal with him. When Jesus came into the house, he took his place at the table and a woman, known in the town as a bad woman, found out that Jesus was there and brought an alabaster flask of perfume and stood behind him crying, letting her tears fall on his feet and then drying them with her hair. Then she kissed them and anointed them with the perfume. When the Pharisee who had invited him saw this, he said to himself, "If this man were really a prophet he would know who this woman is and what sort of a person is touching him. He would have realized that she is a bad woman."
>
> Then Jesus spoke to him, "Simon, there is something I want to say to you."
>
> "Very well, Master," he returned, "say it."
>
> "Once upon a time, there were two men in debt to the same money-lender. One owed him fifty pounds and the other five. And since they were unable to pay, he generously canceled both of their debts. Now, which one of them do you suppose will love him more?"

"Well," retuned Simon, "I suppose it will be the one who has been more generously treated."

"Exactly," replied Jesus, and then turning to the woman, he said to Simon, "You can see this woman? I came into your house but you provided no water to wash my feet. But she has washed my feet with her tears and dried them with her hair. There was no warmth in your greeting, but she, from the moment I came in, has not stopped covering my feet with kisses. You gave me no oil for my head, but she has put perfume on my feet. That is why I tell you, Simon, that her sins, many as they are, are forgiven; for she has shown me so much love. But the man who has little to be forgiven has only a little love to give."

Then he said to her, "Your sins are forgiven."
And the men at table with him began to say to themselves, "And who is this man, who even forgives sin?"

But Jesus said to the woman, "It is your faith that has saved you. Go in peace."
(Luke 7:36-50; J.B. Phillips translation)

The story clearly expresses that love or compassion flows from having been forgiven. The woman was aware of her estrangements (at least some of them). She was aware of her forgiveness as heard by her in the teachings and attitudes of Jesus. She loved him and all the rest of her life because she had accepted this forgiveness. As Jesus said, "It is your faith that has saved you." That is, her acceptance of her acceptance by the Awesome Forgiving Infinite Presence is what had turned the key in her life from fleeing Spirit to living Spirit, from fleeing Awe to being an Awed One.

In Simon's case, he would have had more compassion in his life if he had been more aware of his forgiveness. There is no reason to doubt that Simon was a righteous man in terms of the ways that he understood righteousness. But since he considered himself to be mostly righteous, he needed little forgiveness. Therefore, he had little love for Jesus or for this woman. But the very parable that Jesus told him was aimed to teach him something about himself that he did not know—namely, that in addition to his formal righteousness he was also a self-righteous bigot holding this woman in contempt rather than celebrating the transformation that her excessive behaviors were manifesting. The story does not say whether Simon accepted this opportunity for salvation. But if he did, then he was saved because: (1) he became aware of his bigotry and contempt, (2) he noticed that even this shameful attitude was forgiven, and (3) he accepted this forgiveness—that is, trusted in the forgiving God that Jesus loved and represented.

So again, how do we move from bondage to freedom, from darkness to enlightenment, from indifference to love, from sin to Holy Spirit? Spirit healing is never an achievement but always a gift that is given through the action of the Awesome God of history, and this gift is given in the following manner:

(1) awakening our consciousness to specific sicknesses in our current flight or rebellion from Spirit being,

(2) assuring us of our welcome home to the life of health in spite of all our departures, and

(3) providing us the freedom to answer the call to embrace this restoration.

While answering this call requires our action, even this answering action is a gift of the Awesome Otherness and not our achievement. It is our free act of trust that heals us. But this act of trust is not something we can boast about; it is not like believing a doctrine or obeying a moral precept. The act of trust (or faith) is a surrender to the Infinite Reality that has caught us in a "gracious grip."

And how is Jesus part of this rescue from sin both in the first century and now? Jesus is the Awed One, and it is the Awed One who (1) communicates to us the actuality of our Awelessness, (2) communicates to us the actuality of our forgiveness, and (3) beckons us to seize our freedom to trust in this forgiveness. I have illustrated these three dynamics with New Testament stories in order to show how the community who wrote the New Testament remembered Jesus' ministry of healing. But after Jesus' death, it was no longer the historical Jesus who was doing this ministry. It was his followers who remembered and used these stories about Jesus as well as new stories of their own to do the sorts of things that Jesus did. In this sense they had become Jesus; they were his resurrected body. They were the Awed Ones. Today it is still the Awed Ones in our lives who assist us to see our estrangements, assist us to become aware of our forgiveness, and who beckon us to the life of trust. All Awed Ones are in Jesus Christ. Even if the Awed One is a Buddhist teacher or a Muslim poet or a Native American shaman, that Awed One is in Jesus Christ. Jesus Christ symbolizes the all-inclusive healing event. As healing event, Jesus Christ is a cosmic dynamic that is everywhere present as the way Spirit healing takes place. Jesus, the historical person who lived and died in his place and time, manifested this cosmic dynamic and thereby revealed it to his followers. This is why they called him the Christ. He was the Messianic coming because he manifested the quality of Messianic aliveness and led others to manifest it as well.

Does emphasizing Jesus as savior mean that only Christians are rescued from sin? No, every religion that has survived the centuries has surely brought healing to the Spirit lives of many of its practitioners. Need we find this surprising? No. If the healing dynamic which took place through Jesus, the Christ, is indeed a cosmic dynamic, then this dynamic should be showing up in many different ways in many different places. And so it does.

Does emphasizing Jesus as savior demean other religions? No. Christianity remains one religion among the many. Christianity in all its forms is only one finite set of religions. And all the gifts and awarenesses of these Christian religions are limited. Christians always have much to learn from other religions. And by being loyal to a Christian lineage, Christians also bring gifts into the planet-wide interreligious dialogue. We have no more reason to demean Christianity than any other heritage. Every religious heritage has its perversions, and those perversions are surprisingly similar. Though religions differ greatly in their finite teachings and practices, in both their perversions and their wholesome expressions of Awe, we can discern extensive overlapping. So let those of us who have opted for a Christian practice treasure the worldwide diversity of religious expression. If as Christians we wish to excel, then let us seek to excel in being supportive of the gifts that each religion has to offer us and our planet.

Jesus, the Christ, as the Exemplar of Authenticity

Not only was Jesus remembered as a healer or savior, he was also fictionalized by the New Testament preachers and writers into a literary figure that was meant to exemplify the authentic life for Christian followers. We are all invited by this New Testament literature to identify with this fictionalized Jesus and embody his qualities in our living. We are invited to follow Jesus in the sense of being an Awed One who Awes others and does all else that Awed Ones do.

It may seem strange at first to identify with the Jesus we see on the pages of the New Testament, for this Jesus walks on water, commands the wind and the waves, heals all manner of sickness with a word or a touch, and even raises the dead. But if we remember that the Jesus on the pages of the New Testament is a literary figure, then we can identify with him even though these stories are fantastic fiction. Most of us have little difficulty identifying with Spiderman, Harry Potter, or Hermione Granger even though these literary figures do preposterous things. The literature of the New Testament takes the view that the ordinary facts of life are of no avail unless they are illuminated by Spirit. And for these creative New Testament writers, a lively expression of Spirit could only be expressed through a bold use of myth.

So let us look at the mythic story of Jesus as the story of the authentic human, the story of you and me if we choose to make it our story.

(1) Jesus is born. He is a part of the creation just like any other living being. Surely, we can identify with Jesus in being human.

(2) Jesus is born again. The story of his baptism expresses this. The story of his virgin birth also expresses this. Jesus is born through the power of the Infinite. The Gospel of John makes it plain that every authentic human being enters into "a virgin birth" of this very same nature. We must be born a second time to experience Spirit as a living actuality in our lives.

(3) Jesus is commissioned by his Spirit birth to be a mission of compassion to other human beings: healing their physical and emotional lives, advocating sociological justice, and calling individual persons into their Spirit birth. Living this commission in specific historical circumstances is also what it means to be a Spirit person.

(4) Jesus is sacrificed. His life is taken by the forces that do not wish to be healed. And Jesus gives himself willingly to this sacrifice. Indeed, he actively provokes the sick forces of his historical moment with the challenge to change, with the challenge to operate as Spirit beings, to be the authentic potentialities that human beings essentially are. So the sacrifice of Jesus is part of his mission from the start. This sacrifice does not support asceticism or a martyrdom complex. It supports the brash realism of knowing that authenticity powerfully lived will be rejected by most people and actively opposed by any established structure that feels threatened.

(5) Jesus is resurrected in a physical fashion. The worst his opponents can do is not enough to defeat him. He persists like an out-of-control plague. His new body is a community of people who are living in the very same way that he did. We have been taught that the resurrection was some kind of miracle that happened to the corpse of Jesus. But in the actual resurrection narratives of the New Testament, resurrection is not told as a happening to Jesus of Nazareth. No one interviews Jesus on what it was like to be dead or anything of the sort. The resurrection appearances are told as happenings that happen to the disciples of Jesus. Jesus appears to his community. He walks and talks and eats with this community. Indeed, the community claims in a myriad of ways that they have become one with Jesus. Indeed, they have become Jesus. THEY ARE HIS BODY. So when they fictionalize Jesus they are simply expressing in this fiction their own lives as persons who have been "Jesusized."

(6) Jesus ascends into heaven. This myth, understood in its context, is not about going into superspace. The ascension story is simply reaffirming where the authentic human came from in the first place. The authentic human comes from the Infinite; and after being killed and raised again to bodily life, the authentic human still comes from the Infinite. And the authentic human will continue to come from the Infinite until the end of time. The return of Jesus is not a return from some other world next door. The return of Jesus is the expectation that the authentic human being will eventually, indeed inevitably, win the day in actual human history. Such story telling is about an actuality in our lives: you and I (insofar as we are authentic human beings) are on the winning side in the major conflicts of history. Authenticity shall win because it is authenticity and because authenticity is powered by the Infinite. The sickness of not being our authentic being is a fragile, foolish thing, however strong and well established it might seem to be. It is understandable that the earliest Christians hoped that the authentic human would return very soon and that the existing evil state of

humanity would be no more in their own lifetimes. Nevertheless, when it took 500 years for the Roman Empire to finish collapsing, they did not give up their hope. They grasped the opportunity to build Christendom. When Christendom turned evil as well, they did religious orders and reformations and great awakenings and revivals and renewals. And here are we, after almost 2000 years of Christian action, still facing a deeply estranged humanity. It can perhaps be said that evil is as strong as it ever was. Nevertheless, the authentic followers of Jesus still expect to win in the battle with evil–expect to win here on Earth, expect Jesus to come in planetary fullness, and for evil to be no more in the life of any human being or any human institution. And this hope is possible because in our essence we are all Jesus. We are, each of us, the authentic human being. We do not have to evolve into some other life form; we have only to stop running away from being the life form we already are.

These six themes characterize the story that Christians who know their story tell about being a Spirit person. According to this story, experiencing our Spirit-being includes experiencing all these Awesome yet ordinary things: being born, being born again, being commissioned to live this rebirth in active compassion for other humans, enduring sacrifices because of this commission, being resurrected, and being on the winning side of history. Each element of this story is part of what it looks like to breathe the Infinite, to be the offspring of the Divine, to be Spirit, to be an expression of authentic humanity. In the language of this chapter, the Jesus stories picture what it looks like to be the Awed Ones in history.

But I have not yet told the whole story, for the whole story also contains the disciples of Jesus and the enemies of Jesus. We are not just Jesus. We are also the disciples of Jesus. We are naive, foolish, Spirit dumb-dumbs who need to be illuminated, healed, encouraged, and shown how to be Spirit persons. We ask dumb questions. We frustrate the authentic person with our blindness, powerlessness, slowness, and impulsiveness. We go to sleep when the going gets roughest. Under pressure we deny that we ever had anything to do with dangerously authentic humans. We betray authentic humanity into the hands of its enemies with lies and kisses.

We are also the enemies of Jesus. We accuse the authentic human of not fitting into the standards of stability and security we hold dear. We try to trap the authentic human in contradictions. We throw rocks. We stir up animosity against authentic humanity. We wash our hands of the whole affair. We allow and/or carry out attempts to put an end to the historical presence of any successful leader of authentic humanness.

We may also be those disciples or those enemies of Jesus who repent: who, over and over, acknowledge our estrangements, receive forgiveness, and experience the healing of being restored to the authenticity from which we have fallen. Healing the human Spirit is part of the Jesus story.

This Christian story, embodied in the fictionalized historical person Jesus, is an important contribution to the religious treasury of the planet. It is not better than other religious stories, but it can tell us things about being a human being that we may never learn elsewhere. But, however distinctive it may be, the Christian story is not the only story that tells about being Spirit beings. There is no end to what we can learn about Spirit from Shamanic antiquity, from the Goddess heritages, from Hinduism, Buddhism, and Taoism, as well as Judaism, Islam, and many other traditions. In spite of the boundlessness of all these resources, the Christian story has additional wisdom to teach us about being the Spirit beings we are. The Christian story provides its own special benefit to those who choose to enter into its wonders.

I will conclude by telling one more small piece of the Christian story and briefly indicate its Spirit depth. This is my telling of the story in Matthew 15:24-32. The disciples of Jesus are out on a lake in a boat rowing hard for the land. The wind and the waves are against them. But then they see a figure coming towards them walking on the water of the lake. They cry out in fear, "It's a ghost!" But the figure responds, "No, it's just me." They see then that it is indeed "just Jesus." (It is just an authentic human walking on the wild and stormy waters of life.)

"Well, if it is really you," says Peter, "Ask me to walk on the wild and stormy water."
"Come on, then," says Jesus.

And Peter does step down from the boat and walks on the wild and stormy waters of life. But when he realizes what he is doing, when he sees more clearly just how wild and stormy life can be, he panics and begins to sink.

But Jesus reaches out a hand and catches him, and chastises him, "What made you lose your faith like that?"

In order to appropriate this story as the Spirit story it was written to be, we have to ask ourselves such questions as these: What are the wild and stormy waters of our own lives? What would it mean for us to walk on these waters? What is our boat? Where do we feel safe? Why do we feel safe there? Why do we not trust walking the walk that the authentic person walks? Why do we fear the authentic person? What does it mean to say that the authentic person is not a ghost but real like us? What does it mean to stand in our boat and hear the beckoning words, "Come on, then"? When have we experienced stepping down from the boat? Yes, when indeed have we actually walked on the water? And why do we lose our trust that we can do this? Why do we sink? And what does it mean for some authentic human in our external community or in our interior council of "saints" to reach out a hand and catch us?

Each of these questions can drag out of us a whole lake of Awe. Each line in this one story is a boundless resource for becoming the Spirit beings that we are. Every line of the Christian story is such a boundless resource. So, as we consider the vast religious treasury of the planet, let us also consider the gifts of the Christian story. Let us see if we can hear Jesus saying to us, "Come on, then."

And let us further understand that in following Jesus we become Jesus. If others become aware that we are indeed walking on the wild waters of Awe-filled life, if they call out to us from their safe boats of stodgy doctrines and binding moralities, if they ask to join us in walking on the water of the lake, let's say to them in any way we can, "Come on, then."

5.

Mind, Consciousness, Personality, and Spirit

Again and again, I have been challenged to think through how the call of the Awe is related to the challenge to think more clearly, to become more conscious, and to become more psychologically healthy. These four journeys are closely related, for they all take place in the same person. It is also true that Spirit can be distinguished from these other three journeys. Becoming a person who thinks for oneself and thinks clearly is not the same thing as experiencing Awe. Becoming more conscious is not the same thing as becoming more identified with the wind of Spirit. And becoming more functional and strong as a human personality is not the same thing as becoming a mature Spirit being.

In order to deal with these topics it is important to define in experiential terms what we are pointing to in our lives with the words "mind," "consciousness," "personality," and "Spirit." So this is how I will proceed in this chapter. I have constructed four major sections, each devoted to one of these four words. Until I return in the fourth section to the topic of Spirit, this will be a philosophical inquiry leaning on both the scientific knowledge and the contemplative wisdom that have so far come my way. Readers who are primarily interested in the call of the Awe may find these next three sections to be a diversion from the topic of Awe or Spirit. If this is so for you, simply skip to the section on Spirit. Other readers may find the sections on mind, consciousness, and personality to be helpful in sorting out the place of Spirit in human life. This careful sorting has been important to me in my journey, so I want to share it with anyone who might also find it helpful.

1. What is Mind?

The word "mind" is used in many different ways. Some define "mind" to mean the whole of our inner being. I will use the word "mind" to point to only part of our inner being. I will use the word "mind" to mean nothing more and nothing less than our own inward experience of our own biological brains and nervous systems. I will use mind to mean the inward experience of our biological intelligence. Human mind or intelligence is part of our wild nature. It is never fully civilized, domesticated, or characterized by social conditioning. Human thinking occurs within the human society to which we belong, and it is profoundly conditioned by that society. Nevertheless, human intelligence remains a biological process. And like all biological processes, human intelligence is a mystery that our ordering minds cannot fully fathom.

Dealing with the question "What is mind?" is a stretch, because it entails thinking about thinking itself. Confusions can overwhelm us when we are attempting to think about the very process we are using to think with. But recognizing the possible insanity of this quest, I press on to linguistically describe a biological process of which linguistic thinking is one significant but small part.

We usually associate the human mind with order and with bringing order out of chaos. If we are strongly influenced by idealistic philosophies, we may even believe that the human mind participates in a realm of order separate from the realm of matter. I don't agree with that view. I am presenting the view that the human mind is a down-and-dirty biological process right along with eating and breathing and other life-enhancing processes.

I also feel that I must do battle with the widespread notion that there is a fundamental separation between mind and matter. This false polarization has enabled humans to exalt thinking humanity over the "lesser" realm of matter. From this perverse perspective, all that is not thought, not rational, not meaningful in a rational sense, is seen as inferior or evil or even unreal. Such a view of the human mind claims to support virtuous living, but I believe it supports tyranny over the natural world as well as tyranny over our own biological beings. It also supports tyranny over other human beings who are not rational in the same way that we "true" thinkers are rational. Separating mind and matter is a delusion to start with, and it also raises the question of whose "mind" we are talking about.

The human mind is indeed the master of order. Consider the human creativity that has gone into those ever-unfolding libraries of mathematics. Further, it is remarkable that our mathematics can be so extensively congruent with the natural world. Yet however remarkable these ordering capacities are, the human mind is still part of the finite world of evolving, birthing, and dying processes. The human mind does not stand apart from everything else. The human mind is completely immersed in biological reality

When we focus our consciousness on the surrounding world, we find that our bodies are part of that world and that our bodies have brains and nervous systems that can be correlated with our inward experiences. In the surrounding world, few things are as complex as the functioning of our own brains and nervous systems. When we study the human mind from the inside, we also confront ever-unfolding intricacies. Our minds are a depth of reality that is indeed unfathomable to our thinking processes.

Furthermore, our uniquely human mind is but the latest layer of mental functioning in a very long process of mental evolution. The story of the human mind begins with the capacity of those very first single-celled living forms to sense their surroundings and creatively respond to them. The emergence of life from inanimate matter was also the birth of intelligence.

Mind as the Wild Intelligence of the Animal Body

The layers of intelligence that the evolution of life has built are much more complex than can be described in a thousand books. For the purpose of this limited discussion, I am suggesting this simple model: human life has evolved five basic layers of intelligence. This model is not intended to be a complete analysis, but more like an art form which expresses my main point–namely, that the human mind is a layered reality extending back to the origins of life itself. I will describe these five layers of intelligence beginning with what I believe to be the most primitive and then move toward the most recently evolved.

P & P intelligence	The wisdom of avoiding pain and seeking pleasure
Sensory intelligence	The senses (light, sound, smell, taste, etc.) letting the outer in
Image-using intelligence	The ability to remember the past and anticipate the future
Emotional intelligence	The ability to recognize interior states in living beings
Symbol-using intelligence	The ability to abstract groupings of sense-grounded images

All five of these layers of intelligence are now inseparable parts of one complex human brain or mind, but these layers have come into being in evolutionary stages. I will briefly illustrate each layer of intelligence with examples from both animal and human life.

P & P Intelligence

The intelligence to avoid pain and seek pleasure is the most fundamental layer of living wisdom. It was already in operation in the most ancient single-celled living being. P & P intelligence also operates in human beings. We seek nourishment and the pleasure of living, and we avoid pain. For amoeba and human alike, the capacity to avoid pain and seek pleasure is wisdom and requires intelligence.

Sensory Intelligence

Perhaps the outer membrane of the bacteria was the first sense organ, but sensory intelligence, as I want to use that term, flourished with the evolution of the eye and the ear and the smell nodes and the taste buds. Animal life came to be more aware of its environment through all of these complex sensors. This was an advance in intelligence. This was an opening outward into wisdom about the surrounding world through letting that surrounding world in through these informative portals. In relation to smell recognition a dog is much more intelligent than humans. Geese and other migratory animals probably have a sense of direction that is superior to humans. In hand-eye coordination humans are very intelligent.

Image-Using Intelligence

The senses alone would have produced only a blur of meaningless signals if animal intelligence had not also evolved images. By "images" I mean the capacity of the animal mind to store experiences like little movies that can be rerun as needed. These little movies are complete with all the senses: sight, sound, smell, taste, pain, and pleasure. As an animal experiences its current situation through its senses, these little

movies rerun, thus informing the animal of what it has learned in previous experiences of the same sort. Somehow animal intelligence is able
to keep straight three types of imaginal movies: (1) those that have
already happened (memory), (3) those that are currently happening
(the present), and (3) those that may happen next (anticipation).

This basic wonder of image-using intelligence is illustrated by a dog
running and catching a Frisbee in its teeth. The dog's mind has to
remember where the Frisbee was and anticipate where the Frisbee
might go next in order to decide in the present moment where to move
in order for teeth and Frisbee to arrive at the same spot at the same
time. This amazing performance takes place without any use of language or other symbol-using intelligence. The dog just uses images in
accomplishing this. It uses images to accomplish all its other amazing
feats of intelligence. These images operate like little movies in its mind.
They are products of the biological brain. They are mental images.

Human beings also possess this image-using level of intelligence.
The famous baseball player Yogi Berra, so I have heard, claimed that
when he stepped up to the plate to bat a baseball, he did not think; he
just batted. I take this to mean that Yogi used his image-using intelligence to bat a baseball and avoided letting his symbol-using intelligence get in the way. When it comes to batting a baseball, linguistic
thinking is quite secondary. Mostly, what a batter needs to do is watch
the ball into the bat using that fast-acting, imaginal-memory and
imaginal-anticipation intelligence that we humans share with dogs and
cats and other animal species.

Human intelligence at the imaginal level differs very little from that
of all the other mammals. Imaginal intelligence does not use language
or other symbols, but it is a very important layer of our human mental
functioning. We could not walk up a flight of stairs without it. And as
we shall see, imaginal mental functioning is foundational for all later
forms of intelligence, and it is essential for the healthy functioning of
these later forms.

Emotional Intelligence

With the term "emotional intelligence" I am pointing to a capacity that became well developed in mammalian life–the capacity to discern the inward states in other animals. If this capacity exists at all in reptiles, it is very rudimentary. Reptiles do not bond with their own young, and they are not able to read human states of being or to bond with humans as mammals often do. An alligator can only see a human swimmer as food; a dolphin can see this swimmer as a living being with inward states. Emotional bonding and emotional relatedness indicate a form of intelligence. Contemporary research has located this capacity in a distinct part of the animal brain. This brain development is often called the middle brain or limbic brain. Mammals have developed an enlarged middle brain.

Even before a human infant learns to talk or to use symbols in any way, the infant is surprisingly intelligent in reading emotional states in the other humans who are caring for it. The ability to recognize faces and the meaning of facial expressions is amazingly well developed in the very young infant. Both scientific experiments and our common involvements with infants bear this out.

All mammals have this capacity. I saw a female dog with three puppies leave the pups to chase another animal away. The pups wanted to follow, but the mother turned toward them with a facial expression and a sharp sound that stopped the pups in their tracks. They did not move again until she indicated it was all right. Such bonding and communication do not occur in the life of a snake.

Emotional intelligence in the lives of adult humans is very important in our relationships with others, in our decision-making, and in our full appreciation and appropriation of the world about us. Adults whose limbic brains have been damaged have great difficulty making decisions or being present to other people. They may be functional on the reptilian level and in their use of language, but their life of emotional connectedness is gone. Such unfortunate persons demonstrate how important feelings and feeling intuitions are to the overall intelligence of human beings.

Symbol-Using Intelligence

The term "symbol-using intelligence" points to the most recent layer of the human brain and mind development. In writing this book I am using my symbol-using intelligence. I use symbol-using intelligence to do this thinking about thinking and to tell these stories about the whole domain of animal intelligence. Language is the most prominent form of symbol-using that humans do. But symbol using also includes the creation of music, paintings, sculpture, dance, architecture, and the various combinations of these presentational arts with language—such as song, drama, story, and poem. Symbol using is a vast topic not easily summarized in a few paragraphs, but the essence of symbol using is grouping together bundles of images into abstract mental forms. By "abstract" I mean moving a step away from immediate sensory experience. Abstracting is a mental process that creates distance from those more direct experiences of life which use the imaginal rerun and prerun processes.

This movement toward abstraction can mean getting lost in our minds and thus losing touch with our sensations of experienced reality. But abstraction can also expand and deepen our experience of reality. When we use our symbol-using intelligence effectively, we do not lose touch with our imaginal reruns and preruns. Rather, we keep returning to the imaginal level of intelligence with wider perspectives on living our lives.

Here is an elementary example of what I mean by "symbol." The abstract number "four" is a mental entity that no dog ever contemplated even though the concrete image of four puppies or four bones or four chairs might have played a role in some dog's life. But what the dog does not do (which humans do easily) is notice that there is a common quality in four puppies, four bones, and four chairs, which is also applicable to four days, four years, and four stars. "Four" is not an image; it is a symbol, an abstraction lifted from many images. Human beings can play with these abstractions, create amazing patterns of order, and then apply these highly evolved bits of order back into their practical lives.

Symbol-using intelligence enables human beings to create their social fabrics. Social fabrics are symbols organized into practical patterns of expected operation. All cultural forms, political modes, and economic systems are products of human symbol-using intelligence. Perhaps I have said enough to indicate the distinctness and the importance of this form of intelligence that has evolved in the human being.

One Overall Mind

All five of these forms of intelligence operate simultaneously in each human being. These forms enrich each other. They overlap and unite with each other. You or I experience having one mind, not five; nevertheless these five types of intelligence are like layers laid down in our human biology over billions of years. I have used my symbol-using intelligence to build this model of intelligence, but intelligence itself is far more vast than my symbol-using intelligence can fathom.

So how do these forms of intelligence relate to consciousness? It seems obvious that each new layer of intelligence, as it evolved, enabled more consciousness in the individual animal. The human is clearly more conscious than the fish.

There is a close relationship between these five forms of intelligence and the evolution of consciousness; nevertheless, intelligence is not synonymous with what I will point to with the word "consciousness." Furthermore, the five forms of intelligence go on unconsciously as well as consciously. On the one hand, the five forms of intelligence blend into the unconscious body. On the other hand, the five forms of intelligence enable and enrich consciousness.

"Mind," as I have defined this word, points to our conscious experience of these layers of animal intelligence that characterize our biological bodies.

2. What is Consciousness?

Next, what do we mean by "consciousness"? When we sit quite still and observe the experience of experiencing, we can witness our body operating and our mind thinking. In the deepest sort of stillness, we can notice that we are related to the rest of reality through these functionings of our own body and mind. Mind and body are like an ever-active ring of processes on the inside of which we conscious beings somehow sit. We are aware of mind and body. And we are aware of a surrounding world beyond our mind and our body. We are aware that we are aware. Here is a visual picture of what I have just said.

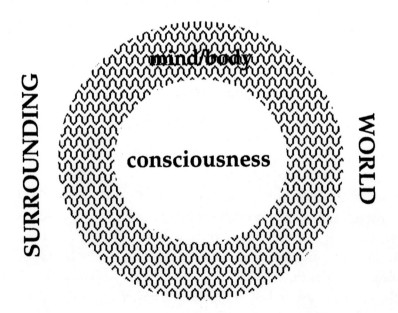

Let "consciousness" be the word we use to point to our centered awareness. Let us associate with "consciousness" and "awareness" two other helpful words, "attentiveness" and "intentionality." Attentiveness is consciousness in its passive mode. Intentionality is consciousness in its active mode. We can be attentive to our thinking mind and simply watch it think, or we can intend to think in self-chosen directions. We can be attentive to the processes of our body and simply watch them function, or we can intend for our body to move in self-chosen directions. Both attentiveness and intentionality characterize our consciousness.

Our powers of intentionality are not absolute; we cannot intend our bodies to fly or to never grow old and die. We cannot intend our minds to think whatever we want them to think. Our minds are like wild animals with their own vast uncontrollable energies. Clearly, our control over our own mind is limited. Similarly, the powers of our attention are not absolute. We cannot pay attention to everything at the same time. We cannot pay attention to anything all the time. We even shut down our attending consciousness entirely and sleep a number of hours every day.

Our consciousness of the surrounding world takes place through the ever-active processes of our mind and body. Consciousness is only directly conscious of the inward processes of mind/body, but these mind/body processes are amazingly good at enabling us to know the surrounding world and to perform meaningfully within it.

As the diagram suggests, we experience three processes going on simultaneously: consciousness, mind/body, and the surrounding world. These three processes are distinguishable, yet they are also inseparable aspects of one overall process of actuality.

So what is consciousness? Consciousness is that centered "you" or "me" that is doing the experiencing.

Consciousness as the Essence of Biological Aliveness

I want to further define "consciousness" as the awake quality of being alive. We experience this wakefulness, this attentiveness, this decision-making intentionality as some sort of "I" who lives inside this vibrant ring of energetic mind/body processes.

We might say, then, that "consciousness" is that factor within living beings that makes living living. A rock does not manifest consciousness; an amoeba does. The amoeba is sensitive to its environment and makes unpredictable or creative responses to that environment. These behaviors are manifestations of consciousness. Consciousness, so defined, is clearly manifest in all simple and complex animal forms. And are plants conscious? Are fungi conscious? Their consciousness is certainly harder for an animal like me to discern or to identify with. Their sensitivities are different from mine, and their responsiveness is slow compared to my constant movement. An amoeba seems more conscious to me than a plant, but I intend to watch and see if my houseplants and garden plants are watching me. Living beings are composed of physical stuff, but the alive part of living beings is impossible to understand with only the concepts of physics.

Yet the fact that consciousness has no physical explanation does not mean that it is part of some second realm of reality. Consciousness is not a lost spark from some supernatural world. Consciousness is a finite actuality. Consciousness even gets tired and needs to sleep. Apparently, consciousness requires energy to remain awake. While consciousness plays a significant role in integrating all the layers of intelligence into a doable practical life, consciousness is also rather lazy. Consciousness is content to let the body automatically do all the good stuff the body will do without needing effort from consciousness. Consciousness comes into play when situations arise that require decisions to be made. Some of these decisions are very serious, having to do with survival itself. Other decisions are not so serious. Consciousness can be unserious, simply playful, enjoying the pleasure of being attentive and being able to make things happen. Consciousness is the capacity to pay attention and the capacity to initiate responses. As such, consciousness is the central hub of being alive.

While consciousness is present in all living forms, in human beings we see consciousness attending to consciousness itself. We see consciousness choosing to be more conscious. We also observe conscious human beings deciding to be less conscious–deciding to go back to sleep. We can see conscious human beings deciding to suppress certain "painful awarenesses" from conscious view. Having done so, consciousness is no longer conscious of the awarenesses it once had. Yet mysteriously, those old awarenesses have not entirely gone away; they persist and threaten to break back into the awareness of the consciousness that has rejected them.

The non-human species do not seem to be blessed with (nor afflicted by) these uniquely human intensifications of consciousness. This human increase in consciousness came into being along with our symbol-using intelligence. It seems obvious to me that the consciousness of consciousness, with all its gifts and perversions, could not have come into being without the enablement of symbol-using intelligence. Nevertheless, consciousness is not synonymous with intelligence, and the consciousness of consciousness is not synonymous with symbol-using intelligence. Consciousness is that enigmatic aliveness within living organisms.

Yet consciousness is not an infinite actuality. The fact that we can speak of becoming "more conscious" or "less conscious" means that consciousness is finite. Something infinite cannot be qualified by less or more. If consciousness were infinite, we could not speak of consciousness becoming more or less conscious. "Spirit," as I am using this word, points to a relationship with the Infinite Presence. So Spirit is not the same dynamic as consciousness. We can become conscious of Spirit, but consciousness of Spirit is not Spirit. But before I look further at Spirit and at how Spirit differs from consciousness, I want to reflect on the subject of personality.

3. What is Personality?

Personality in a human being is a set of habits created by our conscious and intelligent functioning. We may be inclined toward developing certain qualities of personality by our genetic foundations, but these tendencies are given their functional shape by the choices made during our life history. Personality is a complex tangle of habits constructed and practiced over and over by the individual whose personality we are considering.

As personalities we are changing realities. In spite of the continuities that we can discern in our personalities, we can also discern that we are constantly becoming different. The personality I was decades ago may seem almost laughable to the personality that I have now become. And the personality I now am is still changing. Each and every choice I make adds or subtracts from the habits that make my personality what it is. As personality I am in a constant state of becoming.

The Buddha was focusing on this arena when he spoke of giving up our identity with our personality and finding enlightenment in the experience of "no-self." We may have difficulty with this notion of "no self," for we clearly experience our inward reality as characterized by some particular set of personality habits. We know that this tangle of personality habits is not going to simply disappear. The Buddhist experience of enlightenment is not actually about getting rid of our personality; it is about not identifying with our personality. This Buddhist teaching is not very different from the Christian teaching that says, "He who finds his life will lose it, and he who loses his life for my sake will find it." (Matthew 10:39 Revised Standard Version) We might restate this biblical saying as: "She who thinks her personality is her real self will lose the self she thinks she is, but she who loses her personality in following the Awed Ones will find her actual Spirit self."

Yet, after one has identified with "no-self" or "Spirit-self," the personality still exists. *The difference is that we are now detached or non-clinging in our relationship to our own personality.* The patterns of our personality no longer glorify us nor despairingly embarrass us. The constant changing in our personality no longer fills us with boundless dread. The fact that our personality, like all finite things, is passing away no longer concerns us in an ultimate way. Why is this so? Because we are no longer identified with our personality, we have become Spirit. Spirit is who we are. Personality is just one of the passing parts of our ever-changing finite life.

As Spirit selves we will still love our feet, our fingernails, and our personalities. We will care for them and have compassion for them. We may try to have attractive fingernails. We may put our feet in comfortable shoes. We may work to become the sort of personalities that can best communicate with others. These considerations bring us back to our primary question: What is Spirit?

4. What is Spirit?

"Spirit" is often used to point to another realm of existence alongside this ordinary natural realm. This understanding creates a gulf between the world of spirit and the world of matter. Picturing such a gulf brings confusion into our entire thinking about Spirit. I want to avoid the supernatural metaphor in this discussion of Spirit.

"Relationship with the Infinite" is the basic metaphor I have been using in this book to talk about Spirit. But the word "spirit" is also being used in our culture to point to finite processes. Sometimes "spirit" is used to point to a particular quality or stage of consciousness. Sometimes "spirit" means the human capacity to be energetic or disciplined or civilized. I want to avoid using the word "Spirit" to point to finite processes. I want to talk about Spirit with a capital "S." I want to make clear that Spirit breathes Infinite relatedness. I want to depict Spirit as wild and uncivilized. Such a view of Spirit is not new. Human beings have been talking about Spirit in this way since the

dawn of human consciousness. Until "Spirit" is understood as relationship with the Infinite, the Bible and Christian heritage cannot be
meaningful to us.

All our grand religious words are understood only when they are
rooted in our actual experience of our relationship with the Infinite
Presence. "Freedom," "trust," "compassion," "tranquility," "bliss," "joy,"
"equanimity," "peace"–each of these words is understood only when it is
filled with consciousness of our relatedness to the Infinite Presence. Too
often we use these grand words to indicate some form of finite intelligence or some finite state of consciousness. When we use these religious
words to point to finite processes, we are not talking about Spirit with a
capital "S."

Spirit is not the mind or a state of consciousness or a quality of personality. Spirit is not some longed for final orderliness arriving to bless
our chaos-ridden lives. Spirit is nothing we can measure or own. Spirit
is like a wind that blows through mind/body and through consciousness causing these finite processes to shake and move like leaves on a
tree. Like wind, the Bible says, we don't know where Spirit comes from
or where it is going.

Spirit is Awe. And as I have illustrated in earlier chapters, "Awe" happens in our lives when consciousness becomes conscious of the
EVERY-THING-NESS in which all things cohere and of the NO-
THING-NESS out of which all things come and to which all things
return. We humanly conscious beings can become aware of Mystery.
We can stand in a relationship with an Infinite Actuality that we can
neither understand nor control with any aspect of our vast intelligence. To our amazing yet limited minds, the experience of being finite
is itself a mystery beyond all comprehension. And this experience of
being finite, of being inescapably limited, includes experiencing the
Presence of that Actuality which is limiting us and thus rendering us
finite. Our conscious experience of being finite is also our conscious
experience of the Infinite Presence. Our minds may faint in their

attempts to understand such statements, but our consciousness knows that such statements are true.

As a conscious being who is conscious of consciousness and conscious of the fact that my consciousness is finite, I discover that I am a living relationship with the Infinite. This "relationship" is a two-way movement. I am encountering the Infinite Presence moving toward me, and I am responding to the Infinite Presence with movement of my own initiation. "Relationship" means encounter and response. The Infinite Presence is encountering me, and I am responding to this encounter with the Infinite Presence. So understood, human living is an I-Thou dialogue.

Let me be quick to remind us that "I-Thou" is a metaphor or symbol. Literally speaking, the Infinite Presence is not a "Thou," not a big person in the sky. "Thou" means that the "Spirit I" is in a personal dialogue with the Infinite Presence, a Presence that is trusted and thus a Presence toward which the "Spirit I" is open and responsive.

Having this relationship with the Infinite Presence is not optional; it is a given necessity. This relationship is not a belief I was taught in church. This relationship is just the WAY IT IS—or perhaps it would be better to say "the WAY IT MOVES." The Infinite and I are dialogue partners. In my part of this dialogue I may reject, hate, or flee being a participant in this cosmic conversation, but the Infinite does not stop "talking" to me. I exist, willingly or unwillingly, in the grip of the Infinite Presence.

All speech about the Infinite stretches beyond our ordinary uses of human speech. Nevertheless, by using the metaphors of relationship or dialogue I can speak of my encounters with this Infinite Presence and I can speak of my responses to this Infinite Presence. I can say that I "hear" the Infinite "speaking" to me in the events of my life. I can depict my conscious responses as "talking back" to that Infinite Silence that is "talking" to me. This "hearing" and "talking" is Spirit. In some Eastern teachings, Spirit Being and the Infinite Presence are seen as identical.

But in the Western Bible-based religions, Spirit Being is not seen as identical with the Infinite Presence. Spirit is relationship or dialogue with the Infinite Presence.

In our attempts to say what we mean by "the Infinite Presence," we can only speak in paradoxical terms. The Infinite Presence is a Silence that speaks to us in all the sounds and silences of our lives. The Infinite Presence is a Light that shines through all darkness and light. The Infinite Presence is the Unmanifest that is manifest in all manifestations.

Similarly, we can speak of Spirit only in metaphorical and paradoxical terms. All our talk about Spirit is speech about something that the human mind cannot fathom.

Personality and the Tabletop of Spirit

Though talking about Spirit is a stretch, Spirit is not alien to human nature. Spirit is the essence of human nature. Spirit is the Essential Person. Spirit is the "real me." Spirit is who every person is whether he or she has become aware of it or not.

When we think of Spirit as alien, we are viewing Spirit from the perspective of our finite personality. In this section I will attempt to view personality from the perspective of Spirit. In order to do this let us imagine a large tabletop, so large it stretches to the horizons. Let this tabletop represent our Essential Person or Spirit. Next, let us imagine that on this tabletop a child is building a stack of blocks. This child, you or I, is using blocks of experience to build its personality. The stack of blocks represents the personality.

By the age of three or so, each of us has put together the main outline of the personality that will be our characteristic personality for the rest of our lives. These first layers of personality habits have been put together without great consciousness; nevertheless, energies from the Spirit tabletop have been used to put this personality together. Genetic endowments, social conditions, parental presence have influenced this building; nevertheless, the child in you and me has built this personality with freedom accessed from the Spirit tabletop.

The building of personality continues throughout adolescence and adulthood. As further layers of personality habits are added, consciousness of the process increases. At some point our consciousness begins to create an image of the self we take ourselves to be. How does this come about? Let us imagine that each of these blocks of experience has two ends. On one end is printed "object" and on the other end is printed "self." Each block is actually a little drama, a story, a dialogue. There is the I-breast dialogue, the I-mother dialogue, the I-father dialogue and so forth. All these blocks of dialogue are memories, stored packets of experience. Our personality is a building built out of such blocks.

So what is our self-image? Our image of our self comes about when our conscious mind forms a gestalt of the "self" ends of these blocks of experience that comprise our personality. This self-image is then assumed to be "me," my "ego," my "core self." But let us notice what the self-image actually is. It is a mental picture made from a large collection of memories. The self-image is not the ACTUAL SELF that is operating in the living here and now. The full self, the true self, is a more vast and mysterious actuality.

Each of us tends to get trapped in the delusion that "my" self-image or "my" personality or "my" view of "my" personality is the sum total of "me." But this is not so. The real self is the Spirit tabletop, not the little block building, the personality we have constructed during our lifetime. Nor is our real self the self-image that we ourselves have made from our personality structure of memories. Our real self is a big surprise. In the first instance, the Spirit tabletop appears to each of us as a big surprise. The Spirit tabletop has always been the real me; but before consciousness of this tabletop of Spirit happens to us, we do not realize the full grandeur of who we are. Particularly shocking may be the realization that we are the freedom that has built and is continuing to build the personality that we assume to be ourselves. This freedom is not part of the habits of personality: it is the capacity to build further personality and the capacity to take a relationship to the personality we have already built.

Freedom is part of the tabletop of Spirit along with compassion, trust, expansiveness, equanimity, tranquility, courage, joy, and many other Spirit gifts. When we first begin to experience the tabletop of Spirit we experience a type of emptiness or void. We become aware of the fragility and limitations of our personality. We are becoming aware that our personality is not actually "I" but only something "I" have built and am building. This can be terrifying. As we begin to give up our customary self-images and begin to identify with the tabletop as the "real me," we experience this emptiness turning into a vastness or expansiveness. We realize that we are far more than we thought we were. If we open to this profoundly larger "me," this discovery can be exhilarating and strengthening, and our original fear can be seen as a petty trauma of our finite personality rather than a concern of the "real me."

At some point in the journey of becoming conscious of our Spirit Being, a huge shift takes place. At first we experience ourselves as a personality having Spirit experiences. Awe happens to us, like an invasion from some other planet. *But when we begin to significantly shift our sense of identity from our personality to the Spirit tabletop, then we cease to be a personality to whom Spirit is happening and become instead a Spirit Being who has a personality*. This shift is the shift from being a Spirit novice to being a Spirit adept.

But after this shift, our journey of Spirit maturity is not over. A new and perhaps even more troubling journey begins! We experience our personality being boiled in the oil of Spirit. The fantasies we have built into our personality are vaporized. The defenses we have built into our personalities to protect us from reality are burned to ashes. This will seem at first to be a loss, for we thought these aspects of our personality were essential, were indeed "me." The numerous delusions and fantasies and defenses we have built into our personality come to the surface of conscious experience. This can be shocking. But it does not mean that we are falling apart; it means that our personality is being purified or purged of its unrealistic elements. Perhaps the most unrealistic element of all is the belief that the personality is "I." This belief has made the personality into a big defense toward taking in further reality about who "I" am. To part with this false belief can seem like death itself. But it is not death; it is only the death of a false view of the self. It is actually resurrection, an upwelling of the Spirit me.

If we persist in allowing Spirit to be the context in which our personality exists, some aspects of our personality will become golden amidst the vanishing dross. This "gold" is any aspect of our personality that has managed to be successful in relating us to reality—to the reality of Awe-filled being. Spirit is the supremely real, and Spirit will boil to oblivion any aspect of our personality that is unreal. But not every aspect of our personality is unreal. Our personality includes all the functionalities we have learned since infancy: how to drive a car, how to type, how to think logically and intuitively, how to do all the things we know how to do. These functionalities do not disappear with the maturation of Spirit. Rather, they take their places in the Spirit context. Similarly, our bodily sensations and emotional feelings do not end but are digested into the Spirit context. And our centered consciousness—our basic attentiveness and intentionality—does not disappear. This foundational component of our humanity also turns golden. That which was a defensive ego defending its self-image from REALITY becomes a golden consciousness attending objectively to REALITY and intending creative responses.

This entire picture of personality as a human-made building on the tabletop of Spirit is important because it expresses that Spirit is our essential self. Spirit is not alien to our personality but the origin of it and the means of its purification. The purification of personality may never be complete and even if it were completed, such purification would not mean perfection. The personality remains a fragile building, warped, reductionistic, specific, and capable of leading us astray from Spirit. At the same time, our personality is a structure we built from living experience. It is the structure through which we have become conscious and through which we are now capable of experiencing the tabletop of Spirit. Without our specific personalities we would still be infants who are unconscious of both personality and Spirit.

Spirit and the Consciousness of Spirit

Next, I want to clarify that what I am pointing to with the words "Awe" or "Spirit" is not the same thing as the consciousness of Spirit. Spirit is not a dynamic of consciousness. Spirit is not a state of consciousness. Spirit is not pure consciousness, whatever that phrase might mean. Spirit is our human essence, our relationship with Infinite Presence. Consciousness is a finite process.

We can, however, be conscious of Spirit. We can even speak of a journey of Spirit maturation in which we, in the beginning, have only a little consciousness of Spirit. Then as our life journey continues, we can become more conscious of Spirit. We may become persons who are intensely conscious of Spirit most of the time. We have given this journey many names: "sanctification," "growth in maturity," "realization," "enlightenment," and others.

What is actually "maturing" or "growing" as we take this "journey"? Spirit is not growing, for Spirit does not grow! Spirit is not a finite dynamic. What is growing is our consciousness of Spirit. Consciousness of Spirit is a finite dynamic, and consciousness of Spirit can grow in its intensity.

Why is this distinction important? If we do not maintain this distinction we become confused about what Spirit is. We lose sight of the realization that Spirit is a relationship with the Infinite Presence. This relatedness is not a human achievement. It can never be possessed. It does not grow or shrink. Only finite actualities can become less or more. Spirit is not a finite actuality. Spirit is not an accomplishment that we may achieve some day. Spirit is an unavoidable gift from which we may try to flee or in which we may thankfully participate. We can become more conscious of this unavoidable gift, but the gift itself does not change. There are many aspects of Spirit (trust, freedom, compassion, tranquility, etc.), and in any given situation the wind of Spirit may blow one of these aspects more strongly than another. In that sense Spirit experience does change from moment to moment and from decade to decade. But in the larger sweep of things, Spirit remains what Spirit always was and always will be for every human being at any time in past or future.

Further, this gift of Spirit is the same in the life of the religious novice as it is in the more experienced person. It is helpful and usual for the teacher of Spirit topics to be more conscious of Spirit than his or her students. But Spirit in the teacher is not different from Spirit in the student. A student filled with Spirit is in the very same place as the teacher. There is not one sort of Spirit for teacher and a lesser sort of Spirit for student. There is just Spirit which always manifests as a complete humiliation of and a complete glorification of the finite actualities in both student and teacher.

Destructive religious teachings most often come into being through a Spirit teacher who becomes confused about this never-ending humiliation that characterizes each finite human life that is committed to being a manifestation of Spirit. A Spirit teacher who comes to believe that he or she is beyond the normal run of humanity has become a demonic presence, a person who is using his or her Spirit experience and wisdom as a tool with which to pervert the actual experience of Spirit. A Spirit teacher who feels that he or she has arrived at some final place toward which others are merely heading is an arrogant fool who has exchanged the life of Spirit for some state of finite consciousness of Spirit. Consciousness of Spirit is a fine, wonderful, and powerful actuality, but consciousness of Spirit is not Spirit!

One of the great delusions in the religious treasure troves of the world is the notion that a religious body or a religious teacher can transmit Spirit leadership to another person. Christian heritage has practiced the laying on of hands, attempting to pass Peter's leadership along from one generation to the next. Buddhist teachers have also bestowed a "transmission" of their ministries to one or more of their "best" trainees. But Spirit does not obey these attempts of human beings to ascertain or shape where Spirit leadership will occur. Spirit does indeed blow where it wills.

And when Spirit blows, the leader upon whom it is blowing will find that he or she has not become a Spirit leader by any form of transmission or laying on of hands. Spirit leadership happens through a direct calling from the Infinite Presence and by a willing response to be called. This call both perpetually humbles us and perpetually ennobles us. The "call" to be Spirit means entering upon a journey for which there is no end point and a journey on which our continued walking is never assured. The next step can always be a step off the track of Spirit-empowered walking. The fall of Adam is not just a story about some ancient event; it is a living possibility of each and every moment of life for every person who embarks upon the Spirit journey.

"Stand fast therefore, and do not submit again to the shackles of slavery." (A slight rewording of Galatians 5:1) This is the advice given to us by Paul, the Christian apostle to the Gentiles. This advice might be given by every well-informed teacher of every religious heritage to every generation of every culture.

"Standing fast" means remaining aware that we are not accomplishing Spirit or possessing Spirit as a state of consciousness. "Standing fast" means constancy in gratefully receiving Spirit as a gift from the Infinite Presence—a dreadful/glorious gift that is humiliating all consciousness and supporting all consciousness in each and every never-to-be-repeated moment of our lives.

Spirit as Deathless

The reincarnation of the essential self, the immortality of the soul, and the resurrection of the body at the end of time are three religious fictions that the imagination of humanity has created and used to point to the deathless nature of Spirit. As religious fictions these three metaphors express a strange and elusive truth; but as literal descriptions of what happens at death to our conscious being, they are all three false. Our conscious being is finite, which means that our conscious being dies. If we are only interested in literal truth, that is all we need to know.

So how can we express the truth of deathlessness in a way that is devoid of all literalized fiction? We can begin by underlining again that Spirit is a relationship with the Infinite Presence. Spirit is not one end of this relationship—the finite end or the Infinite end. *Spirit is the relationship as a whole.* Spirit is finite consciousness being encountered by and responding to Infinite Actuality. Therefore, Spirit is not Infinite only, and Spirit is not finite only. Spirit is a relationship, a very mysterious relationship that blows through our actual finite human lives. Spirit is both wholly finite or human and wholly Infinite or non-human.

Spirit is deathless because Spirit is not a finite quality, yet Spirit is a human experience because it is also wholly human. Spirit is our essential humanity. This essential humanity differs from that of a rock or a cat. Unlike inanimate objects or other living species, humans can be aware of being this relationship between human awareness and the Infinite Mystery which limits us and is also the Bountiful Source that supports our being and our awareness. A rock or a cat is also in relationship with this Infinite Presence, but these beings are not aware of this relationship. The human can, however, participate with awareness in this deathless actuality which we are calling "Spirit."

The deathless quality of Spirit is more than an abstraction; it is an experience in the living here and now. How can deathlessness be illustrated as an experience that people actually have?

I have been helped to grasp the experience of deathlessness by contemplating the mystery of living in the here and now. In our living experience there is no past; it is gone. The past is only a living memory in the now. And there is no future; it is not yet. The future is only an anticipation in the now. In our actual experience of living there is only now. As we, in this now, contemplate our lives, we notice that everything about our lives is changing. Every part of our life is destined to pass away, yet our deepest being endures through these changes. We live on and on in this enduring now. As we become more conscious of the strangeness of this now, we become more and more able to detach our identities from the ever-changing particulars of our lives and settle into being these strange beings who are somehow alive in this always present now.

Here is another window into the experience of deathlessness. Imagine that you have already died, but have been given a reprieve to return to life for a short period of time. Imagine what it would be like to live in that interval, being already dead and yet still alive. There is nothing to lose. There is nothing to gain. There is just living. Imagine that in that short interval you are assigned to do a dangerous task that might cost you your life. Since you have already died and are destined to die soon, you can act with great courage, with great freedom, and with unanxious presence to the details of this task. There is no fear of failure. There is no fear of death. There is just living.

This bit of fiction describes our actual situation. Once we have identified with being the Spirit beings we are, we have died to everything. So we now live in a reprieve from the deaths we have died. We have only a brief interval before we will die some more. If we can identify with this invulnerable state of being, this freedom, this boundless courage, this complete lack of self-defense, then we know what it means to experience the deathless quality of Spirit.

Whenever a human being fundamentally identifies with Spirit and thereby renounces the centrality of finite identifications, that human being has overcome death. Death no longer has its sting when we no longer identify with the finite processes of our lives. *When we opt for being Spirit rather than just having Spirit happen to us from time to time, we have overcome death.* Death has become for us just one more astonishing experience in our relatedness to the Infinite Presence. We simply stand deathlessly before this Infinite Presence who sends us both birth and death, both limitation and support, both ordinary and extraordinary experiences, both ups and downs, both fate and the freedom to creatively respond to whatever fate we are handed. In surrendering to being this relationship with the Infinite, we are surrendering to being our life in every event that is being sent to us by the Infinite. Such a surrendered mode of aliveness is deathless. No passing thing can assail it.

This all-encompassing surrender includes surrender to the ever-present possibility for us to shape the events that may happen to us and to all humanity in the future. We experience deathlessness in both our encounters and our actions. A glorious singleness floods our life when Spirit has become our devotion, our enlightenment, our sanctification, our life.

Language fails us in expressing this experience of deathlessness, but such talk is present in almost all of our religious traditions. Such talk did not come into being to be meaningless. Religions emerged to express actual experiences. Deathlessness is a real experience. Our hopes for the immortality of what is finite are religious perversions.

Consciousness as the Origin of Evil

There is no such thing as evil Spirit; there is only false consciousness from which all evil emerges. False consciousness is a flight from Spirit, a refusal to be Spirit. False consciousness may be an attempt to forget Spirit or to not notice Spirit. False consciousness can also mean using our consciousness of Spirit to construct a fight with Spirit. In this case we have initiated a defiant rebellion from being Spirit, a conscious refusal to be the dialogue with the Infinite that we are.

Rebellion from Spirit is a tragic affair because there is no escape from the Infinite or from being related to the Infinite. Escape is an unrealistic approach to living. Escape is a preordained failure. This is why escape or rebellion can also be called "despair." It is a fight with the undefeatable, a flight from the inescapable, a murderous attack upon the unkillable. The novel Moby Dick pictures the dynamics of defiant despair in Captain Ahab's compulsion to kill the unkillable white whale.

In the opening paragraphs of *The Sickness Unto Death,* Søren Kierkegaard pictures Spirit as a relationship between time and eternity. This relationship between time and eternity has the capacity to relate to itself. When this relationship is willing to be itself we have the dynamic Kierkegaard calls "faith." I prefer to call it "trust." When this relationship is not willing to be itself we have the dynamic Kierkegaard calls "despair." The reason despair is despair is that we cannot actually be what we are not. So despair is a pseudo-reality, an attempt to make real what is not real. Spirit, Holy Spirit, is the inescapable essence of our being. Despair is the ill-advised, foolish, impossible attempt to do what cannot be done.

This either/or choice between faith and despair does not mean that we are in a neutral place facing two options: trust or despair. Rather, we face the choice of: (1) surrendering to the trust that is our actual being or (2) continuing in our program of despair which means fighting against trust. So our choice is not between two interesting ways of relating to reality. Rather, our choice is: (1) simply allowing reality to be what it is or (2) refusing to do so. In other words, trust is a gift, not a human achievement. Trust is built into reality along with freedom, compassion, tranquility, courage, joy, and other forms of Awe. We don't have to do anything to have these Spirit qualities. We only have to stop resisting them and stop fleeing from them.

Despair, on the other hand, is entirely of our own doing. The source of our despair is not reality, but our flight from reality. Despair is real in the sense that we do have the freedom to attempt this escape and commonly do so, but despair is despair because the escape cannot be actually brought off. Despair is Spirit only in the sense that Spirit is opposing our escape. But the sickness of despair is actually being created by our finite human consciousness. It is not a sickness of Spirit. Spirit cannot become sick. Despair is the mistake of hoping for some self-created certainty to take the place of the uncontrollable actuality of Spirit. The ironic truth turns out to be that our self-created certainties result in our sense of inadequacy, while opting for the uncertainties of Spirit gives us grounding, strength, and confidence.

To the extent that we surrender to being Spirit, despair vanishes, for it had no essential reality in the first place. Despair is simply how reality forces us to experience reality when we do not want to experience reality. All the horrific perversions of which humanity is capable stem from our finite human consciousness taking this wrong turn into despair.

There are only two basic directions for human life to take: (1) surrender to being Spirit or (2) despair over not being able to escape Spirit. One is heaven and the other is hell. This hell is the suffering that the Buddha dedicated himself to relieve. This heaven is the enlightenment the Buddha found and taught. This heaven is also the kingdom that Jesus proclaimed was at the door calling us to repent and enter. And the hell of which Jesus spoke was none other than despair, the hopelessness and horror of being a member of the kingdom of Satan—of being that pattern of futile rebellion from the Infinite Presence. Jesus and Buddha have remained important to human beings for many centuries because they called attention to this fundamental crossroads of human living. Every human being in every age faces this choice: whether to groan on in futile and despairing quest for an impossible life or to surrender to being the realistic Spirit relatedness that each of us already is.

Spirit as Unfathomable

The Awesome is incomprehensible. The Awed Ones are an enigmatic people the boundaries for whom no one knows. And the Awe itself is overwhelmingly more profound than can ever be rationally explored.

The task of describing Spirit cannot be completed in a thousand books. In fact, saying what "Spirit" means in mere human language is impossible. So I will close this chapter with a poem I have written about the impossible possibility of speaking of Spirit.

Inspiration

What is Spirit?
Lao Tzu says:
"Those who say don't know,
and those who know don't say."
Buddha says:
"It is not this;
it is not that.
It is an emptiness
that is also freedom and compassion."
The Bible says:
"It is like wind;
it blows where it wills;
no one knows where it comes from
or where it is going."

We see a chair,
but no one is sitting upon it.
We see footprints in the mud,
but we do not see the walker.
We see the tree under which he sat,

but we do not see the Buddha.
We see the tomb in which they put him,
but we do not see the Messiah.

It is said that words can speak
the WORD of TRUTH;
but words are not the WORD.
And the WORD is not words.

The WORD is SILENT,
yet every noise, every sound
screams with this SILENCE
to those who have ears
of Spirit.

So again, what is Spirit?

Let us never stop asking,
for then we think we know.
Asking means we do not know,
which is true.

When the mind of knowing
surrenders to freedom and compassion,
when the heart of longing
clings no more to this or that,
when the will of achieving
renounces both failure and success,
then Spirit is left
to know and do
its own un-self.

6.

Infinite Awe and Finite Religion

Again and again I meet people who have heard the call of the Awe, who want to live a Spirit life, but who want nothing to do with established religion. I understand this feeling, for I too have found the typical religious organization to be more of an obstruction than a means of healing our Spirit lives. Nevertheless, I want to defend the role of religion in human life and make a case for the importance of religious transformation.

Like economics and politics, religion is an unavoidable and necessary social process. Religion is that social process that has to do with giving expression to Awe or Spirit. Religion may also assist us in maturing our living of an Awe-filled life. As I have discussed in earlier chapters, Awe or Spirit is Infinite relatedness, and this relatedness is like a wild wind blowing through our finite lives. Good religion is like a sail that can catch the wind of Spirit. But the sail must not be confused with the wind. No religion ever catches the whole of the wind. And the wind is never possessed by any religious sail.

In plain words, religion is a social process, and all social processes are finite and transient. Religion is an earthly, fragile, and pervertable reality. No religion can claim absolute certainty. No religion has a scripture written by an Infinite authority. No religious form is immune from becoming obsolete and thus no longer capable of serving the function of expressing Spirit. So every religion has its perversions. Religious perversions have often become greater than the perversions in economics or politics or any other aspect of social life. In some moments of history, the deconstruction of bad religion and the construction of good religion have been the most important aspect of progressive social change. This was surely the case in the 16th century of Western society when Martin Luther and others set the Protestant Reformation in motion.

Jesus, remembered as the Messiah, and Siddhartha, remembered as the Awake One, are two of many mountain peaks in the history of religion on this planet. But thousands of other figures also bear witness to Spirit and to the core heaven-or-hell choice–the choice to identify with Spirit or to refuse to do so. Spirit is an ever-present actuality in human life, and that is why every society has developed religion as an integral part of its fabrics. The role of healthy religion is to express Spirit and to spell out how living a Spirit-committed life can take form in a particular historical setting.

Today, every long-standing religious tradition is facing an immense challenge to move away from religious metaphors, practices, and organizations that have become obsolete. A religious metaphor can become obsolete even though it has served humanity well for thousands of years. This is the case with that very ancient religious metaphor which I call "the transcendence metaphor." The transcendence metaphor is that metaphor in which we picture a spirit realm–a place where God dwells or perhaps where all sorts of gods, angels, and devils dwell. It is understandable why humanity has found this metaphor useful, for Spirit is an experience that seems to be above or beyond ordinary life. But today, transcendence is an obsolete metaphor. Why is this true? It is true because our common-sense scientific knowledge does not allow for a universe beyond the one universe in which we dwell. The experience of Spirit must be talked about in some other way than as "transcending" ordinary life. There is no universe next door. Literally speaking, we know that there is no "up there," "over there," or "out there." And even if we can theorize about other universes, we cannot experience them, so they have no personal meaning in our lives.

We can no longer talk meaningfully about Spirit as an invasion from another universe. But we can talk meaningfully about Spirit as a relationship with Infinite Presence (the Awe we experience in the presence of the Awesome). We are experiencing the birth of a new metaphor. The image of an Infinite Presence shining through each finite process is a functional religious metaphor. Let's call it "the transparency metaphor." All the earlier chapters on Awe and the Awesome have been written with the aid of this new metaphor. The Awesome shines through all finite processes awakening Awe in human beings. Today, the metaphor of transparency can do for us everything that the metaphor of transcendence did for humanity for so many thousands of years.

This shift from transcendence to transparency is a major cultural shift–arguably more major than the Copernican revolution or the Einsteinian revolution in modern physics. Since the dawn of religion in human life, the metaphor of a spirit world has been used. A cultural transition that is abandoning that metaphor is very deep change indeed. This shift from transcendence to transparency, however, is only a shift in the finite fabrics of religion. Our actual experience of the Infinite Presence is the same as it was for Moses or Jesus or Buddha or Mohammed. Nevertheless, this shift in basic metaphor is important. Hanging on to the transcendence metaphor includes hanging on to hierarchical religion. Transcendence and hierarchy are companion metaphors. To see "the Divine" as a supreme realm of meaning above humanity is consistent with seeing humanity as a realm of being above the rest of nature. This above-and-below thinking tends to support the oppression of nature and also the oppression of human beings who are not quite human by someone's "all-too-human" standards.

In some of the creative periods of the past, the transcendence metaphor was used in ways that did not demean nature or natural human life. The transcendence metaphor was certainly used as a means of challenging the final authority of the cultural canopy of the old world civilizations. But today the only way to challenge our cultural canopy is to reject the transcendence metaphor. Scientific secularism has already rejected it. Religious renewal does not need to reinstate it. Furthermore, most attempts to reinstate the transcendence metaphor are unclear that transcendence is a metaphor and always was a metaphor. Today the transcendence metaphor is often taken as a literal truth.

When I say that transcendence was always a metaphor, I mean that religious thinkers like Jesus, Paul, Augustine, Thomas Aquinas, Luther, Calvin, Wesley, and others used this metaphor knowing it dealt with a different sort of truth than the truth of practical reason. Mythic expressions of truth were acceptable before the modern scientific age clarified what was literal and what was literally not literal. For all those thousands of years before the modern age, the mythic expression of religious experience was simply how people talked about their Spirit experience.

For example, it is misleading to suggest that Jesus literally believed in a male Father figure dwelling in a literal place called "heaven." He was simply joining his culture in its customary metaphorical ways of talking about the deep issues of human living. It is feasible for us to reject Jesus' way of talking without rejecting what he had to say. So what did he have to say with this God, the Father, imagery? His point was that the Final Reality we confront is more surprising than a cosmic moral order. We can be "welcomed home" to our authentic lives in spite of all our legally defined failings. This is part of what the metaphor "Father" or "Abba" or "Papa" meant to Jesus. It also meant that the Final Reality we face is trustworthy. Jesus' use of the male metaphor for God was, of course, taken from the then familiar patriarchal family life. Does this imply any sort of put-down of women? No, it just means that he was using for his metaphorical material the everyday life experience of the only family pattern anyone in his time had experienced. We need not expect Jesus to have dealt with patriarchy any more than we should expect him to have dealt with nuclear disarmament. Each time is given its own ethical challenges. We contemporary interpreters of our religious past are not skilled in letting our forefathers and foremothers live in the their own times. Furthermore, we are not skilled in living in our own times. We are certainly failing to live in our times when we attempt to use what our foreparents did as the correct model for our times.

Using the transparency metaphor has to do with living in our own times. In our day if we continue using the transcendence metaphor (especially when we do not acknowledge that it is a metaphor), we create very bad religion. The transparency metaphor assists us in affirming that nature is not a lower reality; rather, the transparency metaphor allows us to affirm nature as that reality through which and only through which the Spirit relationship with the Infinite Presence is taking place. This perspective frees the Spirit person from any need to take an ascetic relationship to his or her own mind and body or to avoid appreciation for the rich fluorescence of nature. Rather, being our Spirit being supports a wholehearted affirmation of our own minds and bodies and of the surrounding natural world. Our mind, body, Earth, and the cosmos as a whole are processes that mediate our conscious relationship with the Infinite Presence. All of nature is made "holy" (i.e., Awe-filled) by the Presence of the Infinite streaming through nature toward that Awe-awareness which is the depth of being human. Furthermore, mind, body, and nature provide the medium through which a human being responds to the Infinite. The transparency metaphor allows us to indicate that Spirit is a deeper state than obsession with the finite realm of passing realities. At the same time the transparency metaphor assists us in sustaining a thoroughgoing affirmation of the natural world.

The transparency metaphor also helps us fight the temptation to talk about our own particular religion as having been sent down from heaven and thus being the true dogma that we must defend from all other religions. Every religion can be understood as a fragmentary, human, finite, and perpetually changing process. In this regard, religion is not different from every other social process. As paradoxical as this may sound, good religion is a finite social process inspired by the Infinite Presence and designed to give expression to the Deathless Spirit of relating to the Infinite Presence.

Religion, so understood, need not be tied to hierarchical forms of organization. Religion that has rejected the transcendence metaphor and embraced the transparency metaphor has thereby rejected hierarchy as well. In the transparency mode of religious formation, religious reflection and organization are wedded to the mysterious, ever-surprising insurgence of fresh Spirit. Such religion can give order to our experience of Spirit and discipline to our religious lives without asking us to bow down to some authoritarian dogma. In the transparency mode of religious formation, our religious ordering is being constantly undone and redone by the ever-surprising blowing of the wind of Spirit. We know that our religious forms do not and cannot fully contain the Spirit they aim to express. We know that it is Spirit that is deathless and not our religious forms.

In the context of the transparency mode of religious formation, a true religious tolerance can be practiced. Once we no longer have any reason to believe in one true doctrine or one true practice of religion, then we can be fully tolerant toward other religious lineages. If we have to defend our correct dogma, we cannot genuinely learn from other heritages. If we have to promulgate some correct dogma, then we cannot genuinely teach people who are practicing other religions about the gifts of our own heritage. True Spirit includes compassion for all beings.

Such compassion extends toward those who practice a religion different
from our own.

✓   As long as we are able to view Spirit as first and religion as second, we
need not demean other heritages in order to affirm our own. And we
need not demean our own religious heritage. Furthermore, we need not
shrink from admitting the weaknesses and horrendous perversions that
have grown up in our own religious heritage. Spirit provides us the
standing place from which we can evaluate those perversions and enact
some genuine repentance that leads toward honest religious renewal.

Further, we can passionately give ourselves to religious renewal,
while remaining modest about what we are doing. As religious reformers we are simply repairing one finite social process among the many
social processes of humanity. We are doing so in order to experience
and communicate deathless Spirit more adequately. But however deep
our Spirit communication, our religious forms are fragile. Such fragility
characterizes every religious tradition in all its past, present, and future
forms. The awareness of religious fragility and an appropriate religious
modesty go together.

Putting Spirit before religion loosens us from the past and supports
our religious creativity. When we are no longer stuck in inherited forms
that must be defended with our last ounce of blood, we can be open to
fresh and more powerful expressions of Spirit. We can indeed create
religion—if not a new religion, then a new version of an old religion. We
can identify with the Buddha and with Jesus and others who have
clearly dared to create religion. If we are Christians, we can stand in the
shoes of Paul and Mark and Matthew and Luke and John and see that
these amazingly creative persons were building fresh religious practice
with every word they wrote. They were not robotic tools in the sway of
a Divine Writer. They were ordinary persons, not unlike ourselves, who
were inspired with Spirit and who were creative as a result of this inspiration. In every religious heritage we notice examples of this fantastic

creativity that Spirit releases. When we answer the call of the Awe, we become participants in this vast story of religious creativity.

I will close this chapter with two of my poems that express the gist of this perspective on religion in a feelingful manner.

Soap and Water

Religion is like soap;
without water it won't wash.
Spirit is water;
it will wash without soap,
but it washes better with soap
if the soap is good soap.

Good religion catches Spirit.
Good religion,
if practiced in a disciplined fashion,
can intensify and mature
the living of Spirit.

But Spirit, like blood,
is the gift of God,
while religion is human-made,
subject to perversion
and obsolescence.

So let us never confuse
Spirit with religion.
Water is not soap,
and soap is not water.

Not a Private Matter

Religion is not a private matter.
Religion is a sociological process.

Spirit is not a sociological process.
Spirit is only known in the secret solitude
of singular persons.

Yet Spirit is not a private matter either.
For Spirit is expressed in public
through outward acts of
freedom and compassion.
Flight from Spirit is expressed in public
through outward acts of
despair, self absorption, and destruction.

If Spirit blows in you,
you are the light of the world.
Do not put your lamp under a washtub
but on a lamp stand
so it will illuminate the house.

Spirit is the same in every age,
but religion changes.
Religion is created by the human family.
Religion is part of human society.

Spirit is not a creation of the human mind or body.
Spirit is not an achievement of the human will.
Spirit is not a perfected personality.
Spirit is a wild gift, like blood, like air.

Spirit is human authenticity
breathed by the Infinite Silence
into our finite processes of body and mind.

Bodies and minds do religion.
Spirit inspires bodies and minds.
Spirit fills the biological processes
        of human beings.
Spirit is a bridge of relationship
between human biology and the Wholly Other
—the emptiness—the NO-THING-NESS from which
        all things come and to which all things return
—the fullness—the EVERY-THING-NESS
        in which all things cohere.

Spirit is not a finite process.
Good religion is a finite process
that expresses Spirit.
Bad religion is a finite process
that only pretends to express Spirit
while providing means of escaping
from being and living Spirit.

Nevertheless, Spirit is inescapable,
even though escaping from Spirit
is the general condition of humanity.
And since escaping from the inescapable
        is a futile journey,
humanity is not happy.
Indeed, despair is the general condition
of the human family.

The despairing only occasionally notice
that they are in despair,
for to notice despair
is the first step toward
moving away from despair.

To be stuck at this first step
of noticing despair
is intolerable.
So most noticers of despair
take a step backwards into hiding
            despair from view
rather than a step forward
toward leaving behind the
understandings and commitments
that are causing the despair.

The unhappiness of despair
is rooted in some specific way
of not being willing to be Spirit.
Happiness is the state of willing to be
the Spirit relationship we are,
being that bridge between our wondrous biology
and the Wholly Other
—the emptiness—the NO-THING-NESS
        from which all things come
        and to which all things return
—the fullness—the EVERY-THING-NESS
        in which all things cohere.

And all this is not a private matter.
Every leaf and every hair
of the biological world
is involved in this public act
of choosing to be the Spirit beings
that we are.

7.

The Authority of Authenticity

Jack Kornfield, a Buddhist teacher and writer, cites this saying of Pope John XXIII:

> It often happens that I awake at night and begin to think about a serious problem and decide I must tell the pope about it. Then I wake up completely and remember that I am the pope.[8]

Such an awareness can be experienced by any of us. When fully awake, each of us is indeed the pope. Or we might say that there is no pope except the ordinary human being who is fully awake. There is no authority other than the authentic human. In our fully awake, deep, inward actuality, each of us is the only authority there is.

Such a view of authority is reflected in the following saying about Jesus:

---

[8] Kornfield, Jack; *A Path with Heart* (Bantam Books: 1993) page 164

And when Jesus finished these sayings, the crowds were astonished at his teaching. For he taught them as one who had authority and not as their scribes.

Matthew 7:28-29 Phillips translation

During the time in which Jesus and his first followers lived, the scribes were respected religious teachers. Many scribes were sincere persons, but they based their teachings on the written words of the heritage. The meaning of the above passage is that Jesus spoke with an inward type of authority unlike the scribes who spoke with the objective authority of the traditions. Today we might say that Jesus spoke with the authority of authenticity while the scribes spoke with the authority of their Bibles, their religious groups, their "pastors," their "Pope," their favorite theologians and philosophical teachers.

If we are honest, we must admit that authoritative religion has injured or offended most of us. The extent of this abuse has been so great that many of us have entirely rejected Judaism, Christianity, the Bible, the Koran, or any other objective authority. Often, the intuition behind such rejections is correct: anything that does not make sense in terms of our own experience of life is an imposition. It is surely appropriate to reject any meaningless doctrine that is being crammed down our throats.

Also, when we do tolerate the imposition of outside authority, this may mean that we are hungry for security–hungry for someone else to tell us how to live our lives so that we do not have to take responsibility for discovering truth for ourselves.

Jesus apparently had discovered truth for himself and therefore spoke from an interior certainty that gave him the ability to reinterpret the heritage, interpret the future, and say something relevant within each and every moment-by-moment happening of life.

Many people today reject the authority of authenticity along with scribal authority. They don't see the difference between the two. They feel that anyone who speaks strongly and certainly is imposing some alien truth upon them. Many people today are relativists. In the arena of religion and ethics, they believe that no one has authority. There are just opinions–your opinions, my opinions, and the next person's opinions. Furthermore, this very popular view claims that one opinion is just as good as the next opinion. According to this view, everyone has the right to his or her own opinion. There is no authority, except someone's opinion. There is no way to challenge anyone to change their opinion, for everyone can say, "My opinion is good enough; my opinion is just as good as any other opinion."

Such thoroughgoing relativism was not the view of Jesus. He spoke with authority, with the authority of authenticity. He interrupted people's opinions with teachings aimed at allowing his listeners to see for themselves that their own opinions were foolish.

Jesus was Not a Relativist

Let us look again at some of the New Testament stories cited in chapter four. Let us notice how these stories depict Jesus as an exemplar of the authority of authenticity.

In the story in which a person rushes up to Jesus and says, "I want to follow you but first I must go bury my father," Jesus does not say, "I understand, family duties are quite important; you have a right to your opinion." Rather, Jesus says, "Let the dead bury the dead; you need to come and follow me."

In another story a person comes up to Jesus and says, "I will follow you wherever you go." Jesus does not say, "Thank you for your enthusiasm. I share your opinion that this is a good cause." Rather, he says, "Foxes have their dens and birds have their nests, but a Messianic human has no place to lay his or her head." Jesus saw through the naiveté in that person's enthusiasm. Jesus was not trapped by naive praise. He simply spoke to what he saw as the truth of each encounter. Jesus spoke with the authority of authenticity.

Jesus' own disciples were not immune to having their opinions contradicted. In the very center of Mark's gospel, Jesus tells his disciples what to expect on the journey down to Jerusalem. He says bluntly that he is going to be rejected by the leaders, captured, and put to death. Peter says, "No, this cannot happen to you." Jesus does not say, "Thank you, Peter, for your concern. You are entitled to your opinion. I understand that it is comforting for you to believe that the Messianic human will always be safe." Rather, Jesus rebukes Peter, "Away with you, Satan. You are thinking as finite humans think, not as the Infinite God thinks."

In story after story Jesus cuts through all naiveté, moralism, and sentimentality and challenges the central life-understanding of the person encountered. Here is one more example: A women in the crowd calls out, "Oh, what a blessing for a woman to have brought you into the world and nursed you." Jesus does not reply, "Thank you for your strong sentiment of affirmation." Nor does Jesus deny the truth in what she says. Here is his reply: "Yes, but a far greater blessing is to hear the word of God and obey it." Jesus cuts through the shallowness of her understanding of who he is and what he is about. He makes it clear in one sharp reply that it is relatively unimportant to be some good person's mother. What is more important is to hear for yourself, whether you are a man or a woman, what is being said to you by the Infinite Silence in this very moment of time. And not only to hear what is said but to act accordingly.

In other words, don't wait around hoping to be some great child's mother. Get going with your own life today, now, immediately. Jesus spoke with authority, the authority of authenticity. And he asked this woman to find her own authority. This also applied to all those standing around, and it applies to you and me who stand in the twenty-first century reflecting on this story.

All three of the Synoptic Gospels paint this unswerving picture of Jesus, the exemplary human being. The exemplary human speaks with authority, not with the *authority of the tradition-bound scribes.* The exemplary human speaks with the *inward authority* of knowing what he or she or you or I actually know about our lives and the lives of those about us.

Opposing Contemporary Scribal Authority

Many contemporary, conservative Christians defend themselves against the address of the above scriptures by saying that Jesus was God, but we are only human. Jesus could speak with authority, but we can't. They say that we have to rely on the authority of Jesus–that is, on the authority of the Bible. This view represents the same type of authority that the scribes represented in Jesus' day. Jesus was fighting against scribal authority. And Jesus embodied the authority of authenticity not for himself only, but for all of us as well. Paul certainly spoke with the authority of authenticity. All the gospel writers did, too. The whole New Testament embodies this fresh attitude toward the authority of tradition. The New Testament writers found support in the Hebrew Bible (what Christians call the Old Testament) for the authority of authenticity. This older tradition was searched for support for the authority of authenticity. The prophets were revered because they spoke with the authority of authenticity. Moses was revered because he spoke with the authority of authenticity. In other words, the New Testament claims that the Jesus-type of authority does not contradict the older tradition; rather Jesus' type of authority is an embodiment of the same type of authority that filled Moses and the prophets.

And this same authority of authenticity can be embodied by you and me as well. *Jesus was a human being just like us.* If the authority of authenticity was part of his godliness, such godliness is a godliness that we too can find ourselves to be. So let us consider what it would mean for us to embody the authority of authenticity. It means that we would always be speaking from our own interior experience and never simply repeating phrases we have only rationally learned. It means that we would have the inward confidence and courage to challenge scribal authority wherever we encounter it.

Perhaps we can illustrate this confidence by considering how we might relate to the conservative Christian forces of our times. How might we respond to members of the Christian Right or their Republican representatives in the House of Representatives when they spout out mean-spirited moralisms that they defend with biblical authority? We might say, speaking with the Jesus-type of authority, that Jesus spent his entire life fighting against such mean-spirited moralism. We might say that Jesus was crucified by mean-spirited moralists very similar to those who dominate modern Christianity. We might point out that it was Jesus' unrelenting attack on mean-spirited moralism that led to his death. We might point out that Jesus considered these moralistic religious opinions so deadly to the people of Israel that he considered it worthwhile to risk his life opposing them. We might say that if mean-spirited moralists are going to continue to dominate contemporary Christian practice, it is going to be over our dead bodies. That is how awakening Christians might speak today with the authority of authenticity.

Opposing the View of the No-Authority Relativists

Perhaps those of us who are willing to embody Jesus' authority of authenticity have an even tougher conflict with those who argue that in matters of religion and ethics, there is no authority at all. Here are some typical words spoken by these no-authority relativists: "One religious opinion is as good as another. Why get upset over conservative Christians or Muslim fundamentalists or atheists or secular humanists or any other religious opinion? Let a thousand opinions coexist in peace. No religious opinion has all the answers. I cannot say that my opinions are better than other people's opinions. This is what love means: to tolerate whatever opinion my neighbor has, to listen to him, and to respect his opinion."

This position is difficult to effectively oppose because it embodies a modicum of truth. Love does mean respecting the other person and his or her opinion-creating capabilities. The authority of authenticity agrees with the relativists that cramming my opinions down other people's throats is the wrong style. Cramming is the style of the scribal authoritarians, not the style that expresses the authority of authenticity. Nevertheless, the thoroughgoing relativist is profoundly wrong. Every opinion is not of equal value. Some opinions express the actualities of life better than others. Respecting people does not mean denying this truth. Respecting people means entering into conflict with their opinions in the context that each person is something greater than his or her current opinions. If a person is totally identified with his or her current opinions, that person is underestimating herself or himself. Challenging someone's opinions can mean asking that person to look at life more carefully or more fully and thereby become more completely the person she or he actually is. Challenging someone's opinions, if done from the perspective of treasuring authenticity in self and in others, can mean true respect for others. Affirming other people's opinions no matter what those opinions are is not respect; it is co-dependence. It is coddling immaturities because we do not have the courage or skill to ask others to grow up.

The relativists are also partly right about the need for peace among all the religious perspectives on earth. Every religious expression is a finite reality; therefore, it is not absolute. It cannot be the standard by which every other religious expression is judged. The Christian way of coming at Spirit is not intrinsically better than the Hindu way or the Buddhist way. At their best, all these long-standing religious traditions have great gifts of Spirit expression for all of us. Tolerance toward other religious groups is a living necessity as well as a mode of respect. Nevertheless, the relativists are wrong (that is, inauthentic) in assuming that there is no way to judge specific religious expressions as good or bad. This is a hard question for everyone in our era: what is it that makes good Christianity good or bad Christianity bad? What is it that makes good Buddhism good or bad Buddhism bad?

Adequate answers to such questions can only be found if we raise an even deeper question: what is the essential purpose of religion in human life? What is religion and why do humans do it? Let me put this very simply: the purpose of all religion is to express Spirit. All religious expressions are finite inventions of limited human beings. *Good religion is a finite expression of Spirit. Bad religion is a finite expression of fleeing away from Spirit.* Spirit, as elaborated in earlier chapters, is a more-than-finite actuality blowing through our lives on its own authority. Real Spirit or Awe can judge all religious expressions as good religion or bad religion.

As the history of religion amply illustrates, all religious expressions are open to deadly perversions. A religion which came into being to express Spirit can be turned into its opposite—into a religious expression which is running away from Spirit, suppressing Spirit, and even giving form to attitudes that are "demonically evil." So the criticism of bad religion is the beginning point for all good religion. An appropriate religious tolerance does not mean the renunciation of all religious criticism. If we wish to make peace at any price and never criticize religion, the following words of Jesus, as recorded in Luke's gospel, are a stinging challenge:

> Do you think that I have come to bring peace on earth? No, I tell you, not peace, but division! For from now on there will be five people divided against each other in one house, three against two, and two against three. It is going to be father against son, and son against father, and mother against daughter, and daughter against

mother, mother-in-law against her daughter-in-law, and daughter-in-law against mother-in-law!

Luke: 13:51-53 Phillips translation

Clearly, anyone who wants to protect his or her current personal opinions from the ever-active assault of truth is not a follower of Jesus. Anyone who permissively accepts whatever opinion other people hold and smilingly gives them "space" to hold that opinion is not a follower of Jesus.

How, screams out the relativist in us all, can we experience this "authority of authenticity" that Jesus manifests? How can we know within ourselves that we have a valid means of evaluating all finite religious expressions, seeing accurately their goodness and their badness?

Looking More Deeply at the Authority of Authenticity

We can begin answering these questions by noticing that life simply has an actuality. In the realm of objective truth as pursued by the scientific method, we assume an actuality that judges one scientific theory to be better than another. We know that all scientific theories are approximate and partial and will one day be replaced by better theories. Nevertheless, we do not, if we are good scientists, claim that one scientific theory is just as good as another. Einsteinian physics is better than Newtonian physics because it interprets our actual, factual experience better.

A few people do misunderstand Einsteinian relativity to mean that any scientific theory is as good as another, but this was not Einstein's view. Einstein saw that all measurements had to be taken relative to an observer who was part of the physical system, but he did not mean by this that there is no objective reality. Einstein was asserting that a view of nature that encompasses the role of the observer is more true to life than the older view that the human observer is looking at the physical world from some abstract rational space.

Many people in our culture, even when they admit that science gives us an approximate sense of objective reality, insist on being thoroughgoing relativists in the arena of religion and ethics. In popular politics we often hear it said that "everyone is entitled to his or her own opinion."

It is true that in religious, ethical, or political pursuits we are dealing with something more than objective truth that can be verified by outwardly observable public experiments. *In these pursuits we are dealing with an inward truthfulness.* In religion and ethics, as in many forms of depth psychology, we are dealing with a living human individual telling the truth or not telling the truth about his or her own deeply inward experiences.

Let me begin with an elementary example. Your cat dies and you say, "I feel sad." That is truthful if you really do feel sad. Then again you might be lying to yourself. Perhaps you are not sad but simply relieved to be rid of the pesky animal. If that is the case, then "relieved" is your authenticity. Or maybe you are both sad and relieved. Or perhaps something else is the case, but your state of being is not a matter of arbitrary opinion. At the same time no outside authority can tell you how you feel about your cat's death. You feel what you feel. Whatever is true is the truth.

The authority of authenticity involves *actualities* even deeper than how we feel. For example, in each personal relationship with the beings who neighbor us, we are either willing to have those relationships or not willing to have them. We may be in deep despair over some or all aspects of our lives, and if we are, then this despair is the truth. Whether or not we are in despair is not a matter of arbitrary opinion. It is a discovery of truth. There may be more truth to be discovered—such as the realization that despair is not the only option, that there is a way out of despair. But if despair is currently characterizing our life, this is the truth with which all rescue from despair must begin. What is the case? What is the actual state of affairs going on in your or my life at this time and place? Such questions can be answered with a level of authority that is more certain, not less, than the certainty of objective scientific knowledge.

But, says the relativist, even our scientific knowledge and our inward awareness have a degree of uncertainty about them. This is certainly so, but let us also notice that this ever-present degree of uncertainty is one of the most certain of all certainties about which the authority of authenticity speaks. The authority of authenticity is not the possession of rational certainties; it is the experience of what is so and what is not so in the living here and now.

What sets the authority of authenticity off from our scientific knowledge or even our codified contemplative wisdom is this: *We have created our relative certainties, but our actual life experience is providing the authority of authenticity.* The writer of the gospel of John was very clear about this. He puts into the mouth of his fictitious Jesus these words: "I do nothing on my own authority, but in all that I say, I have been taught by my Infinite Parent. This Authority who sent me is present with me, and has not left me alone; for I always do what is acceptable to this Authority"– a slight rewording of John 9:28-30.

So if I, like John's literary Jesus, am to live by the authority of authenticity, this means that I am to be obedient to the Infinite Authority that I am experiencing moment by moment in my actual life. All my opinions, all my religious expressions are to be constructed by me to express my actual relationship with the Infinite as obediently as I can. *And if I do this in pristine truthfulness, then you can hear me with your own pristine truthfulness.*

If at any point I am lying about my own experience, then the authority of authenticity is not present. Each of us has grounds within ourselves for rejecting what any speaker is saying, and it is possible for us to do this from our own authentic experience rather than from our current opinions.

Similarly, when we are listening to a speaker who speaks from authenticity, we can listen beyond our own opinions to our own truthfulness about our own experience. In this way the words of the authentic speaker can take root in us. This reception may cost us our current opinions, but we gain fresh awareness of our own true greatness. If, on the other hand, we insist on identifying with our current finite opinions rather than with our own truthful relationship with Infinite Actuality, then we will miss an opportunity to be more fully awake. We may also find ourselves in furious opposition to an authentic speaker who is simply challenging some of our finite and thus fragile opinions.

Infinite Actuality is the authority, and Infinite Actuality is not someone's opinion. Infinite Actuality is THAT to which each atheist, each relativist, as well as each religious practitioner, must bow in obedience. Infinite Actuality cannot be dismissed as a mere opinion held by religious people. Relationship with the Infinite is as certain as death and as plain as being here. The Infinite is that mysterious Void that brings forth all beings and takes them back again. The Infinite is that mysterious Fullness that confronts us with possibilities we cannot fully imagine. The Infinite is the Radical Demand to live openly in the searing blaze of that mysterious Fullness and that mysterious Void.

Jesus bore witness that this always-Present Infinity could be his, your, and my true home (our parentage, our kingdom). We can be at home with this Infinite Presence every single moment of our lives. The Infinite, Jesus said, is like a parent waiting for a lost child to return home from the land of unreality. And when that child returns, the parent runs to meet her, puts rings on her fingers, clothes on her body, kills the fatted calf, and throws a huge party. When another loyal but moralistic family member objects to this seeming indulgence, the parent simply says, "My precious child who was lost has now been found."

When you come home to the Infinite, the Infinite simply greets you with, "Welcome home!" "Welcome home, daughter." "Welcome home, son." Someone precious has returned home. This, Jesus claims, is simply the truth. In other words, Jesus is saying, "This is not my opinion; rather, I have received this saying from the highest authority." And if you and I can agree with Jesus, it is not because Jesus said so but because it is true. Whenever we return home to Infinite relatedness, we find everything just as Jesus said. There is no punishment meted out for our grim and despairing trips into unreality. Those trips were themselves the punishment. Returning home is like a great welcome. Your and my whole past is forgiven. Your and my whole future is open. All of life is suddenly completely good in spite of all its challenges and difficulties. Your and my entire actual person is completely accepted in spite of all those longings and addictions for unreality. This is the truth. To enjoy this truth, I have to actively accept it and live it. I have to resist the temptation to reject it. But whatever I decide, this Infinite Welcome is still the truth. I do not have to make it the truth by some effort of my own opinionatedness. *I simply have to surrender to the Infinite Actuality of this Welcome Home being the truth.*

In conclusion, I want to underline these two themes: (1) the authority of authenticity enters into the ongoing conflicts between human opinions, valuing some opinions over others. This illuminates how the authority of authenticity can be a foundation for choosing all our ethical values and ethical perspectives. (2) The authority of authenticity is beyond the realm of human opinions. Authenticity is not a worldview or a rational construction of any sort. Authenticity is not one opinion fighting against another opinion. Authenticity does not have to do with being tolerant of all opinions or hostile toward all opinions. *The authority of authenticity simply speaks the truth of our own inward states of being.*

And such truthfulness turns out to be deep wisdom, for it includes our being truthful about our relationship with Infinite Actuality. This "relationship with Infinite Actuality" is the essence of all good religion. This mysterious "relationship with Infinite Actuality" includes all those inward states of being we call "Spirit" or "Awe." It is the actuality of this

Infinite Spirit relatedness that validates or invalidates each and every religious dogma, practice, or ethical teaching.

If we understand Spirit as the actuality of Infinite relatedness, then we understand what there is to know about the authority of authenticity. We know how to see for ourselves that the *scribes of authoritarian religion are off the mark*. We know how to see for ourselves that *the relativists of no authority are off the mark*. And we know how to identify with Jesus in his being obedient to that Awesome Infinite Stillness that shouts so loudly. We know how to speak, not on our own authority, but with authority that is backed by THAT which is the FIRST and the LAST and ONLY Infinite Actuality.

So the authority of authenticity is simple–it is merely telling the truth about our own inward experience of the Infinite. And yet the authority of authenticity is complex and ever unfolding. The authority of authenticity is a shocking capacity to see our way through the validity or invalidity of every religious and ethical expression in the entire history of the human species. What a privilege to be able to speak only of what we know and yet to have insight into the meaning of everything! What a blessing to have been given the capacity to speak with the authority of authenticity, an authority that is not like that of the scribes!

In the chapters that follow, I will be applying (to the best of my ability) the authority of authenticity to the study of other-than-Christian religions. In this manner I propose to conduct respectful dialogues with religions other than my own and to thereby deepen my own understanding of Christian heritage. This sort of dialogue can be applied to deepening whatever religious heritage a person has chosen for his or her core practice.

PART TWO:

How Awe Gives Depth to Interreligious Dialogue

8.

One Awed Christian's Approach to Interreligious Dialogue

I was raised Christian and have chosen to remain so. Yet for over three decades, my life has been enriched by Eastern religions, especially Hinduism, Buddhism, and Taoism. These traditions have greatly expanded my understanding of the essence of religion in human life and why human beings do religion.

I have also been intrigued with Native American religious practices, with those of the Australian aborigine, and with the religions of Old Europe before the coming of Christianity. The entire scope of that nature-sensitive religious climate that preceded the dawn of civilizations has captivated me. I have also been intrigued with how some of these early religions used feminine symbolism and appropriated the feminine aspects of human life.

As a Christian I am a Protestant, a spiritual descendant of Martin Luther and John Wesley and those twentieth century theologians who have reinterpreted the Reformation for our time. I have, nevertheless, been fascinated by a wide range of Christian expressions–from Quaker to Roman Catholic to Eastern Orthodox. And I have come to consider Judaism and Islam as members in my family of religions. My life has been deepened by my dialogues with all these traditions.

I do not claim to have mastered any of these longstanding religious traditions. And I will not attempt in this book to summarize the vast diversity that exists within each of these traditions. Instead, I have selected specific aspects of these various traditions–aspects that have enriched my life with Awesome insights and challenges. I will then examine where these encounters interface with my own Christian-articulated experiences of Awe. This method leads to further clarity with regard to my own heritage as well as opening myself more deeply to the wonders of other heritages. I am hopeful that this method will also be deepening for the reader.

I have found that focusing upon experiences of Awe has an uncanny power to illuminate the place of religion in human life. An objective religious survey can be exceedingly informative; but unless the objective approach is combined with experiences of Awe, it misses the essence of religion. Exclusive objectivity overlooks why human beings do religion in the first place.

I do, however, deeply respect objective scientific scholarship on the history and content of the world's religions. I have studied such materials extensively, and I especially appreciate scholars like Huston Smith, Thomas Merton, Joseph Campbell, Mircea Eliade, Heinrich Zimmer, and Thomas Berry–all of whom combine a personally felt approach with extensive interreligious mastery. But interreligious mastery will not be my emphasis in the following chapters. Each chapter provides only a very narrow window into some particular realm of Awe. I will share experiences of Awe that have happened to me through select parts of these other-than-Christian religions. Then I will explore these same topics through the language and wisdom of Christian heritage, which I will continue to view through the Awe window.

I will begin with Islam and Judaism, which are very closely related to Christianity. All three of these religions are children in the same family, even though their members have too often fought one another intensely. Next, I will turn to what I feel are some important enrichments of Western life arriving from the East. I will dialogue with Taoism, Buddhism, and Hinduism. Finally, I will dialogue with that religious antiquity that underlies all these more recent traditions, focusing first on the Goddess recovery and then on our religious inheritance from the tribal societies of precivilization.

In each of these chapters I will explore some of the gifts to me of the religious heritage being engaged. And each of these chapters will attempt to further clarify the breakthrough of Christianity. Dialogue with others often raises fresh questions about ourselves. I intend these dialogues with other-than-Christian traditions to inspire deeper dialogue among those of us who identify ourselves as Christians.

None of these essays will exhaust their selected subjects, but I intend for each chapter to open more widely our appropriation of these boundless arenas for continuing dialogue. Open-ended dialogue is a profound biblical theme. Dialogue among human groups can bring to our awareness how we participate in that vast dialogue with the Infinite. It will continue to be my theme throughout this book that down-to-Earth dialogue with the Infinite characterizes the theologies, the stories, the poems, and the histories that comprise the biblical literature.

These considerations lead me to the conviction that interreligious dialogue is an expression of Christian faith. Closing down such dialogue is, therefore, an act of unfaith–an absence of trust in the trustworthiness of the Awesome Origin of all Awe.

The Children of Abraham

9.

Allah and Yahweh

Islam shares with Judaism and Christianity what we might call a "monotheistic devotion." In their deepest currents these three religions are children in the same family whose similarities are greater than their differences. But in their more narrow and defensive forms these three religions have been hostile toward one another as siblings in a common family sometimes are. In the Christian West, Islam is typically appreciated less than Judaism, less than Taoism, Buddhism, and Hinduism, and less even than the religions of human antiquity. Enabling a meaningful dialogue between Christianity and Islam is a challenge and an important challenge in the context of our current planet-wide conflicts. In this chapter, I hope to show that when Christians see the core breakthrough that issued in Islam, they will also see the core breakthrough of Christianity more clearly. So I want to focus rather narrowly on Mohammed himself and his initial breakthrough.

In Mecca, in the year 610, a monotheistic oneness of devotion broke open in the life of Mohammed. This happened at a time of deep decay in the vital integrity and ethical fiber of southeastern Mediterranean societies. A wide diversity of religious practices–Paganism, Zoroastrianism,

Judaism, Christianity, and others–had decayed into what we might describe as a swamp of shallow magic and superstition.

Mecca, Mohammed's home, was filled with temples and cults, priests and worshipers of many gods. Allah was the name of one of those gods. Allah means literally "the God," but Allah was being worshiped at that time not as the only God but as a very impressive one. Huston Smith tells very well the story of Mohammed's birth of Spirit:

> Through vigils, often lasting the entire night, Mohammed became convinced that Allah was far greater than his countrymen supposed. Allah was surely not a god or even the greatest of the gods. He was, as his name asserted, *the* God—One and only, One without rival. Soon from this mountain cave was to sound the greatest phrase of the Arabic language; the deep, electrifying cry which was to rally a people and explode their power to the limits of the known world: *La ilaha illa 'llah!* There is no god but God! [9]

There is no god but *the* God. Mohammed was not saying that there is only one valid religion, his own. He was saying something about life, about the way life works. He experienced himself as having seen through to the bottom of something, and after having had that vision he was telling others about it.

So what did "Allah" mean in Mohammed's experience? How is Allah related to Yahweh, the God of Israel, and to the Almighty "Father" of Christian tradition? Mohammed himself related Allah to the ancient Hebrew Scriptures. He embraced the story of creation and the story of Adam and Eve. He saw Abraham, Moses, the prophets, and Jesus as prophets of Allah. He saw himself as bringing together in a fresh form something that was primordial.

---

[9] Smith, Huston; *The Illustrated World's Religions*, (HarperSanFrancisco: 1991) page 149

My own appreciation of Islam took a leap forward when I saw that there was, in the Islamic breakthrough, a vigorous opposition to all bad religion. We can sense this if we read that primal sentence of Islam with the following pause.

There is no god,   (long pause)   but *the* God.

Let me put this even stronger: **there is no god PERIOD.** (Now pause for several minutes to take this in. Imagine yourself renouncing every understanding of the word "God" or "Goddess" that you ever heard. Feel, if you can, the refreshing emptiness of being rid of all superstition and all escape from your real life to some false superworld. Feel, if you can, the absolute end of all religious sentimentality, all pretentious religious rationalism, and all shallow and irrelevant moralism. And then after this long contemplative pause say:) **but *the* God.**

Now of course, if the phrase *"the God"* brings nothing more to your mind than all the bigotries and superstitions of the current Islamic world or Christian world or Jewish world, nothing has been gained. But if Muslims, Christians, and Jews could together recover the real essence of their monotheistic heritages, then we would have something.

In all three traditions, the One God speaks. Through the metaphor of speech the One God reveals what is required to be a full human being. But today, all three traditions tend to take this metaphor of speech literally. Words in the Bible or the Koran are understood to be the very words of God. This literalism brings the "speech" of Allah or Yahweh down to the level of human speech. The Speech of the One God becomes merely a human tradition. We end up worshiping a tradition, not the One God. This is called idolatry or infidelity in all three traditions.

In order to break past this barrier, we have to reflect on something very basic in our own experience. We know that only finite realities speak. To talk about the Infinite speaking is metaphorical talk: that is, we are using the material of our finite experience in an attempt to express something about our experience of the Infinite Presence. The

Infinite Presence does not literally speak. The Infinite is Silent. When we go to our favorite "holy place" and cry out to the Infinite what do we hear? Silence!

When the monotheistic heritage was first invented, "the speaking God" was a metaphorical way of pointing to the action of this Infinite Silence in the ordinary course of events. The Infinite Silence speaks not in human words but in the events of history. Words are the human interpretation of this wordless speech of the Infinite Silence.

So let us listen once more to this contemplation of the primal sentence of Islam.

There is no god,   (long pause)   but the Infinite Silence.

Christian Idolatry

Surveys show that most of us who claim a Christian identification say that we believe in one God. Yet very few Christians live in intimate contact with that Infinite Presence whose existence is as obvious as life and death itself. The radical monotheism of the Christian Bible is perhaps the most misunderstood aspect of Christian tradition. Most liberal Christians actually practice a belief in two Gods. One of them they call "Nature," and the other one lives in another realm, "Supernature," and intervenes in Nature in ways that assist human beings to deal with Nature better. In this completely unbiblical perspective, the death of a child is an event of Nature not directly related to the God in heaven who loves us and wishes us well. We pray to this heavenly God to help us deal with the death of this child, to comfort us, to give us courage, or whatever it is we think we need or want. When we are thinking in this context, we do not even consider how the death of this child is an action of the ONE GOD or how it could possibly be true that this ONE GOD loves us, or even whether or not this ONE GOD is the proper object for our worship. We simply ignore the book of Job in which it is clearly said that Yahweh both gives and takes away. Surely, we say, it must be an obsolete religion that would view ALL EVENTS as the action of the ONE GOD.

Thinking in this vein, most of us who call ourselves Christians do not grasp the severity of the Islamic cry, so let us contemplate a few more rewordings of this primal sentence:

There is no magical heavenly assistance PERIOD. There is just the Infinite Mystery that gives and takes away.

If we heard that clearly, we might also discover that part of what the Infinite Mystery gives to us is our own vital courage and freedom to respond to that Mystery in creative living.

There is no smiling, friendly Being up there, out there, or over there in some supernatural place PERIOD. There is just THAT WHICH IS.

If we heard that clearly, we might also discover that part of WHAT IS is our own most personal relationship to THAT WHICH IS. Indeed, being this relationship with the Infinite is our human dignity and our human glory, distinguishing us from all the other forms of life on this planet.

If we keep on listening to this Islamic sentence, we might finally understand that there is also no escape from suffering and death and ethical responsibility PERIOD.

There is just the creative submission of our self-centered ego to the WAY LIFE IS. Or there is the opposite—our rebellious infidelity to the WAY LIFE IS, our self-centered reliance on phony gods of our own creation.

There is no god PERIOD. (Oh, the wonder and the healing of this thoroughgoing atheism.)   (long pause)   There is just the Inescapable Infinite Presence. (Oh, the stability and groundedness that comes from rooting our living in THAT which can never pass away.)

There is no god, but *the* God.

Our contemplation of this phrase can open a window into the glorious sternness of Islam. Looking through this window we can understand why Mohammed's teachings created such hostility in many people and such passionate conviction in others.

The core teaching of Islam is an all-out rejection of all gods and goddesses, indeed of all religion. Religion is not God. Islam is a religion that undermines the ultimacy of all religion. Islam, which means "peace with God," does not mean peace with superstition, magic, or any sort of otherworldly foolishness. Peace with God means submission to the inescapable. And this submission is religiously practiced with prayers five times a day, the giving of alms, a month of dawn to dusk fasting each year, and a pilgrimage to Mecca at least once in a lifetime. The Islamic style is not passivity. It is a vigorous opposition to all excuse-making religion, to all passivity and sloppy living. Islam, at its best, is an unrelenting, realistic discipline acted out in the broadest overarching context. And this context is the same context I have been attempting to indicate with the terms "Awesome," "Mysterious," and "Infinite Silence."

In the light of this central illumination, Mohammed accomplished an astonishing reinvigoration of a languishing culture that was swamped in passivity and religious excuse making. Contemporary Christianity could use such a reinvigoration. But in order for this to occur, contemporary Christians require a rebirth of awareness about their own heritage of radical monotheism.

Those of us who have puzzled over why contemporary Christianity is making so little difference in the arenas of cultural reinvigoration, human justice, and ecological transformation may find our answer in these considerations. We have lost our radical monotheism in the swamp of modern enthrallments with the works of humanity. A vital Christianity would reject these enthrallments as idolatry, as rebellion from the One God.

The Paradox of Human Freedom and Divine Determination

All radical monotheism–Jewish, Christian, or Islamic–is a sort of atheism. It is a non-belief in what most human beings have chosen to worship as God. Instead of a god to help us out of our downs, radical monotheism sees the action of God in both the ups and downs of living. Everything is created by God and everything that happens is the action of God. Radical monotheism might be characterized as a submission to fate, except that the word "fate" has been used in another context to mean another sort of thing. Radical monotheism, fully understood, is not fatalism where "fatalism" means passivity or lack of freedom to change things. In all three of these prominent Middle Eastern expressions of monotheism, human freedom has been emphasized as much as the Infinite Determiner of all things.

We are determined, to be sure, but we are also determined to be free. And our free acts figure into how the Determiner will determine us next. This paradox has been discussed, understood, and misunderstood in all three traditions.

While Islam has emphasized submission of our pride-filled ego to the Infinite Determiner, vital Islam has not interpreted this submission to mean passive indecisiveness in our daily living. Far from it. The peace of Islam is not quietude but peace with our own radical freedom, with being a Spirit being who is willing to act and often acts differently from everyone else around. The vitality of the Islamic style is unexplainable if we think that submission to Allah means complete passivity.

This same paradox of radical human freedom and Divine determination exists in Judaism and Christianity. To paraphrase the famous prayer of Reinhold Niebuhr, monotheism includes a proper passivity to what cannot be changed and a proper activity toward what can be changed and the wisdom to know the difference.

Early Islam made vast changes in the cultures to which it spread. Its correction of female infanticide, its kindness to the poor, its reconciliation of racial differences still challenge the most enlightened modern societies to realize that all oppression could be ended.

We must not judge any religious movement by its periods of decay or by its incompletenesses at specific times in its development. Early Islam, like many other religious movements, is an illustration that a deep Spirit renewal, practiced in a disciplined fashion, can be the source of massive social change.

In our times most manifestations of Christianity, Judaism, and Islam cannot be described as vital movements of Spirit sweeping through society and resolving the fundamental issues of our era. Rather, we are experiencing defensive bigotries rebelling against the actual course of events in the name of some obsolete rigidity. It is true that all three of these religious communities are laced with sporadic spurts of heroic relevance, but these spurts seem to die back into the ongoing, tragic momentum of our currently unrealistic societies. This momentum includes our headlong stampede toward ecological ruin, deep injustices, and whole populations of people who are more inclined to sectarian violence than to Spirit sainthood.

What is missing in contemporary Christianity, Judaism, and Islam is precisely what has characterized the strongest periods of all three of these religions—a radial monotheism religiously practiced in a disciplined fashion. Today, in all three traditions, monotheism has decayed into something theoretical—an idea that needs to be defended from the secular climate of our times. Belief in One God has, for the most part, ceased to mean loyalty, passion, or commitment. We have lost the energy for bold opposition to religious superstition and secular foolishness. I am suggesting that a vital monotheistic Islam would manifest opposition to the defensive, irrelevant, and destructive forms of Islamic religion as well as to every other form of escapist religion. I am suggesting that a vital monotheistic Judaism would manifest opposition to the defensive, irrelevant, and destructive forms of Jewish religion as well as to every other form of escapist religion. I am suggesting that a vital monotheistic Christianity would manifest opposition to the defensive, irrelevant, and destructive forms of Christian religion as well as to every other form of escapist religion. What a time in human history this would be if vast numbers of all three of these religious groups recovered that scathing monotheism which was initiated by Moses, matured by the prophets of Israel, and elaborated by Jesus and Mohammed!

Is the Worship of Allah and Yahweh the Same?

Let us use the ancient Hebrew word "Yahweh" for the monotheistic oneness that Jews and Christians have in common. Then we can ask, "Are there no differences between the worship of Allah and the worship of Yahweh?" Yes, there are. Just as there are differences between the Jewish and Christian covenants with Yahweh, so there are differences between the practice of submission to Allah and loyalty to the covenant with Yahweh practiced in Judaism or in Christianity. But we can learn to see these differences as enrichments of a common thrust rather than as opposing religious positions. Rather than discredit each other and even kill each other, we can learn from each other the glories of a common emphasis.

Islam rejected the small pilgrim-people emphasis of Judaism and set its sights on the transformation of entire civilizations. In this regard it was more like medieval Christianity. Some of us who favor small group Christianity have dismissed the medieval, civilization-wide form of Christianity as a complete perversion of the true faith. But we need to look more carefully at the gifts of Islam and of medieval Christianity. At their best these forms of religion took on the whole of a human society and intended to infuse that society with Spirit. "Small group and whole society" is not an irreconcilable conflict but a glorious polarity in which both poles can be affirmed. On the one hand, Spirit intensity always dawns first in a small group and that small group must then make its own preservation and the preservation of its Spirit breakthrough a priority. But also, Spirit that is really Spirit is a gift to all human beings. A religion that ignores the issues of cultural revitalization, political/economic justice, and ecological viability is not a religion that is in tune with the full meaning of radical monotheism. A full practice of radical monotheism includes compassion for *all*, not *some*, of the human family.

But neither Christianity nor Islam can return to its medieval ways of doing religion. Christendom is gone. So is "Islamic civilization." So is Jewish nationhood. We now live in secular environments in which many religious expressions are present. We must integrate into our vision of the future the realization that diversity, not uniformity, in religious practice is going to be the rule in every society. The medieval practice of supporting, and even dictating, a religion through the use of state power has worn out its welcome on this planet. We who are the Spirit-inspired members of any religious heritage must now teach tolerance and individual integrity rather than use state power to manipulate or impose religious victories. We can indeed conduct vigorous campaigns to call forth the deepest Spirit responses of any and all human beings, but religious imposition by state power is out of date. We might say that a state imposition of religion is opposed by the One God whose action in contemporary history is making diversity inevitable. Whether or not my religion is the best religion is an arrogant question. A much more modest question needs to be asked. Does my religion have gifts to contribute to myself and to the social whole? If Christianity is not needed anymore, then let those of us who were raised Christian become Jews or Muslims or something else. Let us stop defending the "truth" of our petty religious inventions. Rather, let us recover "Truth" as something given by the Infinite Silence–a Truth that needs no defense–a

Truth that simply needs to be put on the road in the service of all humanity.

In this book I am discussing many religions, but I am focusing on the gifts of Christianity. I am critical of bad religion wherever I see it, but I do not really know how to tell Muslims and Jews how to renew their gifts and contribute them to the world. I have more than enough to do renewing and contributing the gifts of Christianity.

In this chapter I have emphasized the gift of radical monotheism, a gift commonly carried by vital forms of Christianity, Judaism, and Islam. Yet each of these three long traditions carries gifts not emphasized by the other two. For example, the Trinitarian description of the experience of God is a gift carried by Christianity that is seldom appreciated by Jews and Muslims. Indeed, the Trinity is also poorly understood by most Christians. I want to close this essay with a few reflections on this uniquely Christian expression.

The Trinitarian understanding of God is not a dilution of radical monotheism into the worship of three Gods. Sometimes, literalistic Christians picture Father, Son, and Holy Spirit as sitting side by side in heaven. This is another confusion of religious poetry with literal scientific statement. The triune insight has to do with three simultaneous components of one experience. All three of these components are present whether we call that One God "Allah" or "Yahweh" or something else. The triune insight, as I have explored it in earlier chapters, is one experience with three faces: The Awesome, The Awed One, and the Awe itself. The Awed Ones are those who trust the Awesome Otherness and do not flee but stand present to the inspiration of Awe and thus live their lives accordingly. Whether this Awed One is Moses or Jesus or Mohammed or you or I, being an Awed One is part of the dynamics of every experience of God, the Awesomeness, and of God, the indwelling Awe. So understood, the Trinity is not merely a Christian dogma; it is a universal dynamic in the composition of the cosmos.

In its triune vision Christianity has seen something about experiencing the Awesome and has told about it. When a member of some other religion also sees this truth, it does not mean that they have become a Christian; it only means that they see what Christians, at their clearest, are talking about in their triune talk. Muslims and Jews do not have to oppose the triune thinking of Christians in order to worship One God. They can just say, "Oh, I see what you mean. I never noticed that before." Or they might say, "I have noticed that as well, but I have used other language for it." In other words, we do not need to get bogged down in interfaith battles over right doctrines.

I am attempting in these essays to envision a new type of dialogue between human beings who are open to the Truth–who have seen what they have seen and who tell each other what they have seen. If interfaith dialogue can proceed in this fashion, then the horrific estrangements between Christians, Jews, and Muslims can be overcome. We who are the "awake" members of these three traditions can see ourselves as partners in the awakenment of our Spiritually drowsy cultures. We can reclaim our family ties as the common offspring of Abraham.

10.

Mosaic Lawfulness
and Pauline Liberty

Judaism and Christianity have more similarities than differences. Jesus and Paul remained Jews their entire lives. Early Christianity can be viewed as a sect of Judaism. We might say that Paul taught a "Christ way" of being Jewish. It was after the destruction of the Jerusalem temple in 70 C.E. that these two varieties of Judaism began to separate into two distinct religions. The Christ way of being Jewish had attracted large numbers of Gentiles into its fold and had developed a more open relationship with Greco-Roman culture. Those Jews who were developing the Talmud took the approach of protecting the Hebrew heritage from Gentile dilution. These two different choices set the stage for two different strains of religious development.

Yet even today Christianity and Judaism remain two branches of one religious tree. The spectrum of differences among members within each heritage tends to be greater than the overall difference between the two heritages. From the beginning Christians retained the ancient Hebrew writings as part of their Scriptures. The Gospels of Mark,

Matthew, and Luke are best understood when we see them as fresh ways of interpreting the older writings. The word "Testament" is another word for "covenant." The exodus covenant was seen by early Christians as foundational for the new covenant they were articulating. Their departure from the popular religion of their times was interpreted by Mark and others as a new exodus.

Many Christians today tend to exaggerate the difference between these two "covenants." It is not always understood that these two covenants were covenants with the very same Infinite Thou. Numerous Christian thinkers have claimed that Jesus and his followers improved upon the God of the Old Testament. In the mid-second century, Marcion of Sinope created what he felt was a purer form of Christianity. He insisted that the Old Testament God was different from the loving Father of Jesus Christ. Marcion rejected the Old Testament God and wished to form a type of Christianity based upon a more "spiritual" God that Marcion believed he found in Luke's gospel and Paul's letters. Most contemporary New Testament scholars hold that Marcion's view of Luke and Paul was inaccurate; Luke and Paul are as deeply rooted in the Old Testament writings as the rest of the New Testament canon. Classical Catholic Christianity rejected Marcion of Sinope as a heretic, but Marcion's impetus has never fully died out. Today, many Christian-identified persons still distinguish their God of Love from the Creator of the material world with all its change, death, and decay. It is still taught in Christian churches today that Christians have a fundamentally different view of God than the Old Testament Yahweh. Nevertheless, it is my vigorously held view that the most fruitful dialogue between Jews and Christians can be pursued when we understand that the Exodus covenant and the Jesus/Messiah covenant are covenants with the very same Infinite Actor in history. I am convinced that such a perspective is vividly present in the letters of Paul and the gospels of Mark, Matthew, and Luke. In all these writings faith in Jesus as the Christ is expounded as a breakthrough that enables the transformed person to see more clearly what the old Exodus was all about in the first place. In his letter to the Romans, Paul makes the astonishing claim that Abraham was a person of faith (and he meant Christian faith) and that Abraham thereby stands in judgment on those other Jews who, through their reliance on legal achievements, can no longer be counted as Abraham's true descendants.

Paul and other New Testament writers sometimes say that Moses brought us "the law" and that Jesus brought us "freedom from the law." Phrased in this way, these two Spirit breakthroughs sound like opposites. Yet, Moses and the law are fully affirmed by both Jesus and Paul. How can we contemporary Christians reclaim Moses as our Spirit ancestor?

Moses, the ancient lawgiver, gave "us" the law in the context of "our" having been delivered from Egypt. This deliverance was an interior deliverance as well as an outward sociological escape. Moses, as a religious inventor, was not inventing law itself, but rather a new kind of law based upon the worship of the Infinite Actor who had delivered "us" from slavery in Egypt into the freedom of being the children of God. When I say "Moses" I realize that the actual historical person of Moses is a dim figure clouded in hundreds of years of legendary elaboration. But for my purposes here, it does not matter whether the ten commandments of Moses were actually written by Moses or by the followers of Moses. A breakthrough in law writing was made, and this breakthrough was a departure from slavery under a hierarchical social system and a movement toward freedom. This freedom was to be manifested by the entire social group and by each individual in that social group. This freedom was a Spirit reality–the freedom of being a responsible agent in relationship to the Awesome Wholeness of Being. The Mosaic freedom was more than responsibility to a finite social law; it was responsibility to an Actuality larger than any social order. This responsibility is incapable of being reduced to a legal practice.

So I want to look afresh at the Ten Commandments with the understanding that they are not moralism or legalism but historically specific Spirit teachings about freedom.

The Ten Commandments

In Egypt, as in every ancient civilization, social law was written to maintain a hierarchical social order. The aim of such law was to protect the existing social hierarchy from replacement by its own potentially rebellious masses. Such social law taught acquiescence, not freedom. Social law, in the Mosaic tradition, meant something very different: it was a freely taken covenant made by all the people of the social group. This law made particular their promise to obey as their God an actual Infinite Presence that was active in their lives. This "God" was not simply a personification of Egyptian society. For Moses and his Spirit descendants "Yahweh, your God" was a symbol that pointed to the Infinite, to the Primal Source of all nature, of all social groups, and of each and every event in the actual course of history. Obedience to such a God was at the same time an affirmation of human freedom. And Mosaic freedom was not freedom for rulers only; it was freedom for every member of the covenant group.

I will cite each of the 10 commandments, as listed in the 20th chapter of Exodus, and explore them as teachings about freedom and how freedom needs to be manifested in social living.

> I am Yahweh your God who brought you out of Egypt, out of the land of slavery.
> **[1] You shall have no other Gods to set against me.**

In other words, worship the God who got you here. This was religious law. It was the basic axiom for the religious discipline practiced by the followers of Moses. Having a God or Gods means having an object of worship, a mode of meaning, direction, or purpose—a way of understanding What-Is-What in a foundational, all-inclusive fashion. The Old Testament writers were clear that many potential objects of worship existed. Neither the existence of these Gods nor the existence of Yahweh was the issue. The Old Testament writers did not discuss whether or not Yahweh existed. Of course Yahweh existed. We were delivered from Egypt, weren't we! We were led out of the land of slavery, weren't we! Whatever name is given to the Reality that delivered us, there is no question about the existence of that "Deliverer." Learning more about this Almighty Actor took place across the centuries as this community continued in its worship. The meaning of "the Almighty" was better and better articulated as the community of Israel accumulated more experience. But the Old Testament writers never needed to argue for Yahweh's existence, because this Infinite Presence was a daily experience. Yahweh was not the idea of monotheism. Yahweh was not an idea of any sort. "Yahweh" was nothing more than or less than a "holy" name which pointed to that mysterious other-than-rational, other-than-human, All-Powerfulness in the actual flow of events. The radical monotheism of the Hebrew Scriptures had nothing to do with the existence or non-existence of a Supreme Being. Radical monotheism was then and is now about finding meaning and purpose for living that inescapable relationship with the unifying and mysterious Allness that everyone is confronting. The alternative to such radical monotheism is finding meaning and purpose in something finite and passing–such as a nation or pleasure or one's own pride-dominated ego. The call to worship Yahweh is a call to obey the Awe of freedom. Obeying freedom and obeying the Awesome are one and the same obedience.

[2] **You shall not make a carved image** for yourself or the likeness of any thing in the heaven above, or on the Earth below, or in the waters under the Earth. You shall not bow down to them or worship them: for I, Yahweh your God, am a jealous

God. I punish the children for the sins of the fathers to the third and fourth generations of those who hate me. But I keep faith with thousands, with those who love me and keep my commandments.

If we worship something finite, then we do not worship the Infinite. These two forms of worship "oppose" one another. We either worship the finite and hate the Infinite or we worship the Infinite and reject worship of the finite as something silly, foolish, and dangerous. What does it mean to say that the Infinite keeps faith with those who love the Infinite and keep the commandments of the Infinite? It means that being realistic to the extent of worshiping the Infinite reaps a reward from this Final Reality. Worshiping the finite is unrealistic because the finite passes away. Worshiping the finite enslaves the human Spirit and betrays the worshiper to a destiny of being let down in the end by an object of worship that passes away. Worshiping the Gods of Egypt was worshiping the finite because those Gods were personifications of Egyptian civilization. Such worship is enslaving. This is the basic Mosaic insight: the Infinite has set us free; so let us worship the Infinite rather than return to slavery in some new form. To say that the Infinite God is jealous is not a theory about the emotional life of a Supreme Being: it is a mythic expression of our life experience that worshiping the finite has dire consequences in the course of historical events. Since all historical events are the action of the Infinite, these dire consequences can be called "the jealousy of the Infinite."

> [3] **You shall not make wrong use of the name of Yahweh your God;** Yahweh will not leave unpunished the person who misuses this name.

This commandment is about something more serious than swearing. The word "name" has the overtone of "reputation." The Infinite has a reputation among human beings just like each human being has a reputation. The Infinite God has a name that we, the worshipers, need to defend. We remember the deeds of the Infinite. We tell stories about the acts of this Almightiness. We have created a meaningful heritage about what worshiping this Infinite Almightiness means. This heritage, these meanings, this reputation of the Almighty, this "name" is vulnerable to misuse. And misuse is an important matter because it undermines the worship of the Infinite not only within our own worshiping community but also for our entire planet.

This commandment, rather than being trivial and unneeded in our modern setting, is a crucial challenge for Christians and Jews alike. For example, Christian-identified persons are misusing Christian heritage to the extent that Christians and non-Christians alike are being provided with excuses to reject or trivialize this heritage. Those who tie Christian faith to having belief in a literal seven-day creation or a literal resurrection of Jesus trivialize this entire heritage. Christian heritage is further misused by tying it to rigid moralisms about birth control, abortion, and sexual orientation. The reputation of this heritage has been further disgraced by rampant sentimentality such as meeting one's saintly grandmother in heaven and many other feel-good trivializations. All this literalism, moralism, and sentimentality are examples of a wrong use of Yahweh's reputation—that glorious reputation which the best of Judaism and Christianity has built up over the centuries. The extent of this misuse has been so great that the very name "Christian" has become a source of embarrassment to many of us who deeply honor this tradition. The name or reputation of the Jewish and Christian object of worship has been misused and such violations are destructive of Awe-filled living.

[4] **Remember to keep the Sabbath day holy**. You have six days to labor and do all your work. But the seventh day is a Sabbath of Yahweh your God…

In this commandment the religious law of Moses turns to the issue of time. A religious practice requires time. Our work for survival and for our physical and cultural enrichment can surely be done with six-sevenths of our time. If we are going to be serious about being a fresh start in worship, we need *time* for grounding ourselves in our love for the Infinite, *time* to get used to our own profound depths, *time* for preserving effective religious heritage for future generations, *time* for nurturing ourselves toward the full stature of a wholehearted responsiveness to the Infinite. So here is how I would reword this commandment for people today: "Remember to set aside *time* for a religious practice that nurtures your best potentials." Doing so is an act of freedom. Not doing so loses freedom to the busy drift of contemporary diversion, sloth, and greed.

[5] Honor your father and your mother…

This commandment rounds out the specifically religious half of the Ten Commandments and provides a transition to the next five commandments, which are the social components of that law. This commandment indicates something more than caring for the elders in our biological line. It implies caring for the elders in our religious community. It implies that those who built this religious culture and passed it on to us deserve our respect. This is part of our worship: to honor the people who created, lived, renewed, and transmitted to us this worship. This commandment stands opposed to our modern idolization of youthfulness and novelty. It is indeed important for us to face the future, but it is also important to face that future with the wisdom of the ages–with the wisdom of our true elders.

[6] You shall not murder.

Clearly, the wilderness band of Moses could not survive and carry its spiritual gifts on to succeeding generations if its members resorted to killing one another. A small desert band is vulnerable to total chaos if even a few people are allowed to get away with murder. Such a truth is relevant today for any inner-city housing project, any city street, any suburban sprawl, any rural village, or any planet-wide interaction. In Mosaic teaching, the murder restriction applied to every member of the community; whereas in other societies of that day, the murder of a slave or an underling had far less restriction than the murder of an aristocrat.

Moses did not apply this commandment to the subject of warfare. This commandment is not about not killing human beings under any circumstances; it is about restraining murder within the social group. What is the difference between killing and murder? Killing can be done to protect a community of people or to advance in history critical values that benefit all the peoples of the Earth. Murder is a disruption of these same practical values that certain kinds of killing may support. It is clear that the Israelite people never thought of this commandment as a prohibition of warfare. We must not read our modern idealisms of non-violence back into the Mosaic heritage. Sometimes nonviolence is the best practical strategy; sometimes it is not. Sometimes warfare is necessary in the service of overall justice. Killing can sometimes be the ethical action of not allowing murder to take place. However confusing this may seem to our contemporary moralism, this commandment is best understood as a teaching about the practical need to find within ourselves the freedom to restrain self and others from murder within the social group.

[7] You shall not commit adultery.

In the patriarchal social format, each woman was some man's trusteeship. She was some man's wife or some man's daughter. Moses was not given the vision to oppose this patriarchal social format. We had to wait until our century to see clearly that practicing the patriarchal format is incompatible with worshiping the Infinite. Nevertheless, Moses and his followers, operating within their taken-for-granted patriarchal context, prohibited the misuse of women. The commandment was primarily addressed to men—don't take as sexual partner a woman that has not been given to you as wife. This moral directive, like murder and stealing, was simple common sense for the situation in which Moses and his descendants had to live. This was practical social law, but law constructed within the context of responding properly to the Infinite. In the typical hierarchical society, a poor man's wife or daughter was often fair game to a more powerful male. But for Moses loyalty to the Almighty included ordering sexual relations more equitably. Our contemporary "ordering of sexual relations" may be different from that of these ancient people, but finding the appropriate moral order for our sexual partnering is still a necessary requirement for equitable social life. Freedom for men and women means restraining ourselves and others from chaotic sexual practices.

[8] You shall not steal.

As with life and sex, the goods of each person are to be respected. This practical honoring of our fellow human beings is another crucial part of what worshiping the Almighty includes. And if we want to embody the wisdom of this terse statement today, we must surely apply it not only to shoplifting but also to wealthy investors who use our modern economic structures to take wealth from the powerless. Freedom means restraining ourselves and others from stealing.

[9] You shall not give false evidence against your neighbor.

Similarly, honoring the neighbor means respecting the neighbor's good name, reputation, and protecting him or her from false punishment. Applying the wisdom of such honoring of the neighbor in our contemporary societies would include changes in our willingness to mislead others through propaganda and advertising. It would also exclude the stereotyping of races, cultures, and religions. Freedom means speaking the plain truth and thus restraining ourselves and others from false statements about our neighbors.

[10] You shall not covet your neighbor's…anything…

This commandment sums up the inner meaning of the last five commandments. Not only are we commanded not to outwardly take what is our neighbor's; we are also commanded not even to covet it, desire it, or wish for it. We are commanded not to covet a life different from the one we are being given by the Almighty. This does not mean that we should not pray, work, and scheme for something we want. But it does mean that we are not worshiping the Almighty when we wish we were a different person, having different gifts, possessions, and opportunities than those we do in fact have or may honestly and realistically acquire. Each life has its limits. Our responsibility is to accept those limits, for those limits are the action of the God we worship. Having accepted our limits, the actual possibilities within those limits can also be claimed as part of our authentic lives. Coveting means fighting against the Almighty for a life that is not ours–a life less limited than ours or even for a life that is not limited at all. A deep death to our ordinary egoism is implied by this commandment. The deep and inward profoundness of the "don't covet" commandment is seldom explored. Also seldom explored is the truth that not coveting is the freedom to be the freedom which each one of us already is.

One of the interesting qualities of these Mosaic commandments is that they blend together what we might call religious and secular law. Today we tend to keep separate the rational forms we use for governing religious practice and the rational forms we use for governing the general social order. But for Moses religion was part of the social order, and the social order was an outgrowth of a religious perspective that undergirded both religious practice and social order. The first five commandments are aimed at constructing a social practice of religion that keeps in history the consciousness that also undergirds the last five commandments. There is indeed just one commandment: obey the Almighty; obey the God who delivers us from slavery—who delivers us to the actuality of our freedom and into the awareness that this freedom is our authentic humanity. This commandment to love God includes the corollary commandment to love, with the same level of concern with which we love ourselves, the beings whom God is giving us as neighbors. These two commandments characterize the teachings of the New Testament writings as well.

In the narrative of the twentieth chapter of Exodus, the verses following the giving of these commandments indicate that the people heard thunder and saw lightning. They heard a trumpet sound and saw a mountain smoke. They trembled and kept their distance. Such phrases are symbols for an experience of deep Awe. The first hearers of the commandments, according to this account, were smote with profound dread. The commandments meant changes in their normal mode of thinking and behaving, and these changes were experienced as radical, far-reaching, perhaps more than a person could bear. Moses, in this story, tries to assure them that the commandments are friendly—that they are gifts from the Almighty who means them well; but the people keep their distance anyhow.

In the history that followed, these commandments were frequently resisted as well as obeyed. Some recent scholarship indicates that the historical Moses may have spent much of his life struggling to overcome even crass practices like human sacrifice within his new social experiment. Centuries later the prophets still struggled with their national aristocracies over simple issues like giving minimal respect and support to the poor in their midst. Indeed, we are still struggling with every one of these commandments in every society on Earth.

It is important to underline one more time that it was not Moses alone who wrote the Mosaic law. The legal creativity in the first five books of the Hebrew Bible has often been attributed to Moses, but these five books of the Bible actually contain the working out of the Mosaic impetus over many centuries. We do not know precisely what the historical Moses did and said. Historically speaking, Moses is now a vague memory about 3300 years deep into our past, but I find it quite plausible to assume that the Moses who was so vividly remembered by his communal descendants was somehow the sort of person that they fictionalized.

Furthermore, I find it encouraging that the descendants of Moses had no qualms about expanding upon the law of Moses and applying it to their ever-changing lives. The wonder of this ongoing freedom in legal creativity is lost from view when we envision every sentence that is attributed to Moses as a rational form channeled to Moses in a magical fashion. All law, including the Mosaic law, was written by human beings for specific times and places. The "divinity" within the Mosaic law resides in its being a departure from hierarchical law-writing. Mosaic law writing, at its best, was an act of free obedience to the Almighty Actor in history.

These reflections on Moses and Mosaic law-writing help us understand why Jesus and Paul and the other New Testament authors valued Moses and respected this heritage as "the law of God." When Jesus and Paul gave honor to the law of Moses, they were not picturing the sort of law writing that is typically taught in law schools today. They saw law as spelling out the meaning of obedience to the Almighty. This is why such a fiery conflict could arise for them around issues having to do with the law. In the view of Jesus and Paul, the essence of the Mosaic law was being violated in the name of a meticulously strict obedience to superficial aspects of the law tradition. The law, according to Jesus and Paul, had become an idol, an object of worship taking the place of worshiping the Almighty. Such religious legalism included neglecting those weightier matters of love and justice that flow from a true worship of Yahweh. So the law, which was meant to specify obedience to the Almighty, was, according to Jesus and Paul, being used by their meticulous, legalistic contemporaries as a means of rebellion from the Almighty. Paul had come to hold this viewpoint only after years of persecuting this very perspective in the name of his own strict obedience to the law.

Pauline Liberty

To fully understand the law controversy in the New Testament, we have to see the capacity of the law to serve these two contradictory functions: (1) the law can be used by our Spirit authenticity to give form to that authenticity, and (2), the law can be used by our estrangement from authenticity to justify that estrangement with self-righteous observances.

We are using law in this second way when we view the inherited law as telling us what is good so that we can achieve goodness by our own efforts. From this perspective Spirit health comes about in the human species through human effort in obeying the law. But such a perspective does not deal with the profound depths of human estrangement. It simply covers over hidden interior estrangements with outward goodnesses. Like hanging good apples on a bad apple tree, outward goodness does nothing to heal the actual relationship of the whole person in that person's whole response to the Awesome Overallness.

In both Jesus' teachings and Paul's writings, we find clear expression of the first viewpoint: the inherited law is understood as expressing authenticity and thereby awakening us to our estrangement. As socially empowered law, the law actually restrains our estrangement. In both ways the law, if it is indeed good law, teaches us about our estrangement from the Awesome Overallness. It does not, however, heal that estrangement. Spirit health comes about apart from the law, through the death of the ego and our resurrection to Spirit living. The law may play a role in the death of the ego, but the realization and acceptance of forgiveness is required to effect a resurrection to authentic wholeness. When we have been restored to Spirit health, we can then recognize the validity of the law as an expression of Spiritual health and as a form that can be used in acting out our health.

Furthermore, when we are experiencing Spirit health we are able to be conscious of the fact that the law (all law) is finite and, therefore, a partial or incomplete expression of Spirit health. Spirit is always in the position to write new law, better law–better in the sense of more adequately expressing authentic Spirit.

Jesus was remarkably creative in his handling of the inherited law. "The Sabbath," he said, "was made for people, not people for the Sabbath." Behind this statement is the perspective that all law is made to serve humanity, not to enslave humanity in rigid forms. Law, even when it expresses obedience to the Wholeness of Being, is human-made. And anything that is human-made can be remade. Upon what basis is law to be remade? Or, what makes a good law good? The answer to such questions in both Judaism and Christianity is: "Loving God and neighbor."

The apostle Paul was also remarkably creative in his handling of the inherited law. He had a fight with Peter over requiring Gentiles to eat kosher food. He fought, at risk to his very life, with Jewish Christians who wanted to require Gentile Christians to undergo circumcision. On the subject of eating food offered to idols, he made an extremely illuminating ruling. He said that the person who had no qualms about eating such food was strong in his or her faith. But Paul admonished the strong Spirit person to act with love toward the weak Spirit person, the one who still did have qualms about such eating. Paul held that the strong should eat no meat at all rather than offend the weak and cause them to stumble in the living of their faith. No example could more clearly illustrate Paul's perspective that Spirit love is the foundation for all action and that law is secondary and needs to be flexibly formulated and applied.

The detailed particulars of Paul's life situation have little importance for us today. What is important is Paul's willingness to be creative with the inherited law. Love is the underlying reality that Paul does not question, and love is not law. Spirit love can mean using or not using, improving or not improving the inherited law. Spirit love can mean creating new law to govern new situations. For circumcised Jews and uncircumcised Gentiles to be part of the same religious group is a splendid example of new law.

Of all Paul's flexible rulings, the ones that are most controversial today are his rulings on the roles of men and women in the Christian community. For example, on the wearing of hats and speaking in church, Paul went along with the patriarchal etiquettes of his day. Clearly, these are choices that Christians need not make today. Today we can see the destructiveness of the patriarchal patterns for both men and women. But Paul and all his male and female companions were so immersed in patriarchal oppression that it was literally invisible to them. To his credit Paul never denied that women were full members of the Spirit community. And I believe he meant his patriarchal etiquettes to be love for his situation. Furthermore, contemporary Christians have Paul's example of legal flexibility to use in correcting the very rulings Paul made about the roles of men and women. Paul saw law as something that could be changed. I groan when I hear conservative Christians proclaim that whatever rules were used in the New

Testament churches must be used today. Such a perspective is just plain silly as well as un-Pauline.

So with these practical contexts in mind, let us look more closely at what Paul meant by "the freedom for which Christ has set us free." We are all habituated in some set of moral principles, rules, customs, or laws. Our interior psyche as well as our outward social patterning has some sort of moral organization built into it. In most cases our parents have gone to some trouble to instill in us the desire to be good persons so that we may get along better in our lives and perhaps also make our parents proud of us. This superego, as Freud called it, functions in every human life. And as Freud also pointed out, this superego can conflict with doing our best practical living. What Paul is saying about this universal human situation is that our superego (our social conditioning) is finite. It is human-made. Such law only becomes "holy" insofar as it truly expresses the Spirit of actually responding in trust to the Infinite Actor. If we trust the Infinite Actor, then we can also love the Infinite Actor and this love includes loving all the finite beings among whom the Infinite Actor is giving us our lives. With this context clearly set, loving our neighbors will then include creating and obeying social rules with which we order our living together.

But when we face our concrete ethical choices, which comes first, love or law? Love is prior. Love gives us the freedom to obey the law, to violate the law, to create a new law, or whatever is necessary to accomplish love. For example, Paul would not agree with those who have made an "always applicable" law out of non-violence. Paul's perspective implies that there are situations in which killing someone is the proper response of love. Paul clearly had no qualms about speaking boldly and even insulting people when he deemed it appropriate. He used satire, chastisement, and wild imagery, whatever it took to love the situation as he perceived it.

The law, any law, practiced as a means toward becoming a good person, is not freedom and not love. It is moralistic sentimentality and perhaps self-indulgent arrogance. If you or I have been restored to our trust of the Infinite Actor, we do not need to become good persons. We are good persons already in every way that matters. We do not have to seek goodness; we have only to be the authenticity we already are with as much creativity and boldness as we can muster. If this entails violating our superego or the laws of our society or the customary morality of most people, then so be it. Such liberty does not mean indulging our finite drives. Indulgence is not freedom but another sort of bondage to our self-centered ego. Furthermore, the ego, according to Paul, can be appropriately limited by appropriate laws. Appropriate law is a means by which the Awesome Infinite Actor opposes egoism; therefore, such law can rightly be called "holy and good." But for those who have died and been raised into that Spirit life which Mosaic law was intended to express, there is no law. The resurrected life follows the far more radical non-law of love.

Some Non-concluding Comments about Jews and Christians

There are practicing Jews who see Paul's point clearly and who affirm freedom and love over the specifics of the Mosaic law. And there are huge numbers of people who practice a Christian religion who are enslaved in Christian forms of legalism which are similar to the legalism of those Jews and Jewish Christians with whom Paul battled. It is also true that legalism crops up in the writings of the Christian and Jewish Bibles. The battle between legalism and freedom has been a recurring theme within this long and complex heritage. Both Jews and Christians still face the challenge to see that freedom also means freedom from the written heritage and thus freedom to reinterpret that heritage in the context of our current callings to respond to that Infinite Actor in our own times.

So we might say that there are "true Jews" and "true Christians" who share many common understandings. Both types of true worshipers trust the Awesome Infinite Silence and dialogue with this Infinite Actor in the events of contemporary history. Both pursue this dialogue through prayer and through communion with other worshipers. Both affirm the Awesome Infinite Silence as the master context for loving with freedom every human being and every other creature given existence by the Infinite. Both see themselves being in a covenant with the Infinite, a covenant which renders them vanguard servants within human history, a people called forth to bring truth and justice to all the nations of the earth.

Does all this similarity mean that we have only one religion, not two? No, we clearly have two separate heritages, one centered in the Exodus covenant and the other centered in the Jesus-the-Christ covenant. Christians can discover, however, that their new covenant is a renewal of the old covenant and that the old covenant was an interpretive foundation for shaping the new covenant. Christians need not reshape their entire symbol system to make the original Exodus story their primary center of illumination. And Jews need not reshape their entire symbol system to include the Christian symbols. Rather, both Christians and Jews need to consider the possibility that humanity has been and continues to be best served by the presence of two separate religions. Each heritage carries values that the other heritage is somewhat more tempted to neglect.

While both religions are rooted in a covenant to trust the Infinite Silence, the two ways of formulating this covenant are significantly different. The Jewish way of formulating this covenant emphasizes the need for making the covenant particular in a specific religious practice. So Jewish identity and preserving Jewish culture is a major concern of Jewish practice. Christians, on the other hand, tend to emphasize the universal elements of covenanting with the Infinite Silence and thus minimize the importance of particular religious expressions. This has made Christians considerably more flexible in the forms of religion they have invented and, when true to themselves, more loose within the religious forms they practice. At their best, Christians have even become aware that trusting the Infinite Silence is religiously contentless, that the essence of Christianity is not a religion at all, but an attitude toward living that is creatively critical of every religious formulation.

But when this Christian universalism is combined with modern individualism, many Christians have lost all sense of being a vanguard people who need to sustain their communal intensity with a rich and nurturing religious heritage. One of the deepest challenges that Christians face today is to reconstruct their religion for these times. This challenge is being neglected in part because many Christians who are awake enough to see that Christianity needs to be reconstructed are doubtful that a religious embodiment of Christianity is vitally needed. Jewish practice is less open to such individualistic scattering. Though many Jews also abandon their heritage, they are, nevertheless, more inclined to deeply value a nurturing religious heritage. Christians today might take lessons from those diligent Jews who insist on being Jewish in some specific and meaningful manner. Jewish diligence preserves the truth that Spirit without religious embodiment is subject to loss and is unlikely to be fully matured.

Jewish people tend to be more tempted to the opposite extreme–namely, to pursue a rigid practice of religious forms that have ceased to have contemporary meaning. Such Jews might take lessons from those Christians who see clearly that the authentic human has the power and the flexibility to thoroughly reconstruct religious practice.

I do not mean for these generalizations to be taken too rigidly. Many Jews and many Christians have found ways to hold a constructive balance between universality and particularity, between Spirit and religious form. I am only attempting to look through the complexities of these two heritages to the underlying tendencies that make them different. Further, I believe that the difference I have identified is a creative difference. Spirit without religious form is flimsy living. Religious form without Spirit is frozen living. We need both contentless Spirit and religious content to flesh out a healthy program of living…

While the creative difference between Jews and Christians is valuable, I want, nevertheless, to emphasize further the underlying commonness. Jews and Christians do have slightly different "religious genes," but they are children of the same womb. And what is common to both Jews and Christians is a great gift to the Spirit health of the human species.

Here is a summary statement of those common gifts as I see them. Both religious traditions focus upon being in covenant with the Awesome Infinite Silence present in all events. This covenant is a commitment to trust and to listen to the Infinite Silence speak in the actual course of historical events. Having heard this contemporary Speech of the Infinite Silence, the covenanted persons are committed to obey what is heard. This obedience is both an obligation to respond appropriately within the external situations of human living and the obligation to respond freely and creatively–to respond without certainty of right or wrong. In this covenant with the Infinite Silence, the covenanters never know for sure what the Infinite Silence is saying, nor do they know for sure what obeying the Infinite Silence means or what the consequences of their obeying will be, but they proceed in radical freedom and creativity and keep listening for this Mouthless Voice to speak again in the course of historical events.

Whatever our religious heritage, we can stand in the sandals of Jews and Christians and see if we can also hear in the events of our times the Speech of the Infinite Silence.

The Asian Enrichment

11.

The Unspeakable Tao and the Messianic Secret

Before Buddhism arrived in China, the sages of Confucian and Taoist wisdom had already captivated the religious sensibilities of this vast area. Lao Tzu is the name given to the original wisdom teacher of the Taoist tradition. Lao Tzu is said to have been born in 604 BCE and is credited with writing the *Tao Te Ching*. Although scholars doubt whether this work reached its final form until the second half of the third century BCE, someone began this ancient tradition. It is our historical consensus to call this someone Lao Tzu.

One of the gifts of Taoism is its affirmation of balance between opposing realities that, in the West, are often seen as conflictive. Nature and society, masculine and feminine, mind and heart–each set of such realities is seen in the Taoist view as two parts of a whole in which one part does not exist without the complementary reality of the other. For example, nature and society are not opposing realities at war with each other, a war which one or the other must win. Rather, true winning means finding that balanced styling of human behavior that appropriately affirms both nature and society. In these times of ecological crisis such wisdom has great relevance. Balancing male and female energies is also supported by these Taoist insights.

How is this preoccupation with balance a Spirit practice? Consider this example. Suppose you are a rather dry social engineer who is reluctant toward being a passionate lover of nature. In the lingo of Taoism, you are living your active, thoughtful yang without accessing much of your passive feelingful yin. Taoism challenges you to make a trip to that place of consciousness where you can see the whole–in this case, see the validity of both the yang of social engineering and the yin of nature bonding. Having arrived at consciousness of the whole, you can see that you are not just one thing, "yang," but you are also its opposing dynamic, "yin." You are not just active, dry, social engineer; you are also passive, moist, nature lover. Now you can return to your "yang" (your active, dry, social engineer) with a new sense of balance. You are now detached from the yang you thought you were by seeing that life is also yin, and so you can return to being the already familiar yang but with a respect for yin in others and in yourself. This Taoist breakthrough is an expression of deep potentialities within human existence. And these are the same potentialities that others have called "Spirit", "the breath of the Infinite," or "enlightenment."

Taoist balancing is not a sentimental view; it is characterized by a certain sternness. Taoism tends to be maverick wisdom, always challenging the status quo and its common-sense rationalizations. In its relations with Confucian wisdom, Taoism is clearly the more disestablishment perspective. In spite of its challenging style, Taoism brought a balancing impetus to the religious life of the Orient. In ancient China it was probably Taoism's "holistic balancing" that allowed the members of Chinese culture to become Taoists, Confucians, and Buddhists all at the same time. Likely, it was the wisdom of Taoism that enabled the social practicality of Confucian wisdom and the intensely solitary radicalities of evangelizing Buddhism to meld into a singular Oriental practice that balanced these tensions.

This amalgam of religions as it migrated to Japan evolved into Zen Buddhism, which is now so popular among Western people. Zen Buddhism might be called Taoist Buddhism, for it holds in common with Taoism many of those qualities which Wes "Scoop" Nisker dubbed "Crazy Wisdom" in his book by that title.

Some of the most outlandish or "crazy" aspects of Taoist wisdom come into play when this heritage deals with the Eternal Tao. In this arena Taoism becomes a head-on assault upon the common sense of virtually every culture on Earth. The Eternal "Tao" or "Way" points to the Way-Life-Is in its ultimate wholeness. Taoism's deepest challenge to human living is its challenge to style our human way of living in accord with this Eternal Way. But the Eternal Way is mysterious, unspeakable, continually uprooting us and challenging us. If we are looking for a secure and orderly way, or for a rationally comforting way, or for a sentimental way, the Eternal Tao is not the way we are seeking. Let me illustrate this with some poetry from Chuang Tzu.

> Tao is beyond words
> And beyond things.
> It is not expressed
> Either in word or in silence.
> Where there is no longer word or silence
> Tao is apprehended. [10]

And Lao Tzu put this even simpler in this brief cryptogram about the Eternal Tao.

---

[10] As translated by Thomas Merton in *The Way of Chuang Tzu* (New Directions: 1962), page 152

Those who know don't say.
Those who say don't know.

When these words are applied to any ordinary matter, they are simply meaningless. Apply them, for example, to knowing how to lay floor tile. In connection with tiling my house, I have read an entire book on laying floor tile. I assumed that this author knew what he was talking about and was talking about what he knew. If he cannot say how to tile my floor, then I don't want to read his book. And if his very act of saying how to lay tile proves that he does not know how to lay tile, then laying tile is a very strange matter indeed.

So, if this Lao Tzu cryptogram is not about practical things like how to lay tile, what sort of "knowing" is this saying indicating? Let us assume that this saying is expressing wisdom about what it means to be wise in that dimension of human experience that every vital religion came into being to express! Let us suppose that all religious knowing is about knowing the Final Mystery of it all. And how can you know Mystery? You can't. And yet you do. You can have a personally direct encounter with Mystery. You can indeed know that you simply do not know.

So those who know Mystery can't say what they know; nevertheless, they know that they know Mystery. If, however, they say something about what they know to others, they know that they cannot expect others to find what they say to be obvious.

But Lao Tzu's saying is even more tricky than it first appears. For if we humans literally never attempted to say what we know about the Mysterious Way that life is, then there would be no religions whatsoever. Even Lao Tzu's saying would not exist. For this saying is itself an attempt to say what cannot be said. Literally speaking, Lao Tzu violated his own teaching. He said this saying! According to the saying, Lao Tzu thereby proves that he does not know what he is talking about.

But Lao Tzu does know what he is talking about, and he expects the students of this saying to grapple with it until they also know. For Mystery is both something you can know and something you do not know at the same time. Further, each person has to know Mystery for himself or herself. No one else can know the unknown for you or for me. Each of us, all alone, has to know the unknown for ourselves.

The Christian Secret

Students of Christianity have frequently had the impression that the Christian tradition is a rather blatant tradition, requiring assent to intellectual propositions that are assumed to be quite objective and obvious. But this is a misreading.

Nothing is more central to the Christian heritage than the issue of whether or not Jesus is the Christ (that is, the Messiah). Yet in the gospel of Mark, which is the first of the four gospels to be written, a great effort is made to indicate that the Messiahship of Jesus is a secret. In the very first chapter of Mark a man possessed by an unclean spirit shrieks, "What do you want with us, Jesus of Nazareth; have you come to destroy us? I know who you are–the Holy One of God." Jesus rebukes this spirit. "Be silent," he says, "and come out of him." In other words, Jesus says to the demons, "Shhhhh, quiet, don't tell anyone; it's a secret." In the very center of the Gospel of Mark, Jesus asks his disciples who they say that he is, and Peter responds, "You are the Messiah." In the very next line of Mark's gospel we read, "Then he (Jesus) gave them very strict orders not to tell anyone about him." In other words, "Shhhhh, quiet, don't tell anyone; it's a secret." In the very next chapter, three disciples go with Jesus to the top of a mountain where Jesus is transfigured into a blazing white figure talking with Moses and Elijah. After this incident Mark says, "On their way down the mountain, he (Jesus) enjoined them not to tell anyone what they had seen until the Son of Man had risen from the dead." In other words, "Shhhhh, quiet, don't tell anyone;

it's a secret." Then at the very end of Mark's gospel, the three women who have just witnessed the empty tomb of Jesus are pictured fleeing from this experience in great dread. And the very last line of the original gospel of Mark contains these surprising words, "They said nothing to anybody, for they were afraid."

Clearly Mark's view of the Messiahship of Jesus is something different from those contemporary Christians who insist on blocking our view with huge billboards proclaiming that "JESUS SAVES." In Mark's view the amazing significance of Jesus is a secret, a secret known only to those who have experienced the resurrection, whatever "experiencing resurrection" might mean. And those who **have** experienced the resurrection are so terrified that they do not say anything to anyone.

I want to suggest that sensitive Spirit persons, whatever their religious background, are capable of sensing in Mark's literary madness an expression of that crazy wisdom for which Lao Tzu is rightly famous. Mark is aware of an unspeakable Awe, which is our state of knowing when we confront the Final Mystery. Furthermore, Mark implies that all the following "Christian mysteries" are intimately connected: the healing power of Jesus, the transfiguration of Jesus, the resurrection of Jesus, and the Messiahship of Jesus. All these "happenings" are a secret–that is, not obvious to anyone who might have been there with a TV camera.

Those who *were* there–those who were the very closest to him–were completely mystified. When they thought they knew who Jesus was, he told them about his approaching rejection and death and they discovered that they did not know at all what was going on. "It's a secret," Jesus seems to say. "Don't proclaim your silly doctrines about me until you know the secret." So what is this secret?

"Those who say don't know. Those who know don't say." Each of us has to discover for ourselves what it means to experience the resurrection of Jesus. Each of us has to discover for ourselves what it means for Jesus to be just Jesus and at the same time the Holy One of God, the

Messiah, the savior of the world, the light of the world, the true food for our souls, and almost every other plaudit known to the religious imagination. All this is a secret. It is just plain meaningless to place it on a billboard. Only in the Awe-filled secrecy of your or my own personal life can these significators of Jesus of Nazareth have any meaning whatsoever.

So what does it mean to call Jesus "the Messiah"? To raise this question is a huge advance in Spirit maturity for most Christian-identified persons.

Jesus, plain Jesus, is just a human being like any other man or woman. In the story about those three disciples who saw Jesus transfigured, Moses and Elijah appear, light shines and a voice says, "This is my Son, my Beloved, listen to him." But in the very next sentence of Mark's gospel are these amazing words, "And now suddenly, when they looked around, there was nobody to be seen but Jesus alone with themselves."

The significance of Jesus is the result of a Spirit transformation within the person doing the viewing of plain ordinary Jesus. In all likelihood Jesus was an amazingly lucid, bold, and provocative person. It is hard to believe that all that fuss could have been made over a person who was not an exemplary religious teacher. But there are many exemplary religious teachers. Why call any of them by some boundlessly exalted epitaph?

Furthermore, Jesus died a criminal's death. He was rejected by the religious authorities. He was abandoned by his best friends. If anyone wanted to live safely within the climate of those times, Jesus should have been forgotten entirely. Nothing was more absurd to the religious imagination of that cultural setting than the notion of a crucified Messiah.

Let us stop to note that at that time, the taken-for-granted meaning of "expecting the Messiah" was expecting an event in history that would make human life good, healed, just, fulfilled, righteous, complete. In that regard what good was a dead, disrespected teacher, however wise he may have seemed to some people? In first century Judaism, the

Messiahship of Jesus simply did not make sense. To most people today, Jesus' Messiahship still does not make sense. Have our lives been made good, healed, just, fulfilled, righteous, complete by this young man and his early death? Have they? Well how? Life is the same as before. Injustice continues. Wicked people still sit in high places. And every form of human estrangement continues to manifest its presence on this Earth. If we are honest, we must admit that we are less "spiritually mature" than we might wish to be. How has anything significant happened here?

Shhhhh, quiet, don't tell anyone; it's a secret.

You or I will not be "in on" this secret until we have ourselves been resurrected through seeing the resurrection of Jesus. And this is a Spirit experience. People standing by may not see that we are resurrected or that the resurrected Jesus has appeared to us. It is a secret.

But we are given hints. We do not have to become something different than we already are in order to become, right now, "The Light of the World" to everyone else on Earth. We just have to stop running away from Reality. We just have to turn around and proceed in the opposite direction from the way that human life is customarily lived. We just have to trust that telling the truth about life is the walk of the Messiah.

Telling the truth? What is Truth?

Those who know don't say.
Those who say, don't know.

It's a secret.

Telling the Secret

My first thought was to simply end this chapter without this additional section. That would have been imitating the style of the Taoist sage: just leaving the listener with a challenging enigma to contemplate until the cryptic nature of the words began to make sense through some fresh interior dawning.

But I have decided to talk on, following the biblical style of running down every possible misunderstanding and then attempting to address that misunderstanding with still further crazy wisdom.

Here is a question that might occur to someone who considers the statement that the Christian message is a secret. If the Christian message is a secret, why have Christians been challenged to tell this secret? In the closing verses of the Gospel of Matthew we read that the gospel message is to be told to all nations. Surely this is the craziest of all crazy wisdom: the good news of Christianity is a secret, and yet we are asked to go into every city and every backwoods of this planet and tell this secret.

In order to understand such crazy wisdom, we must learn to identify with the disciples in their pre-resurrection relationships with Jesus. In every one of the gospels, the disciples are pictured as dumb-dumbs who never quite get it. Relative to the Messiahship of Jesus we hear Peter in the 8th chapter of Mark answering, "You are the Christ" to Jesus' question, "Who do you say that I am?" But Peter at this point does not know what he is talking about. This becomes clear in the very next words of Mark's gospel.

> And he began to teach them that it was inevitable that the Son of Man should go through much suffering and be utterly repudiated by the elders and chief priests and scribes, and be killed, and after three days rise again. He told them all this quite bluntly.
>
> This made Peter draw him to one side and take him to task about what he had said. But Jesus turned and faced his disciples and rebuked Peter.
>
> "Out of my way, Satan," he said. "Peter, you are not looking at things from God's point of view, but from man's!"
>
> Then he called his disciples and the people around him and said to them,

"If anyone wants to follow in my footsteps, he must give up all rights to himself, take up his cross, and follow me. The man who tries to save his life will lose it; it is the man who loses his life for my sake and the gospel's who will save it. What good can it do a man to gain the whole world at the price of his own soul? What can a man offer to buy back his soul once he has lost it? If anyone is ashamed of me and my words in this unfaithful and sinful generation, the Son of Man will be ashamed of him when he comes in the Father's glory with holy angels around him."

Then he added,

"Believe me, there are some of you standing here who will know nothing of death until you have seen the kingdom of God coming in its power." (Mark 8:31-9:1 Phillips translation)

Clearly, Peter does not really understand when he says that Jesus is the Christ. What is it that he does not understand? He does not understand that the Christ must suffer and die at the hands of sinful people. And here is a second thing that Peter does not understand: if the Messiah is indeed one who must meet such a grim fate, what does this mean about our expectations for our own lives if we live in a Messianic fashion? Must we also face rejection in the world? Jesus says a very blunt "Yes!" to this question. Walking in Jesus' footsteps means walking the road to Jerusalem.

Let's put this bluntly for our own lives in the 21st century. If we choose integrity and authenticity, we are also choosing to be rejected by the religious and civil leadership of this world. Why? Using the language of Jesus, this world is ruled by Satan. Using our 21st century metaphors, what do we mean by the "reign of Satan"? And how do we distinguish the "reign of Satan" from what Jesus meant by the "kingdom" or "reign of God"?

Let us consider what it is really like to make some finite reality the fundamental meaning of our lives. Such a relationship leads us to despair. All finite realities pass away. And even before they pass away they let us down as realities capable of providing the final meaning of our lives. Take children for example. If you have made your children the final meaning of your life, you are in for trouble. Children seem uniquely suited to lead their parents to despair. If you have a number of children, it is probable that at least one of them will go completely off the charts of any expectations you had for them—mental illness, criminal activity, drug addiction, enduring sickness, accidental death, unmitigated selfishness, or simply well-meaning failure to live up to your expectations. Children, when made the meaning of your life, are certainly capable of leading you to despair. You might say that when children are the meaning of your life, you are quite realistically doomed to arrive one day in hell. You are living in the kingdom of Satan.

But perhaps you have no children or have never made children the meaning of your life. If so, children are not the finite reality that is leading you to despair. Perhaps it is your spouse or love relationship. Intensely loving someone who intensely loves you back can be one of the highest of all the high experiences known to humanity. And love relationships can also carry you into some of life's lowest lows. Love songs are characterized by both buoyancies and blues. So if you make some love relationship the fundamental meaning of your life, you are heading for despair. You will, sooner or later, for a day, for a week, or for the rest of life, enter into the living hell of a meaningless life. If you are making a love relationship the fundamental meaning of your life, you are living under the stern governance of Satan.

Now Satan is a mythological figure and his kingdom is a mythological kingdom, but this mythology points to a reality—you actually do live in a hell-bent state of being when you make some finite reality the fundamental meaning of your life. It is not having children or lovers that makes your life Satanic. It is having a relationship with your finite children or your finite lover that is "infinitely excessive" and thus inappropriate for happy human living.

Here is one more example. Suppose you are making your nation the meaning of your life. Then one day you come to realize that your country is letting you down in spite of all the sacrifices you have made. Perhaps you discover that your particular class or sex or race or type of person is poorly cared for. Perhaps you discover that the president you voted for is a sexual addict and reckless besides. Perhaps you discover that your representative is a sanctimonious moralist driven by irrational anger and downright foolish thinking. Perhaps you discover that your particular nation leads all others in doing irreparable damage to the natural environments of this planet. Whatever it is, your nation, at such moments, may simply fall from the high pinnacle of giving fundamental meaning to your life. And when this happens you enter a moment of self-conscious despair—despair over the meaninglessness of your life. You have arrived at the destination toward which you have already been heading by making the nation your overarching meaning. You have arrived in hell. And it can now become clear to you that you have been living in a state of human living to which Jesus and his companions were pointing with this strange phrase "the kingdom of Satan."

Finally, I want to state clearly that living in "the kingdom of Satan" is the common state of living for most human beings. Satan (mythologically speaking) actually does rule the world. Each of us (consciously or unconsciously) has made our pact with some finite meaning-giver and erroneously relied upon this unreliable reality for the meaning of our whole lives. We may not even be clear what our finite meaning-givers are until they are taken from us.

So what does it mean for the kingdom of God to dawn in our lives? We sometimes hear the kingdom of God described as something that happens after our deaths or which comes only with the literal end of the world, but such a view is hard-pressed to explain this sentence in the above passage from Mark.

Then he added, "Believe me, there are some of you standing here who will know nothing of death until you have seen the kingdom of God coming in its power."

What does it mean for us to experience the coming of the kingdom of God before we die our physical deaths? It means that we have died to the kingdom of Satan in our actual modes of living. It means that we have ceased to find the meaning of our lives in the finite things that come and go and begun to trust instead the Infinite Source, Sustainer, Limiter, and Ender of all finite things. The Infinite will never let us down: the Infinite will go on being the Infinite infinitely. As Paul put it, nothing can separate us from the affirmation of the Infinite.

What does trusting the Infinite have to do with Jesus being the Messiah? Well, the false Messiah is the one who comes to save us from the Infinite. The false Messiah claims to help us cope with the Infinite. The false Messiah claims to help us manipulate the Infinite to get the finite treasures we are actually concerned about. Jesus was no such Messiah. The footsteps of Jesus lead to the city of those who expect the false Messiah. And when Jesus challenges these false expectations, they plot to get rid of him. They put him through whatever wringers they find handy for destroying him. Do you want to follow Jesus? Then take up your cross. The cross is the walk of the true Messiah. Anyone who challenges the kingdom of Satan will have to endure the wrath of that ever-present reign of energies. If we are not willing to walk this walk, then we are opting to be a willing part of the kingdom of Satan. We have sacrificed our integrity, our authenticity (in biblical language, "our soul") for the comforts of fitting into the satanic world. According to Jesus, such a choice is worthless. It is like trading our whole lives for a bowl of soup. So this is the challenge that Jesus extends to us:

The person who tries to save his or her life will lose it; it is the person who loses his or her life for my sake and the gospel's who will save it.

What good can it do a person to gain the whole world at the price of his or her own soul? What can a person offer to buy back his or her soul once he or she has lost it? If anyone is ashamed of me and my words in this unfaithful and sinful generation, the Authentic Human will be ashamed of that person when He/She comes in the Father's/Mother's glory with holy angels around Him/Her.

(A slight rewording of Mark 8:34-38)

Now why might Jesus' disciples or we be ashamed of Jesus? He did not fulfill our expectations. He had a very short ministry, and then they killed him. Compared with Jeremiah who lived a long life and wrote several scrolls, Jesus was a dud. If we expect Jesus to prove our belief system to the whole world with some irrefutable miracle, we will be disappointed. For the resurrection and all the rest of the so-called miracles of Jesus are invisible to the ordinary world of humanity. To see Jesus' resurrection, virgin birth, healings, transfiguration, Messiahship, ascension to the place of final honor, and his inevitable victory, we have to be resurrected, we have to be virgin born, we have to walk the walk of Jesus to the city of Satan and challenge Satan in the core temples of his reign. The significance of Jesus is a secret known only to those who walk this walk. Only those who are walking this walk will see the holy angels shouting and singing their choruses of glorious Awe around the Infinite Mystery and around all the honored exemplars of human authenticity.

We cannot truly understand the New Testament term "Messiah" unless we are willing to be the Messiah, not the ordinary Messiah for whom almost everyone hopes, but the Jesus Messiah, the scandalous Messiah, the Messiah who walks the dangerous walk into the teeth of evil and remains the victor. If we don't have the stomach for this walk, then we should renounce the name of Jesus and his Christ title and thus refrain from polluting these symbols with our misunderstandings.

That Jesus is the Christ is a well-coded secret. And telling the secret does not end the secrecy, for each of us must discover the truth of this secret for ourselves. It seems that we must discover over and over that

Jesus, with all his seeming shortcomings, actually is the true Messiah leading humanity to its true authenticity.

SHHHHHHHHHHHHHHHHHHHHHHHHHH. Don't tell anyone.

Those who know don't say.
Those who say, don't know.

Also, tell everyone.

12.

Buddhist Enlightenment and Christian Salvation

The dialogue with Buddhism going on in my life and in Western culture is so important that I have chosen to spend two chapters on it. In this chapter I will compare the basic personal transformation of Buddhist enlightenment with the basic personal transformation that Christian's call "salvation." In the next chapter I will explore how these two heritages speak of Spirit love or compassion.

The Four Noble Truths

Siddhartha Gautama, like Jesus, was a real person whose life was given mythological expansion by his followers. Buddha, a title he took for himself, means "to be awake." The original teachings of the Buddha were astonishingly simple. I will paraphrase the four noble truths, as I understand them:

(1) Life's shoe pinches us in many places: the birth trauma, illness, old age decrepitude, the fear of death, being separated from what one loves, and being saddled with what one hates.

(2) Why? Because we are driven by the specific patterns of our finite personalities and this drive pulls against life as a whole. We are off center. We crave to satisfy or enlarge the power of our finite self and this craving is the real cause of our deepest pain.

(3) The cure for our torment is to be released from the narrow limits of our craving self into the vast expanse of our universal life.

(4) And here is how this is done. In association with those who are already finding enlightenment and can instruct us in this path, we need to practice:

1. right knowledge
2. right aspiration
3. right speech
4. right behavior
5. right livelihood
6. right effort
7. right mindfulness
8. right absorption

The challenge to understand these "four noble truths" (including the eightfold path) has filled thousands of books and has been the lifetime quest of millions of avid practitioners. These deep dynamics are not capable of exhaustive description in a few paragraphs. Furthermore, Buddhist teachers tell us that we cannot merely talk about these four truths; we must personally experience them for ourselves. Indeed, many say that only a disciplined personal inquiry using the tool of meditation can unlock the wonder of these teachings. In the following paragraphs, I will be expressing some of the truth of these teachings as I have experienced them so far. Mainly, I want to counter a few common misunderstandings and point toward the essential truth that has made this heritage so long-lasting.

It is incorrect to assume that the Buddha was saying that our core problem is our ordinary pains and frustrations that derive from our

finite limitations. Rather, our core problem is our customary relationship to these ever-present limitations. We suffer despair over life's limitations because we, in identifying with the cravings of our finite self,
insist that our self be unlimited in a universe that constantly limits us.
This craving attitude toward life, the Buddha is saying, causes our deepest suffering. It is this craving attitude, not life itself that is the core
problem. But this is not an easy problem, for our cravings are deeply
rooted. Do we not all want a painless and pleasant life? Do we not all
want only success and never failure? Our deep cravings manifest as
clinging to what we have and what we want. These cravings also manifest as aversions to any reality or challenge that frightens or displeases
us. We begin our life's journey unaware of how our lives are enmeshed
in cravings and aversions and how these deep-seated attitudes make us
miserable. As we become aware of this misery, we can also become
aware of the possibility of a realistic life that is also happy and effective.

Strange as it may seem to many Western people devoted to the individual self, the Buddha taught that happiness is found in disidentifying
with the self. The Buddha did not deny the importance of the self or
the personality; he only taught us to be more realistic about its reality
and function. "Self" is something that has developed over the time of
our lives. It is a pattern of habits. It is a system of memories. It is not
who we are in the living here and now. The Buddha saw that the self is
finite. The self is a passing reality, just like any one of our thoughts or
any one of our feelings. Change encompasses what we call our "self."
We sometimes acknowledge this when we say that we are a different
"person" today than we used to be. We may also be a different "person"
in the future. The Buddha's point is this: as long as we identify with and
defend this passing "person" as the core "me," we will experience need-
less suffering. The Buddha taught that there is a way out of this suffering. There is a way out of the trap of cravings and aversions.
"Enlightenment" is the name for this liberation, this happiness, this
way out.

Another misunderstanding is to assume that the Buddha was saying that our natural desires for food, comfort, companionship, love, sex, or contentment are the problem. Rather, these natural desires have their appropriate place within the enlightened life. They are transformed by enlightenment from cravings into meaningful aspects of the comings and goings of our living. The core problem of human life is cravings that strive to make some of our natural desires unlimited. Our problem is that we want always to experience what is desired and never to experience what is undesired. The impossibility of this hope is our suffering. The Buddha's teachings illuminate how we are trapped in this "suffering," but the Buddha is not saying that our natural life is bad.

Although this trap or cravings is deep, it need not be permanent. The trap of craving and aversion is an off-centered way of living that can be overcome by wholehearted willingness to do so. So understood, the Buddha was an optimist not the pessimist he is sometimes accused of being. Actually, he was a down-to-Earth realist who proposed a practical solution to our customary, though often unacknowledged, grief.

Noble Truth Four: the Eightfold Path

Key to understanding this eightfold path is understanding the practice of meditation. Steps seven and eight of the eightfold path focus directly on the practice of meditation. Step one is becoming aware of being trapped and of our need for liberation or enlightenment. Steps two through six are about wholehearted commitment to becoming enlightened. Then steps seven and eight describe meditation, the practice of inquiry into our own specific traps and into the way that we might be released.

Step seven introduces the important term "mindfulness." Mindfulness means paying attention. Mindfulness is not what western philosophy would call "thinking." Mindfulness is an act of intentionality or freedom. Mindfulness means paying attention, not thinking something through.

In the Buddhist vocabulary "mind" tends to mean our entire inner being, not merely our rational intelligence.

Mindfulness practice begins by simply noticing our breath and noticing our body's sensations. The Buddha was a splendid psychologist; he noticed that our experience begins with bodily sensations. Our thoughts and feelings reflect interpretations being constructed by the self, which is consumed with cravings and aversions. In order to inquire beyond our self-produced sense of reality to the actual reality we are experiencing, we need to notice our bodily sensations. Then we can also be present to the detailed comings and goings of our thoughts and feelings. When we are mindful of our thoughts and feelings in the context of being mindful of our bodily sensations, we are enabled to inquire beyond the boundaries of our self-constructed maze of cravings and aversions. Mindfulness is a method of inquiry that can lead us into deeper and more inclusive awareness. Mindfulness meditation is a finely tuned mode of contemplative inquiry. Just as scientific research has blossomed in the West and is spreading to the rest of the world, so Buddhists have initiated a blossoming of contemplative inquiry that is also spreading to the rest of the world. Both scientific research and contemplative inquiry are sophisticated modes of seeking truth, modes that are rooted in the actualities of human existence. Both modes of truth seeking apply to all religions and can be practiced by those who have no religion at all.

In paying attention to our bodily sensations, thoughts, and feelings, we are exercising our intentionality—our freedom to observe our lives, our freedom to be more than the flow of our thoughts and feelings, our freedom to be more than the automatic acting out of our cravings and aversions. Mindfulness of our sensations, thoughts, and feelings makes us aware that these finite-self dynamics are not the deepest "I" but are simply parts of the passing flow of life. The deep truth of our lives is not found in our thoughts and feelings but in realizing our more fundamental "being."

Mindfulness, however, does not seek to rid us of particular sensations, thoughts, and feelings. Rather, mindfulness means paying attention to all these inner processes, paying attention to our usually unconscious, mechanical existence, paying attention to the elemental trap of our customary living. The practice of mindfulness does not seek to change things but to focus our attention on seeing the processes of our own life and to see them for what they are: passing realities. Mindfulness prepares us to experience the deep truth that we are truly strange beings. If we can be an "observer" of our own inner processes, then our lives are something more expansive than these inner processes.

The full dawning of this deep "observer self" changes everything. It shifts the operating center from the finite self to what some traditions call the "Great Self." Buddhists frequently use the term "no self"—a term that holds the truth that this deep shift of identification entails a loss of identification with the "finite me" (the personality or ego) which we have customarily considered ourselves to be. Over time, mindfulness enables us to identify with being our deeper being, thus experiencing the whole of living in a different way. This result is the meaning of step eight on the eightfold path: **right absorption.** "Enlightenment" means being "absorbed" into this "no self" or "Great Self" and thus being delivered from the "limited self" we often think we are.

Enlightenment happened to the Buddha under the Bodhi tree. But enlightenment also began to happen to the Buddha many years earlier when he began his quest. And the Buddha's enlightenment was not completed in one flash. A continuing practice of meditation characterized the Buddha's post-Bodhi-tree living. Three times a day the Buddha withdrew from his duties to meditate. Three months a year he retreated from his teaching and joined his monks in meditation practices. The Awake One remains awake by practicing wakefulness.

This brief description of the Buddha and the core teachings of Buddhism is only an introduction, but perhaps it is sufficient to compare Buddhist enlightenment with Christian salvation.

Christian Salvation

So how is Buddhist enlightenment the same or different from Christian salvation? If we assume that Christian salvation has to do with a literal immortal soul going to a literal heaven after death, then Buddhist enlightenment is something very different. But let us assume that the word "salvation," in the original biblical witness, was another word for "healing" and that the essence of this "healing" is being healed of our "sin" where "sin" means our estrangement from real life. Further, let us assume that this "healing" begins here and now, setting us upon a journey of healing that continues for the rest of our lives. So understood, Christian salvation and Buddhist enlightenment overlap strongly.

So how does this Christian "healing" relate to overcoming the problem of cravings and aversions of which the Buddha spoke? In New Testament usage "sin" means something more profound than the violation of moral precepts. What I consider to be the best of Christian theology interprets "sin" as the underlying estrangement of our entire lives from the authenticity for which human beings are constituted. If we take this view, we discover that "sin" points to the same basic problem the Buddha was addressing. The similarity becomes even more obvious when we consider how Buddhism broke down its analysis of the basic problem into these three poisons: delusion, craving, and hostility. "Sin" in the best of Christian tradition has also been described as delusion rather than realism, as craving the finite rather than loving the Infinite, as hostility toward our neighbors and toward the Ground of our Being.

Thus Buddhist enlightenment and Christian salvation are both about overcoming the same basic problem in human living. It does not matter that different words are used and different aspects of this complex problem are emphasized. The same problem is being addressed.

How do the means of overcoming this problem differ? At first, it seems that we have a big difference in this arena. Buddhists tend to emphasize persistent human effort and the indefatigable practice of meditation. Christians tend to emphasize trust in grace–a deliverance that comes to us from outside ourselves.

But let us examine the experience of "grace" carefully. Grace happens like this: we are rolling along in our "sin-dominated" drift when we are interrupted by a Message that convicts us of our foolish living and asks us to repent, (that is, to *die* to our estrangements from reality). This Message asks us to trust that if we do repent, we will be forgiven and restored to our authentic aliveness. This Message demands a response from us: "yes" or "no." This response is more than an intellectual assent to "correct" doctrines. The "yes" response means a movement of our whole lives into a life of trusting this Message and learning to trust this Message more and more. As we *make this movement*, we find that more and more of our finite-personality-oriented living dies and more and more of our Spirit potentiality emerges.

Thus, in our actual living of the dynamic of grace we find that human effort is not absent. Faith, or "trusting the Infinite," is a passionate action of our deepest being. Such trusting is manifest in disciplined solitary exercises, in persistent group life, and in intentional ethical living. And this action of "trusting" is an integral part of the dynamic of grace. Without the trusting response, the grace happening is not happening.

And if we carefully examine the dynamics of Buddhist enlightenment, we find a witness to action upon us from the outside. First, there is the action of the Buddha's teachings–the "wake-up call" that these teachings may be for us. Next, the Buddha's teachings ask that we be part of a community of meditators who continue to confront us with wisdom that we did not have when we began our meditation effort. And, most important, the enlightenment, which is our goal, turns out to be nothing more than being the being that we always were in the first place. Such enlightenment cannot properly be called an "achievement"; rather, it is our actual life reappearing through its own innate power.

Enlightenment is the gift of our actual lives. So all the strenuous effort of Buddhist practice simply places us in the way of receiving the gift of enlightenment. As one Buddhist teacher put it, "Enlightenment is an accident. The practice of meditation makes us more accident prone."

Also, the style of Buddhist meditation is not about forcing enlightenment. In healthy Buddhist practice we do not willfully construct a new self for ourselves; we simply pay attention to the old self, to the craving finite self, in order that the essential "no self" or "Great Self" might reappear. The enlightened person knows that he or she has not created this essential enlightened being. Enlightenment is a gift. Hence, the story of enlightenment is much closer to the Christian story of grace than it might seem to our surface understandings.

But from what or from whom do we receive the gift of enlightenment? Buddhism, in its pristine beginnings, did not answer this question. The Buddha was not a theist. He dismissed or ignored supernatural beings of all sorts. Yet the Buddha did not deny that the gift of enlightenment was being given by The Mystery-of-it-All. The Buddha certainly supported being a person who trusted in the basic goodness of Being. The Buddha did not blame the basic structure of Being for our unenlightened suffering; he blamed our clinging, our finite obsessions. Buddhism implies that the basic Ground of our Being is "gracious," that Being stands ready to give us enlightenment.

While the Buddha clearly placed the responsibility for finding enlightenment upon the individual person, he also acknowledged the need for outside action upon the ego-identified human being. He was himself an active teacher who knew full well that human beings need a teacher. So the actual experience of Buddhist practice is not inconsistent with the healing ministry of a teacher or Christ figure. And the Buddhist trust in the goodness of Being is basically the same movement of Spirit indicated by a proper interpretation of the Christian trust in God.

The tension between the grace of an outside actor and need for human effort is not the basic tension between Christianity and Buddhism. Rather, grace-and-effort form a polarity that is known within each of these heritages. Nevertheless, it remains true that most Christians, though not all, emphasize grace over human effort. And most Buddhists, though not all, emphasize human effort over grace.

The I-Thou Dialogue

A much deeper difference between Christianity and Buddhism enters our screen when we notice Christianity's emphasis upon the action of the "God of history." Christianity emphasizes an I-Thou dialogue rather than silent meditation. I, the Christian practitioner, am encountered by the Infinite Thou, and I respond to this Infinite Presence. Traditionally, Christians have not spent hours every day in meditation like the Buddhists. Rather, they spend hours every day in dialogue. They dialogue with Scripture or with this or that contemplative object or teaching. In the dialogue of prayer Christian worshipers are exercising their deep freedom—asking for fresh futures from the Infinite Thou before whom they envision themselves to be living. Prayer does not control history, but it prepares the praying person to be a co-creator with the Infinite Thou who does control history.

So while Christians, in their unique history, may have been meditative and mindful, they did not often teach a practice of mindfulness meditation. Instead, they taught a practice of *dialogue*–dialogue with the Infinite. Abraham, Isaac, Jacob, and Joseph might be characterized as primordial dialogues with God. Moses, the prophets, the psalm writers, Jesus, Paul, the gospel writers, and other Christian luminaries can also be understood as model dialogues with the Infinite. When Christians dialogue with a specific human "saint," they enter into that person's dialogue with the Infinite Thou. In entering into these dialogues, we Christians seek to hear the Infinite Thou speaking to us, and then we speak back. We pray our passionate prayers to an Infinite Thou and then we "listen" for answers from that Infinite Thou as these answers are given in the actual course of historical events.

This religious method of dialogue with the Infinite may seem strange to many Buddhists, and it is also neglected by many Christians. Nevertheless, it is a practice with deep historical roots, and it has been experienced as a means to Spirit health by many Christians, Jews, Muslims, and others. Indeed, many Buddhists have also practiced a form of religious dialogue with the Buddha and other teachers. Some Buddhists even practice dialogue with God-like personifications of The-Way-It-Is. Like contemplative inquiry, interior dialogue is a universal dynamic available to all human beings. An emphasis upon the practice of meditation does not necessarily exclude the practice of dialogue. And an emphasis upon dialogue does not necessarily exclude meditation. Christians and Buddhists can learn from one another how to enrich their practices.

The We-Thou Dialogue

Somewhat more strange to Buddhist practitioners is the Jewish and Christian preoccupation with an ongoing dialogue between God and the People of God. While Buddhism has created strong monastic communities and many Buddhist movements have espoused progressive social ethics, the emphasis of Buddhism has seldom strayed from the enlightenment of the individual person and that person's profoundly individual journey of maturation. Judaism and Christianity, however, have emphasized peoplehood, social ethics, and the dialogue of a "called" people with an Infinite Thou operating in the events of history. Humankind as a whole is viewed as being in an ongoing dialogue with this Infinite Thou. The People of God are those people who listen first and respond first on behalf of all the other people of the planet. The People of God, by being those most sensitive and responsive to the universal "We-Thou dialogue," become, thereby, servants of all people, leading all people into an appropriate listening and responding to the events of history. These images are foundational in Jewish and Christian heritage.

When both Jews and Christians are loyal to that common heritage, social ethics is not merely an outgrowth of their spirit maturation; it is an integral part of their basic religious practice. In social life God is encountered, and in social life ethical responses are made to this encounter with the Infinite Thou in social history.

This view of "God's historical action" provides a fuller context for understanding the term "grace" in the Christian vocabulary. God acts in history by sending prophets of doom who awaken the sleeping. God acts in history by sending prophets of encouragement who heal the despairing. God acts in creating us. God acts in rescuing us from slavery. God acts in awakening us with tragedies. God acts in maturing us with challenges. Something is always going on, and the Christian's challenge is to discern what is going on, give it a name, and then communicate this interpretation of events to others. This interpretation of events is pictured as a "Call" or "Word" from God–a specific Message to respond appropriately to the historical challenges coming our way.

These images can seem bewildering not only to Buddhists but to many Christians. Nevertheless, these images are foundational for a vital resurgence of Christian practice.

The Christian Experience of God

In much Christian discussion the idea of "God" is in a state of deep confusion. This confusion leads to a rejection of Christian heritage by many Buddhists, Christians, and others. Whether liberal or conservative, Christians tend to use terms like Yahweh, Jehovah, Father, Almighty, Lord, King, and even Mother or Sophia to point to a literal personal being. All of these terms are metaphorical language that points not to the characteristics of some literal Supreme *Personal* Being but to the qualities of our *personal* relationship with the Infinite. Even the term "Thou" is a metaphor. The Infinite is not *a being alongside other beings* but the Source, Sustenance, Limitation, and Ending of all beings. To say that we are in personal dialogue with the Infinite is not to say that the Infinite is a literal Person. Surely, it is time for Christians to openly embrace the fact that the very idea of an Infinite Person is a metaphor–which means that we realize that the Infinite is far more than "a person" in the usual sense of this word. Similarly, "Father" is a metaphor: it does not point to an elderly, male, and possibly bearded, super-someone, but to our relationship of trust toward the Infinite. In our trust, we experience the Infinite as having a parental quality. Saying "Father" or "Mother" to the Infinite is stating our trust, not describing the Infinite. In our trust, we experience ourselves as having the dignity of Sons or Daughters of the Infinite.

The entire biblical story comes alive when we understand, in a fully realistic fashion, what we mean by "God's action." Everything that happens is God's action. Did we make it through the sea into freedom in the desert? God's action! Did we find a way to reorder our legal life so that we live in obedience to Infinite Reality rather than obedience to a social hierarchy? God's action! Did we, under Joshua and others, conquer a place for ourselves in the social history of this planet? God's action! Did the Assyrians and Babylonians conquer our fearful little nation-states? Again, God's action! Were we carried off into exile? God's action! Were we allowed to reestablish our religious culture? God's action! And so on until the present moment.

When the Hebraic Bible speaks of God's Word, we must not picture an Infinite Someone channeling human words into the mind of some passive scribe. Rather, all vocalized words or words on paper are human words; the Word of God comes as historical actions in the past, present, or future course of events. Words on paper are human interpretations of God's actions. In a literal verbal sense, God does not speak. The

Infinite is silent. "Revelation" is a paradoxical thing: it means hearing the Infinite Silence speak. Revelation is the human interpretation in human words of the actions of the Infinite Silence who never speaks. Can the actions of the Infinite indeed be trusted? Are the actions of the Infinite love for humanity? On this subject the Infinite is silent. But the Bible is not silent. The actions of the Infinite are interpreted as care for us, as love, as happenings that promote our Spirit well being, as outcomes that are part of our holy calling. For example, the unknown prophet whose writings appear in the latter chapters of Isaiah interprets the sufferings of Israel's conquest and exile as part of God's love for them. According to this view, Israel's suffering is not entirely a consequence of Israel's sin; rather, it is part of the job description of being a servant to all the nations of the Earth. Israelites were challenged by this prophet to affirm their previous hardship and to embrace the further hardship of returning to their land and rebuilding their religious culture as a service to all people.

God Acting in the Jesus Event

The New Testament writers used the tradition of the suffering servant as a means of interpreting the crucifixion of Jesus as another act of God. In this mundane yet horrible death they saw a manifestation of the active love of the Infinite Silence toward humankind. New life was being given to those who accepted the universal truth in this sequence of events. Part of that new truth was the grim realization that a truly authentic person will be opposed by the very people this authentic person is choosing to serve with the call to authenticity. This always was and still is God's arrangement of things: the suffering servant manifests God's love toward those who are as yet enemies of God. So the true Messiah is not a political leader who objectively rids of the world of all the enemies of God. The true Messiah suffers the scorn of the enemies of God and in doing so communicates that these very enemies can be restored to the family of God.

"While we were yet enemies," the early Christians said, "the true Messiah laid down his life that we might live the very quality of life that he was laying down." In other words, the action of God encountered in Jesus (when seen as the Christ) crucifies our egoism and releases us to be that freedom which lays down our own lives toward the further healing of human estrangement on this planet. We were crucified with Christ and we were raised up with him to newness of life. And this is not of our own doing. We have only to trust that these doings of God are our deliverance. Furthermore, deliverance is what our God, the Infinite Silence, is doing in each and every event of our personal lives and in each and every event of our social histories. The Infinite Silence is at work in each and every event, reconciling precisely those who are living in illusion, addicted to finite processes, and hostile toward the Infinite and toward most of their finite companions. This is the meaning of "salvation" in the New Testament witness: we are being delivered from our narrow self-centered living into the trust, freedom, and compassion of servanthood on behalf of all people.

If we understand Christian salvation in this manner, then Buddhist enlightenment is also salvation. The words "salvation" and "enlightenment" each hold a broad range of meanings. Some of these meanings may be more fully elaborated in Christianity, and other meanings may be more fully elaborated in Buddhism. Religious groups are like the blind men who were reaching out to feel the same elephant. Some felt a tail, some a trunk, some a leg, some a wall of flesh. Buddhist enlightenment and Christian salvation, are describing overlapping parts of the same elephant.

God Acting in the Buddha Event

Perhaps the most surprising result of this mode of thinking is the possibility that Christian theology can say that the God we worship also sent us the Buddha. The Infinite Silence acted (and is still acting) in our lives by sending us the Buddha to teach us meditation, to teach us to observe with disciplined intentionality that we are not merely our thoughts nor our feelings but a relationship of liberty and enlightenment with the Infinite Ground of our existence. Looking through these glasses, we can see that both Jesus and Siddhartha came to know that if human beings choose to willingly and actively be the relationship to the Infinite which they actually already are, then these human lives can be lived with equanimity, joy, and compassion no matter what circumstances these persons confront. So the Buddha, like Jesus, was the action of the Infinite Silence reconciling the very same humanity to the very same Infinite Reality. Such statements sound strange to many Christians, because they have not yet fully understood the universality of the Christian breakthrough.

Christians may find it strange that Buddhists can be so still and silent and somewhat heedless of active verbal dialogue with the Infinite Silence. Buddhists may find it strange that Christians can be so industrious in seeking out, in every passing event, the meaningful doings of the Infinite Silence. Yet, while these emphases are different, vital Christians and vital Buddhists find themselves operating on the same playing field of life. We find ourselves espousing the same lovingkindness for the same deep values of being authentic human beings and building new societies fit for authentic human beings to live in. We are, I believe, entering into a time when Buddhists and Christians are learning from each other how to be better Buddhists and better Christians. And by "better" is meant something so similar that it fills me with Awe to contemplate it. A better Christian or a better Buddhist is someone who is better at dying to the narrow self and better at living the liberty of our unachieved human authenticity.

13.

Buddhist Compassion and Christian Love

In this second dialogue with Buddhism, I want to focus on the qualities of Spirit love. "Love" in the Christianized West has been much spoken about but often reduced to a dutiful niceness or a sentimental feeling. What I consider to be the best of contemporary Buddhist teachings are refreshingly realistic. Dialogue with the Buddhist understanding of compassion can assist Christians to see that the "love" spoken of by Jesus, Paul, John, and the rest of the New Testament is deeper than the love we so often hear about in popular Christianity.

Metta—Buddhist Compassion

Contemporary Buddhist teachers have added the Pali word "metta" (lovingkindness or compassion) to my religious vocabulary. "Metta," as I understand it, means *gentleness* like the rain that falls on *all* not just *some* places. And "metta" means a deep *friendship* towards ourselves and towards all others–a friendship that actively persists in **all** circumstances, whatever the feelings or thoughts or states of consciousness characterize our experience.

Compassion (or metta) is expressed in this story about the Buddha. When he reached nirvana, the Buddha realized that he had no need to do anything more. His happiness was complete. Yet in his happiness he chose to become a teacher of suffering humanity and not rest until every person had found their true happiness.

In the teachings of Buddhism we find a meditative practice that has been used through the ages in assisting people to journey toward a fuller realization of metta. There are many versions of this metta meditation practice, but I like the one used by Henepola Gunaratana in his book *Mindfulness in Plain English*. The practitioner of this metta meditation begins by embracing the challenge to befriend his or her own self.

> May I be well, happy, and peaceful. May no harm come to me. May no difficulties come to me. May no problems come to me. May I always meet with success. May I also have patience, courage, understanding, and determination to meet and overcome inevitable difficulties, problems, and failures in life. [11]

Next, the practitioner of this meditation moves to the challenge of reading and experiencing these same words when said about friends, family members, or teachers. Next, the practitioner says the same words inserting the stranger or the person about whom we feel neutral. Finally, the practitioner reaches the full depths of metta by saying these same words about our enemies, the persons from whom we experience opposition and toward whom we may feel aversion, anger, or fear. Try this for your own enemies:

---

[11] Gunaratana, Henepola; *Mindfulness in Plain English* (Wisdom Publications: 1991) pages 101-102

May my enemies be well, happy, and peaceful. May no harm come to them. May no difficulties come to them. May no problems come to them. May they always meet with success. May they also have patience, courage, understanding, and determination to meet and overcome inevitable difficulties, problems, and failures in life.

To envision having such compassion for our enemies takes us into the depths of what metta means. To actually experience such a state of consciousness makes one clear that metta is a deep sort of love, a strange love that is different from "love" as commonly understood. A love that makes no distinction between the quality of affirmation for self, others, friends, or enemies is something deeper that a human feeling. Metta is manifested in many different feelings.

Our most common use of the word "love" has to do with special feelings we have toward special persons or animals or things. We feel "love" for someone or something. In this common usage of the word "love," we only love special people, people who have qualities that we love. When we say, "I love you," the person to whom we say this is supposed to feel singled out, special, even complimented for his or her special qualities, qualities which have evoked our love. So when love has to do with loving everyone, both friends and enemies, such love seems weird or even impossible. It is impossible to have positive feelings toward every person. It is impossible to be best friends with every person, just as it is impossible to feel sexual attraction for every person. Metta love does not fit into our common views of love. It is something entirely different.

Also, when we say, "I love you," we hope that this love is returned, that the other person will say, "I love you, too." We think of love as a sort of currency that we give to people and that we get back. We worry about having enough love given to us. We may even worry about giving enough love to our children, spouse, or friends. Metta is not like this. Metta is not a currency. It is not something we can give someone. Metta is a state of being that encompasses everyone. Metta

is a state of connection with everyone, a state given with our existence. We don't have to accomplish metta; we just are metta in the
depths of our actuality.

Feelings are not a state of being. Feelings are simply aspects of the
finite flow of life. Feelings come and go. Feelings are not the essence of
the liberated self. Most feelings are rooted in our finite personality, in
our various relationships of craving and aversion. We may also have
feelings that accompany our deep states of being, but these feelings are
only expressions of these states of being. Feelings are not the essence of
metta. Metta is a Spirit actuality; it is part of our liberated being.

The metta contemplation on loving enemies makes clear that metta
is not about feelings. Toward enemies we have feelings like aversion,
anger, and fear. It is befitting and normal to have such feelings toward
those persons who are our persistent enemies. But these feelings are not
our metta love or our lack of it; they are just our feelings. The opposite
of metta love is being obsessed with our anger, acting out our anger,
being burnt up with anger or with our guilt for being angry or for acting out our anger. When these strong feelings are running our lives, we
are not operating out of metta love. And this condition is not improved
by trying to do better, by attempting to control our anger, by suppressing our anger, by wishing we did not feel anger, by holding our anger in
contempt, or any other mode of supposing that feeling anger toward
enemies is not befitting. Anger is as wholesome as any other emotion.
Anger is only a feeling; it is not Spirit compassion or the lack of it.
Anger can even express our deep passion for justice and respect for others and for ourselves. The deep compassion called "metta" operates in
the midst of anger or affection, delight or disgust, longing or fear, exu-
berance or grief.

Buddhist sages advise us to simply notice our feelings and view them
as part of our circumstances, like the sky and the earth. In order to enter
into our true happiness and into our deep metta love, we need to learn
how to observe our feelings as we would observe the birds, the squirrels,

or the butterflies. We might be angry at the squirrels for emptying the bird feeder. We might be delighted with the colorful butterflies and their erratic movements. But neither this anger nor this delight has anything to do with our metta love toward the squirrels and the butterflies. The deep self observes but does not identify with the passing world of events or the passing world of our feelings. The deep self observes the tendencies of the finite self to identify with or to unconsciously act out these feelings. The deep self observes the process of observing all these passing aspects of living. This deep self is an openness, a freedom, a no-self-ness, an empty space from which this strange compassion for all beings arises. If we do not surrender into being this deep self, we do not love in the metta sense of love. If we do surrender to being this deep self, then loving in the metta sense is as automatic as the sun shining.

How, then, does this metta love relate to our feelings of warmth and affection and delight in other people? Metta love affirms these feelings, for metta love affirms all aspects of living. The presence of metta love may even enhance and emphasize such feelings. Yet metta love must not be identified with warm, affectionate, delight-filling feelings. Metta affirms these so-called "positive" feelings no more than it affirms our so-called "negative" feelings. Feelings are feelings. Negative and positive are evaluations made by our finite personality. Metta love is extended to all feelings just as this deep love is extended to both friends and enemies.

This perspective allows us to observe our feelings with realism. We can notice with equanimity that all our feelings of falling in love, sexual pleasure, mate-bonding, child-bonding, friendship-bonding lead us, in the course of our ongoing lives, into other less pleasant feelings like sadness, disappointment, frustration, and grief. This is simply the nature of all human feelings. Gladness and sadness are part of the same feeling process. Desire and frustration are part of the same feeling process. Deep bonding and grief are part of the same feeling process. The whole feeling process is neither good nor bad; it is just the feeling process.

Buddhist liberation liberates us from our binding cravings for good feelings. This liberation roots our identity in the essence of our full human actuality.

So metta, Buddhist compassion, is neither a feeling-denying asceticism nor a feel-good indulgence. Metta is a middle way, a complete detachment from and a complete affirmation of all feelings and all aspects of being. Metta is our essential lovingkindness toward the entire unity of reality within which we are constituted.

Agape—Christian Love

"Agape" is the Greek word most often used for Spirit love in the New Testament. Paul and other New Testament writers used different Greek words for friendship and for emotional and sexual bondings. In contemporary Western culture we tend to be enthralled with our personal love-relationships and preoccupied with maximizing our finite pleasures and powers. We tend to avoid serious inquiry into Spirit as a "relationship with the Infinite" and what this might mean as an actual experience in our everyday lives. Therefore, we have become unclear about the meaning of "Spirit love" or "agape," which Christian tradition has given so high a place in describing Spirit maturity. The Buddhist teachings on Spirit love, summarized above, can assist Jewish- and Christian-trained Westerners toward more clarity about what Western traditions have to say on this crucial subject.

For example, in that collection of sayings we often call "the sermon on the mount," we find Jesus speaking these words:

> Love your enemies and pray for your persecutors; only so can you be children of your heavenly Father, who makes his sun rise on the good and bad alike, and sends the rain on the honest and the dishonest. If you love only those who love you, what reward can you expect? Surely the tax gatherers do as much as that. And if you greet only your brothers, what is there extraordinary about that? Even the

heathen do as much. There must be no limits to your goodness, as
your heavenly Father's goodness knows no bounds.

(A slight modification of Matthew 5:44-48.
New English translation)

In Christianity as well as Buddhism, the acid test for the presence of
Spirit love arises in relationship to our enemies. Jesus does not teach
that we should not have enemies. He is clear that his commission to
preach and teach and walk in his footsteps will create enemies. Having
enemies is simply one part of living our life in right relationship with
that Infinite Source of all things, including our enemies. This enemy-
providing God is seen by Jesus as "heavenly Father," as Infinite Parent, as
the perpetual affirmation of "my" True Self. This "Divine" affirmation
streams through every natural and historical event, including the presence of enemies in our lives.

In the Matthew's passage cited above, Jesus makes it clear that if
we do not love our enemies, then our inner life is simply the ordinary
life of unawakened humanity. Dishonest, money-grabbing sell-outs to
the Roman tyranny love those who love them. The religiously untu-
tored masses do as much. To find the "reward" of being our true selves
in the Family of the Infinite, we must do more. Spirit love means
being as generous as the Infinite is generous—namely, being generous
with all beings, affirming all beings, friends and enemies alike. Such
teachings cannot be squared with an understanding that Spirit love is
a comfortable feeling.

In the first letter of John, we find further clarity on the relationship
between loving our finite neighbors and loving God [The Infinite].

We love because [the Infinite] loves us first. But if [you] say, "I love
the [Infinite]," while hating [your neighbor] you are a liar. If [you]
do not love the [neighbor] whom [you] have seen, it cannot be that
[you] love [the Infinite] whom [you] have not seen.

(A slight rewording of 1 John 4:19-20
from the RSV translation)

With our physical eyes we have not seen the Infinite; we have seen only the finite neighbor. But as we look hard at the finite neighbor we can sense this unseen "Infinite Neighbor" standing behind and meeting us through the finite neighbor. An Infinite Presence is present in the finite neighbor who is being sustained and limited by this Infinite, Mysterious, All-Encompassing All-Powerfulness. And this Infinite Neighbor is not a figment of our imagination. The Infinite Neighbor is an active actuality, an ACTIVE SOURCE from which all things are arising, an ACTIVE TOMB into which all things are returning. So all things, in their coming and in their going, are messengers to us from this Active Infinite Awesomeness. Awe itself is the message each finite messenger is bringing to us. Our friends Awe us. Our enemies Awe us. If we do not love the Awe being sent and the Awesomeness that sends it, then we do not love our friends or our enemies with Spirit love. And if we do not love these visible, coming and going, finite friends and enemies in a Spirit way, then we do not love that Infinite Neighbor whose Invisible Presence we do not see. This is the challenge in John's stern teachings.

John also clarifies that we are involved in this entire loving dynamic because the Infinite Neighbor loved us first. We love in a Spirit way only because we have received the Ultimate Message that the Infinite Neighbor loves us (loves us in creating us, loves us in awakening us, loves us in forgiving us, loves us in welcoming us home to our Eternal relatedness, and loves us in sending us both friends and enemies). If we do not trust this love for us, we cannot return love to the Infinite. And if we cannot love the Infinite, we cannot love our neighbors in a Spirit way. In the theology of the Johannine letters, these three dynamics are inseparably linked: (1) trusting that boundless love coming to us from God, (2) responding in love toward God, and (3) being love for all our neighbors. Any understanding of love that does not fit into these dynamics is not "Spirit love" according to the Johannine letters. The rest of the New Testament supports this view.

In his classic devotional book *The Dark Night of the Soul*, St. John of the Cross has helped me further understand Spirit love. After describing a long journey through many levels of dark night, John speaks of love commenting on this bit of poetry, "On a dark night, kindled in love with yearnings–oh happy chance!–I went forth without being observed, my house now being at rest." Here is the word picture that John is painting: on this darkest of nights, my house of finite relationships is at last asleep, so I can arise and elope with my Beloved. In John's vision darkness has consumed all our customary self-images and all the finite relationships that comprise our personality. On this darkest of all nights, John sees that the dark night is friendly–that this friendly dark night has put all our finite relationships to bed. They are asleep. They may awake and rule our lives tomorrow. But for now they are asleep. They do not run our lives at this moment of darkest night. So we arise in this night and join the Infinite in boundless love–a yearning for union with the Infinite which is also a yearning for the life in which we experience full Spirit love for ourselves and for all beings. What a poem!

When we are dead to our ordinary self-centered consciousness, our ordinary thinking, our ordinary feelings, our ordinary willing–then we can arise in our essential freedom and resolve compassion, kindness, patience, and an aggressive honoring of our own bodies and personalities and the whole finite world around us. We can now affirm everything that exists. We can affirm each neighbor, not because that neighbor is delightful to us or desired by us, but because that neighbor is part of an ecstatic happening: the advent of Spirit love as a natural, real, Awe-filling aspect of our lives.

Does this mean that we no longer take delight in some people more than others? No, but there is a detachment relative to our delight. Does this mean that we no longer desire some people? No, but there is a detachment relative to our desire. Does this mean that we no longer feel aversion toward some people? No, but there is a detachment relative to our aversion. Does this mean that we no longer feel anger toward some people? No, but there is a detachment relative to our anger.

But this detachment does not mean a rejection or a suppression of our feelings. Spirit love loves both our delightful neighbor and our delight. Spirit love loves both our desirable neighbor and our desire. Spirit love loves both our distressing neighbor and our aversion. Spirit love loves both our anger-provoking neighbor and our anger.

Surely this is a strange type of love! Does it even exist? Here is the witness of Paul in his famous thirteenth chapter of his first letter to the Corinthians:

> This love of which I speak is slow to lose patience–it looks for a way of being constructive. It is not possessive; it is neither anxious to impress nor does it cherish inflated ideas of its own importance.... Love knows no limit to its endurance, no end to its trust, no fading of its hope; it can outlast anything. It is, in fact, the one thing that still stands when all else has fallen.
> (Paul: I Corinthians 13:4, 7, & 8—J.B. Phillips translation)

This passage makes it clear that Paul's agape-love is not describing ordinary delight, desire, affection, friendship, or emotional bonding. All these finite forms of love do lose patience, become destructive, are possessive, try to impress, cherish inflated ideas, and do not last. The agape-love of which Paul speaks is part of the ecstatic experience of the Infinite, part of the death of the ordinary ego and the resurrection to Spirit aliveness. Love, so understood, is part of the entire experience of God. Paul concludes that such love is the greatest of all the Spirit gifts.

This emphasis upon love is not unique to Paul; it pervades the entire New Testament. In Luke's gospel Jesus is asked a question about how to live eternally. Jesus responds:

"What is your reading of the [Scriptures]?" He (the questioner) replied, "Love the Lord your God with all your heart, with all your soul, with all your strength, and with all your mind; and your neighbor as yourself." "That is the right answer," said Jesus, "Do that and you will live."

(A slight modification of Luke 10:26-28—
New English translation)

In the 20th Century H. Richard Niebuhr expressed the centrality for Christians of Spirit love in one concise sentence: "The purpose of the Church is to increase among human beings the love of God and neighbor." Throughout its two thousand years of tradition, Christian love has been related to loving and being loved by the Infinite Presence that is confronting us in every moment. This Infinite relatedness gives Spirit love its detachment from our enthrallments with the finite modes of loving. And Spirit love also includes engagement in every aspect of finite life, including all the finite modes of loving–affection, delight, desire, etc. So understood, Christian love and Buddhist compassion clearly overlap.

How are Buddhist Metta and Christian Agape Alike?

Both metta and agape point to an inwardly detached yet actively engaged relationship with the neighbor. Neither view is ascetic in the sense of condemning the various forms of love that bind us to some of our neighbors and distance us from others. But in Spirit love the bonds of our binding loves are broken. A detachment is operating. Engagement is also operating, but this is a detached engagement, a healing of the absorption or obsession that can characterize all the forms of finite loving. The finite forms of love have been broken and reconstructed in the context of that Spirit Love which loves the enemy as well as the friend–the horrific person as well as the delightful person–the opposing person as well as the helpful person–the evil person as well as the saintly person.

Both Buddhism and Christianity bear witness to such a love. Having two such witnesses strongly indicates that such love is an actuality in human existence. Why else would these surprisingly similar witnesses exist in two religious traditions that arose in great geographical and cultural separation from one another? Both Buddhists and Christians have borne witness to experiencing Spirit love in every century since these long-standing traditions began. No sense can be made of either tradition unless we assume that at least some of those who treasured these teachings on Spirit love actually experienced what they were talking about. Yet, however strong the case may be for the existence of Spirit love, the real proof is to experience this state of being for ourselves.

How do Metta and Agape Differ?

This is a hard question, because Buddhism and Christianity say similar things about Spirit love. We can, however, discern differences in emphasis. Like the blind men who were feeling different parts of the same elephant, Buddhists and Christians have had slightly different perceptions of Spirit Love.

Christians have emphasized engagement in social issues. Though Buddhists also engage in social issues, Christians have tended to be more preoccupied than Buddhists with the overall responsibility for making general social history. Through the centuries, Christians have organized bodies of people for social engagements, such as an order of nuns doing education or a slavery abolition movement. Both Jewish and Christian heritages emphasize the "called community"–the creation of an historical force called to impact the overall secular fabric. This "called community" has engaged in the dual task of bringing Spirit deepening to individual lives as well as working for justice in the social systems of humanity.

Buddhism has also been vigorous in its religious creativity, traveling across cultural boundaries to support and deepen human lives; however, Buddhists have tended to focus on individual persons rather than upon social justice. Today there are many "engaged" Buddhists, like Thich Nhat Hanh, do not fit this generalization. Nevertheless through the ages, Buddhist practice has tended to be more like a psychology than a sociology. Christianity, though also an inwardly probing religion, has been surprisingly sociological and communal in its emphasis. "The kingdom of God," "the kingdom of Satan," "the body of Christ"–these are all sociological concepts. Contrary to the view of individualistic Christians, "salvation" in the New Testament means entering a healed sociological body with concrete responsibilities for the whole of human destiny. This communal nature of Christianity includes finding the proper rational forms (religious laws) for life together and the proper rational forms (social laws) for reconstructing justice.

Even today many Buddhist and Hindu oriented Spirit teachers working in Western societies tend to downplay the sociological expressions of Spirit love. For example, though I find A.H. Almaas to be one of the most helpful Spirit teachers living today, I was surprised by the psychological bias in the following passage:

> ...spiritual teachers rarely get involved with social reform. They aren't against it, but they recognize that it will not solve the world's problems since those problems are based on cognitive distortions. [12]

"Spiritual teachers rarely get involved with social reform" may describe Asian Spirit teachers but it is a misleading statement when applied to most renowned teachers in Christian history. All these persons were both spirit teachers and social reformers: Moses, Amos, Hosea, Isaiah, Jeremiah, Jesus, Paul, Augustine, Hildegaard of Bingham, Thomas Aquinas, Luther, Calvin, Paul Tillich, Dietrich Bonhoeffer, H.

---

[12] Almaas, A.H., *Facets of Unity (Diamond Books: 1998)* page 58

Richard Niebuhr, Reinhold Niebuhr, Martin Luther King Jr., and Bishop Desmond Tutu to name only a few in the long history of Christianity.

Perhaps all of these Christian teachers would agree with Almaas that the world's problems are based on cognitive distortions and that lasting solutions require something deeper than rearranging the social furnishings. Yet they would all say that the Spirit person loves the neighbor not only by leading the neighbor into deeper Spirit realization but also by challenging the social status quo and releasing energies toward specific changes in social practice. For all these Christian Spirit teachers, the practice of Spirit love seeks transformation in the inner lives of individual persons but also considers such loving incomplete without the companion practice of organizing whatever awakened forces of humanity are available into a response of criticism and reform toward the reigning forces of the existing social establishment.

The social structures of the Christian religion have also been a key preoccupation in Christian history. In the best of Christian thinking, the structures of the church are seen as practical means for carrying out the mission of love for individuals and for social structures. For example, the renowned fourth century theologian Augustine in his classic book *The City of God* forged a theological context for the political structures of both church and state. The social structures of the next eight hundred years of European life are rooted in this theological work. Similarly, the greatness of the twelfth century theologian Thomas Aquinas is fully grasped only when we see that he reassembled (within Aristotelian thought) the old political foundations of church and state laid down by Augustine. Even revered contemplatives like Teresa of Avila, Hildegaard of Bingham, Benedict, and others were also inventors of social and religious forms. They saw no conflict between sociological responsibility and assisting individual persons into the deep waters of Spirit experience.

The Protestant reformer Martin Luther was also a political person. He organized the German princes into a protectorate for his reformed mode of Christian community. He saw the need to fight the inherited fabrics of church and state. Though all this political maneuvering may seem obnoxious to some Christians and Buddhists, Luther and other Protestant reformers believed that even the horrors of war were in their situation ethically necessary in order to put into history this rebirth of Spirit Love that Luther and his followers had rediscovered. This down-and-dirty attitude toward participation in the ambiguities of history is a strength, not a weakness, in the Christian practice of Spirit love.

I also want to point out that this preoccupation of Christians with religious institutions and historical justice has been a place where Christians have developed their deepest perversions. Spirit love is never synonymous with any particular social or religious form, and confusion about this truth has led to horrific perversions. Defending institutional security is not the same thing as making bold ethical adventures in Spirit love. When Christian churches opposed scientific advances, they were preferring sociological safety to Spirit love. The public burning of supposed heretics illustrates the extremes into which such sociological defensiveness can degenerate.

The Buddhist practice of Spirit love has tended to be rather consistent in preserving the clarity that all rational forms and all social patterns are part of the passing scenery. None of these human-made rational forms are entirely valid for expressing Spirit love. Love is not a rational duty or a social pattern. Love is a vitality flowing from the True Self. Luther, in his analysis of freedom, was also clear about the deeply interior origin of Spirit love. But Luther was a social ethicist to an extent that few Buddhists would be inclined. The Buddhist emphasis on the transience of social formats is quite correct. Luther's social teachings were appropriate only for his own time and may not have been entirely adequate even then. This temporal quality is true of all moral teachings in all times for all religions. Spirit must take on rational form, but it can never be fully contained within the rational forms that are constructed to express it. Spirit is infinitely wild and cannot be domesticated. Buddhists have tended to emphasize this wildness of Spirit, and thus not take rational forms super-seriously. This tendency is consistent with Buddhism's emphasis upon individual healing. And when Buddhists do launch social action movements, they tend to remain in touch with the need those movements have for the individual nurture practices needed to sustain them. Clarity on the fragility of rational and social forms is a strength of Buddhism.

Nevertheless, the sociological emphasis within Christian heritage is also an enrichment of our understanding of Spirit love. Luther's understanding of Christian love and liberty allowed him to do exaggerated things that gave history a timely push. Seldom do Buddhist social thinkers grapple as vigorously as many Christians do with the ethical ambiguities of social action. Spirit love for the Christian ethicist includes searching out the key temporal crises and forging widespread consensus on appropriate general social responses to these historical challenges. Christian traditions provide two thousand years of reflection on the sociological implications of Spirit love. If social ethics is our concern, Christian heritage is the "richer" place for our research.

Buddhism excels in making inquiry into our personal depths through effective solitary exercises. Who is to say which emphasis is the more important? Both are clearly needed and both are practiced by both Buddhists and Christians. The Buddhist emphasis and the Christian emphasis on Spirit love are not contradictory. Each tradition has the capacity to enrich the other. As a Christian I can ask my Buddhist companions to help me expand my personal participation in Spirit Love. At the same time I can invite my Buddhist companions to join me in creating a consensus on how best to embody Spirit Love in a rational, social program for planet Earth in the 21st century. Buddhist Metta and Christian Agape touch two parts of the same "elephant" of Spirit Love.

14.

Coitus with Shiva and the Virgin Birth

Hinduism is a very ancient heritage. Hindu culture contained the taken-for-granted quest for Spirit aliveness that was assumed by Buddhism, Jainism, and the other younger religions of sub-Asia. The most ancient writings of Hinduism were created between 1000 and 700 B.C.E., but the roots of Hinduism go further back, disappearing into an ancient Dravidian culture that was highly developed by 2500 B.C.E. The enduring style of Hinduism was forged when Aryan peoples conquered the cultures of Dravidian antiquity. These two cultures mixed, creating something that did not exist before and that exists nowhere else. States of consciousness became their preoccupation. Thinking has been important in Hindu practice, but unlike Greek culture Hinduism never characterized the human being as basically a "thinking" animal. Hinduism never embraced the hope that the mysteries of the cosmos could be understood through rational efforts. In the Hindu perspective the mature person was understood to be united with "THAT" which was fundamentally mysterious. The "SELF" of such a person was also seen as mysterious, just as mysterious as THAT Whole Mystery with which SELF was united.

At first look, the lush mysticism of Hinduism can seem totally opposite to radical monotheism. If Judaism, Christianity, and Islam emphasize singleness, Hinduism seems to emphasize manyness. Hinduism honors a wide variety of gods and goddesses and an almost endless tangle of myths and legends. No one path to spiritual maturity is promoted; rather, inward insight of almost any sort is welcomed into the mix. But alongside this lush manyness, we also see an emphasis upon singleness. We hear Hindu sages witnessing to a deep experience of "SELF" in which the "SELF" is "ONE" with the "Wholeness of Being."

In the Upanishads, the ancient philosophical writings of Hinduism, the mysterious Wholeness of Being is named "Brahman." The Spirit Self is called "Atman." A window into the Hindu vision of Spirit singleness is provided by this phrase: "THAT YOU ARE." In this phrase "THAT" points to the Wholeness or Brahman–to the outwardly experienced Beingness that manifests itself to us in every specific "that." The term "YOU" points to the inward deeps or Atman–to the inward Witness that is our consciousness of all states of consciousness. And the third term "ARE" indicates a union between the Spirit Self and that mysterious Wholeness.

"THAT YOU ARE" is best understood as a cryptic challenge whispered into a novice's ear by some smiling guru. The phrase is not a philosophical conclusion, but a challenge to look into your direct experience of the overwhelming Fullness (THAT) and then to also notice yourself (YOU) doing this looking. Notice that "YOU" the "Looker" are just as mysterious as "THAT" toward which YOU look. The SEEN and the SEE-ER are one interlocking mysteriousness. The SEEN and the SEE-ER are ONE.

So how does this Oneness expressed in the Brahman-Atman unity jibe with honoring so many gods and goddesses? Hinduism, in its most mature expression, is lucid about the limitations of all religions, all gods and goddesses. Religion is seen as a human means to an End that is beyond religion. Religions are finite containers or paths; Spirit is boundless. No religious myth or practice can exhaustively express or contain Spirit. No religious path is the only way to Spirit. And when the fullness of Spirit is our conscious state, religion drops away like some finite booster rocket that merely brought us to this Infinite state of being.

Within this mature Hindu perspective, religion does not become a rigid set of doctrines that one can or must defend from heresy. Rather any religion, any myth, any practice that expresses a bit of Spirit is welcomed into the lush Hindu garden of religious means. To many Westerners this seems strange. On the one hand Hinduism is awash with religion—with myths and symbols and rituals and healing practices—and yet in the final analysis Hinduism sees all religion as a toy or a tool. Religion is merely a means for finding what is truly important: fullness of Spirit as a direct experience—a direct experience that reveals the crass and limited nature of all religion.

When we contemplate this perspective deeply, we see that it is more similar to radical monotheism than we might assume. Consider these two phrases: "There are no gods but *The God*," and "All gods and goddesses are finite myths that assist us to be conscious of our Essence." These two statements, though different, contain the same evaluation of the gods. The gods are not ultimate. The Ultimate is beyond the gods.

In Islam the Ultimate is called *"The God."* In Christianity the Ultimate is called "Father, Son, and Holy Spirit"—The Awesome, the Awed Ones, and the Awe itself. In Hinduism the Ultimate is found in the experience of the Brahman-Atman unity. These three sets of metaphorical expressions all point toward an experience of the same mysterious Wholeness, the Mystery of Being itself. In the next chapter I will describe my understanding of the Hindu journey toward the realization of the Brahman-Atman unity, and I will compare this experience with the I-Thou dialogue in Christianity. In this chapter I will explore two bits of the vast wonderland of symbolic lushness to be found within Hindu heritage.

Lush Symbols for Learning to Look Within

One of the gifts of Hinduism is that ordinary but profound life experiences are expressed in interesting, lurid, and elaborate forms of religious story and religious art. I will illustrate this by sharing an experience I had visiting Elephanta Island off the coast of India, near Bombay. This island is basically a huge rock, the inside of which has been carved into a cave of art. Two huge stone elephants mark the opening to this human-made cave. Inside is a large open room with a huge head of Shiva on the far wall. This is the famous three-faced head: one face expresses severity or wrath, the face on the opposite side expresses mercy or compassion, and the central face expresses equanimity or perhaps impassiveness. The hugeness and forcefulness of these three faces startled me into contemplation, and the more I looked at them the more I became aware that these three dynamics are indeed parts of my experience of Being and parts of my own capacity for Spirit living. The whole experience was mildly dreadful, but also intensely fascinating.

Around the corner to the right was another room, a relatively small room, maybe 12 X 12 X 12 feet. And in the middle of the floor, carved out of the solid rock rose a penis about four feet tall and a foot in diameter. Suddenly I realized that I was on the inside of woman and Shiva was penetrating my space with his member. The solid rock of Earth was being penetrated by Being as a whole. The stark simplicity of this room further enhanced the impression. No decor on the walls. There was nothing in the room but this big penis. Clearly, whoever carved this place meant to create Awe in me and in whoever else came here with a bit of curiosity about the fundamental dynamics of being alive.

Then it dawned on me that being in this stone room was being in the place of Spirit conception. This is how Spirit begins in human life:

penetration by the Infinite. I recalled from my own Christian tradition
the story of the virgin birth. In this story the Spirit human is also conceived by the Spirit of God in the dark interior of woman. Finite
humanity is penetrated by the Infinite. When properly understood, the
virgin birth in Christianity is not applicable to Jesus only: each of us
can be virgin born. The Gospel of John is clear about the universality
of the virgin birth. For John, it is not through our physical birth but
through a "second birth" that human beings become "children of God;
not born of any human stock, or by the will of a human father, but the
offspring of God."[13] So in this strange Hindu cave I was given a fresh
and graphic symbol for our universal and "virgin" Spirit birth. The
rock of my finite humanity is being entered by the penis of Infinity.
What a picture! Being conceived into the Spirit life is a cosmic coitus
between the visible hereness and the invisible Wholeness.

Let us contemplate further this picture of your or my elementary
Spirit birth. I am the Earth. I am the rock of my planet in biological
expression. And I am penetrated by Shiva's penis—that is, I know that
my life is not everlasting but is sustained by and penetrated by that
which is everlasting. Furthermore, I identify with Shiva's penis, for this
cosmic penetration of me is also me. In my essence I am Spirit, yet my
own Spirit happens to me, the time-developed personality, as a penetration from beyond the boundaries of my personal organization. I am
entered by the Awesome and filled with Awe. This is the virgin birth.
This is also coitus with Shiva. The Christian and Hindu symbols are different, but the experience symbolized is the same.

As I walk out of this cave, I again pass the huge heads of Shiva,
which remind me that I am Shiva's severity, mercy, and equanimity.
And as I leave the cave, I realize that I identify with those human beings
who spent their lives carving this ancient cave. Though I am a
Christian birthed and formed on the opposite side of the planet, I am

---

[13] John 1: 12-13

also, surprisingly, a member of some larger family that includes these ancient Hindu artists.

Not only Hindu sculptors but also the myth writers of Hinduism have created a lush garden of religious means. As a second illustration of Hindu lushness, I will tell part of an elaborate story about a Hindu holy man named Markandeya, who even as a mature Spirit person kept having odd experiences. [14]

Markandeya was passing through the peaceful and familiar villages where he taught religion to the people who lived there, when suddenly he stepped into a hole and fell out of the cosmos entirely. He ended up swimming in a black sea. There were no stars, moon, or sun in the black sky. There was nothing but blackness from horizon to horizon.

Markandeya thought he would surely die in this grim place and cried out for mercy. Then he noticed a vast sleeping being swimming in the water near him. He recognized it as the "god" who represents the entire cosmos. This sleeping being awakened, reached out with one hand, grabbed Markandeya, put him in his mouth and swallowed him. Now Markandeya found himself back in the familiar landscape of his ordinary life.

The story goes on and on; Markandeya makes many surprising visits to this same dark place where he meets luminous beings, learns secrets, and then returns to his ordinary life. I can identify with this story. I have been to the black sea. I know how Spirit is a void, an oblivion, when experienced from the perspective of my familiar life. I can understand how this experience can seem terrifying at first but can become friendly in the final outcome.

I find it encouraging that others have experiences similar to my own. On the other side of my planet in a culture vastly different from mine, ancient Hindus wrote the story of Markandeya. I am further

---

[14] For a fuller rendering of this story see Zimmer, Heinrich; *Myths and Symbols in Indian Art and Civilization* (Harper and Row: 1962) pages 38-52.

encouraged that a sixteenth-century Spanish Christian, John of the Cross, spoke of similar things in his devotional classic *The Dark Night of the Soul*. Yet these past witnesses would not be important to me if I were not experiencing in my own life today this Dark Night, this Black Sea, this Void, this endless No-thing-ness that encircles all things as their Source and as their Tomb. And even this experience would not be important to me if I did not trust that these inquiries lead into the deeps of a trustworthy (yes, friendly) Reality that can be the devotion of my life.

15.

Atman-Brahman Unity and the I-Thou Relationship

"Identification" is a key metaphor in the Hindu system of symbols. Hinduism has been characterized as an elaborate quest to answer the question, "Who am I?" What do I identify as the real me? What state of interior being do I identify as myself? What "me" is the Spirit Me? In Hindu heritage "Atman" is the one-word answer to these questions. In Christian heritage "Holy Spirit" (properly understood) is also a term that points to the real me, to the full essence of being human. But one-word answers are not enough. So I will continue this dialogue with Hinduism by summarizing aspects of the Hindu discussion on "Who am I?"

The Atman-Brahman Unity

"Atman" is a term that suggests that we are more than we usually think we are. For example, when we say "my clothes," we imply that we are distinct from our clothes. So also when we say "my body, my mind, my feelings, or my choices," we imply that we are distinct from our bodies, minds, feelings, or choices. The Atman is that "I" that can say "my" to all these aspects of our existence.

The experience of an Atman self has also been expressed in Hindu heritage with the metaphor of reincarnation. Just as the inward person dies each moment to that moment and moves on to the next moment, so the inward person dies each lifetime to a previous body and moves on to a next body. If we view reincarnation as a mythic expression of an inward experience rather than as a literal description of our sequence of bodies, we find that reincarnation expresses a deep truth: I am more than my relationships with finite things. I am a mystery more mysterious than any of my finite explanations can fathom.

Hindu wisdom views all of us as beginning our life journey bound to the pleasures and successes and duties of time-bound living. But one day we ask, "Is this all there is?" However pleasant or painful our finite life has been, we ask, "Is this all?" However successful or full of failure our finite life has been, we ask, "Is this all?" However righteous or errant our finite life has been, we ask, "Is this all?" And the Hindu sage answers, "No, this is not all." The human being is made for an experience of the timeless—an experience of the grandeur, contentment, joy, and excitement of being "the Great Self" or "Atman." Awake! Be detached; be liberated from time! Be "the Great Self"! And then what happens? Well, life goes on in time, but differently. We can live in time with a detachment from time. We can have pleasure without making the seeking of pleasure the meaning of our life. We can have pain without making the avoiding of pain the meaning of our life. We can take our place in the world without making a place in the world the meaning of our life. We can do our duty to others without making righteousness the meaning of our life. We are timeless. We are Atman.

Hindu thinking goes on to identify the Atman with the Infinite Brahman. Being my Great Self (Atman) entails an experience of identification with the entire grandeur of Being (Brahman). Whatever grandeur there is, I am that grandeur. We cannot understand such statements if we view them as scientific fact, but we can intuit their meaning if we view them as expressions of an actual experience of an inward state of being. The Atman-Brahman unity is an experience that you and I can have, and may have had already.

Here is the most elemental way I have found for saying this truth: "In my capacity for experiencing the Overall Mystery, I am just as mysterious as the Overall Mystery I encounter." I am not merely my body or my mind or my feelings or my personality. I am a "Mystery-experiencer." This is a powerful affirmation of being a human being. I am a profoundly strange being capable of something that does not occur, as far as we know, in any other species of life on this planet.

I have attempted to express this simple but profound awareness in a short poem:

I am an alert deer.
Dread gets my attention
and I can move quickly
in many directions.
I am a surprise
and hard to predict.

A fear of real enemies
is the alertness of a deer,
while my alertness is
dread of a mysteriousness
no deer can know.

And I am unpredictable
in a manner
no deer can match.

Dread of the Unfathomable
is my essence.

Surprise
is my being.

This basic strangeness of being a human being is surely part of what prompted the ancient Hindu sages to create the Atman concept. I have written another poem to illustrate how Hindu seers (and Buddhist seers as well) have expressed the experience of the Ultimate Self.

Who am I?

My mind/body sleeps,
but I do not sleep.
My conscious person sleeps,
but I do not sleep.
My mind/body dreams,
and I watch my mind/body dream.
My consciousness wakes and remembers dreams,
and I watch my consciousness remember.

I watch as the world rises in my awareness.
I watch as my consciousness, mind, and body plan my day.
I watch as my consciousness, mind, and body carry out my day.
I watch as my consciousness, weary of directing the energies
        of my mind and body,
surrenders again to the abyss of sleep.

And I watch, even in dreamless sleep
as my consciousness rests
and as my mind carries on its subconscious work

and as my body pulses on in its sustaining and restorative patterns,
I watch.

Who am I, this watcher?
Who am I, this Witness to my body/mind and consciousness?
Who am I, this Witness to my awareness of the world
        that surrounds my conscious person?

Do I have a face?
My consciousness has a face.
As consciousness I live behind this face.
I present a face to the world.
I concern myself with how the world sees my face,
and about what face to present to the world.

But do I, the Witness to all of this, have a face?
Or am I faceless?
Am I an invisible Witness, without face to present,
unseen by others,
devoid of mirrors in which I may see my own faceless face?
Have I, in being this witnessing, watching I, lost face forever?

Indeed, I have no face!
Is this a horror? Is this a blessing?
Being faceless, I can laugh at my conscious person's loss of face.
I can laugh at my conscious person's humiliations.
I can laugh at my conscious person's experiences of praise.
I can laugh at my conscious person's fears and hopes.
I can laugh at my conscious person's deaths and rebirths.

Yes, I laugh, for I am I, not my conscious person.
I am a deeper me.

I have left behind my conscious person as the definition of me.
But then, I find that I am also the reconstructer of my conscious person.
I recreate my new conscious person as an expression
        of my inexpressible, deeper me.

And I take delight when my expressions reach others–
        allowing others to witness me witnessing them witness me.
I take delight in this comradeship of invisible witnesses–
        knowing that I am known by those invisible faceless others,
        knowing that I know those invisible faceless others
        in the same way that they know me.
I take delight in knowing that we invisible ones,
        watching, watching night and day,
        are a communion of watchers that extends backward
                into the dim antiquities of our species,
        and that extends forward
                into the millennia of human life
                yet unconceived and unconstructed.

And what is our invisible life like?
Is it a blazing light? No!
Is it an absolute darkness? No!
It is just watching whatever darkness
        and whatever light comes and goes.

And what is our invisible life like?
Is it a profound suffering? No!
Is it a profound pleasure? No!
It is just tranquilly watching whatever suffering
        and whatever pleasure comes and goes.

And what is our invisible life like?
Is it a joy unspeakable? Yes!
Is it an incomprehensible peace? Yes!
Is it a freedom from all ego cravings and aversions? Yes!
Is it a freedom to perpetually suffer with equanimity
        the deaths and rebirths of my ego? Yes!
Is it a trust that my ego/body/mind
        (aware and unaware, suffering and pleasuring, dying and
        reborning)
        are servants to me and are allowing me
        to be the witnessing and freely acting being that I am?
YES!

So who am I?
Am I this invisible Witness who nevertheless acts in visible ways?
        Do I need to search further for the true me?
                No!
        Is this unsearched for me good and altogether real?
YES!

While this poem borrows its images from the Hindu heritage, it also describes a state of being that biblical writings point to with terms like "Holy Spirit" or "Spirit of God." Nevertheless, the basic metaphor in the biblical West is different. The basic metaphor of the West is "dialogue" rather than "identification." Instead of identification with the Atman-Brahman unity, Western religions speak of an I-Thou dialogue with the Ultimate.

The I-Thou Dialogue

When I as a Christian speak of Spirit or Holy Spirit, I see Spirit as a dialogue with the Final Mystery rather than an *identification* with the

Final Mystery. In my current Christian theologizing, I avoid symbols that imply the existence of an ethereal substance resident in our material substance. Such dualism is unnecessary to express our actual experience. I do not see myself as an "immortal ghost substance." Nor do I see myself as a "reincarnating entity." I view my Spirit Self as a relationship (an I-Thou dialogue) with the Mysterious Wholeness of Being.

I do not see myself as the *finite* end of this relationship; nor do I see myself as the *Infinite* end of this relationship. *My essential self is the relationship itself.* My consciousness of this relationship is finite, but the relationship itself is more than its finite grounding or my consciousness of it. This relationship with the Infinite is not constructed by me but is established and sustained by the Infinite. I am a derived being in dialogue with the Wholeness of Being. This image has become foundational in my Christian theologizing. It allows me to connect with the ancient heritage of Christianity and with my own times as well.

Within the dialogue metaphor, Awe is inspired by the Awesome without being synonymous with the Awesome. Holy Spirit (Awe) is inspired by the Almighty (the Awesome). Spirit is a gift of the Almighty, a gift with which I can dialogue with the Almighty. Awe is a dialogue with the Awesome. Awe is freedom responding to the Total Demand of the Awesome to be free. Awe is trust responding to the trustworthiness of the sustaining and negating Majesty of the Awesome. Awe is compassion responding to the Awesome as fullness—as the Every-thing-ness in which all things cohere.

In my efforts to renew Christian theology through focusing on the experience of Awe, I also raise the question of identity. I also ask, "Who am I?" But I don't answer this question with images that imply a merger with the Infinite. My identity is not with the Infinite but with the Awe-relationship to the Infinite Awesomeness. Like the Hindu, I can speak of giving up my identification with my finite dynamics, my body, my mind, my personality, my self-image, or my consciousness. But my Christian-rooted vision does not see the essential person as a drop of

Spirit fluid that merges with the whole ocean of Absolute Spirit or Absolute Being. Even though the Awe relationship is joined with the Awesome and is derived from it, the Awe relationship with which I identify in Christian devotion is not the Awesome itself. It is true that there would be no Awe without the Awesome, yet in the triune symbolism of Christianity, the Awesome, the Awed Ones, and the Awe itself are viewed as three separate aspects of one experience. These aspects do not merge. When I use Christian symbols to speak of becoming one with God, I mean overcoming estrangement with God rather than merging with God.

In the East, however, merging with the Infinite has been a way of viewing our deepest human experience (or at least part of our deepest experience). It occurs to me that the metaphor of identification/merging and the metaphor of dialogue/relationship are simply two different finite ways of viewing contact with the Infinite. Perhaps it is unnecessary for one to be judged better than the other. Perhaps both are right in some ways. And perhaps both are also wrong when they claim to be the only way of viewing these matters. This is perhaps another witness to the truth that our experience of the Infinite is unfathomable to the human mind.

Anyhow, Christian heritage is best understood when "oneness with the Infinite" is understood to mean overcoming estrangement through a realization of sonship or daughtership within the family of those who are called out by the Infinite Awesomeness to be the Awed Ones. Teresa of Avila used the symbol of "marriage with the Infinite." This symbol holds the sense of being a derived being while also living in intimate contact with the Infinite. This way of speaking about oneness with God is significantly different from the way many Hindu sages view the Atman-Brahman Unity.

There are, however, Hindu sages who imply that this merger with the Infinite is not the whole story, but only part of the story. The rest of the story has to do with returning from the state of merger with the Infinite to a reengagement with the finite realms of existence. With these sages my Christian theology differs less, yet I would rather say that we never actually leave finite existence and therefore we do not need to return. Instead, we have that two-way movement I call "dialogue." Perhaps the Atman-Brahman unity is an experience I have when my consciousness is exclusively focused on the Infinite end of the finite-to-Infinite relationship. I, however, view that experience as only part of the total I-Thou dialogue. I see my Essential Self not as residing in endless merger but as moving through time as dialogue between the finitely grounded Essential Person and the Infinite Presence confronting me in every moment of time.

Why are these heady reflections important? They are important because they peer into the heart of the dialogue between East and West, between the Sub-Asian set of religions and the biblical religions. For a thoroughgoing understanding and appreciation of the biblical writings, it is important to retain the validity of the I-Thou dialogue symbolism. It may also be important for Christian theology to integrate within its system of symbols the vast experience of the East. I have already suggested a way of viewing the Atman-Brahman unity that can be integrated with Christian theology: "In being a relationship with the Mystery, I myself am just as mysterious as the entire Mystery with which I am a relationship." This statement uses the I-Thou biblical symbolism; nevertheless, it overlaps significantly with the ancient Hindu intuition that created the vision in which Atman and Brahman merged.

I can also learn much from the Hindu description of what it is like to "not be" in the Atman-Brahman unity. Such a state of consciousness Hindus describe as being in a trance—living in a sense of reality that is not fully real. I understand that. I see that most of us, most of the time, live our lives in a trance. Our society provides most of this trance. Our own unique personality development provides further elements of this trance. We grow up in a trance that we take for reality. We think we are being real, but actually we are simply living out the roles of our social conditioning and of our personality development. We are not being our essential reality; we are projecting our trances and taking them to be reality.

Then one day we experience life beyond our social conditioning or life beyond our personality. Perhaps this takes place through a happening in nature like the birth of a calf, or the whirl of a tornado, or the sight of a vast canyon, or the eclipse of the sun. Perhaps it is a happening in a scientific laboratory. Perhaps it is an encounter with another culture. Perhaps it is a surprising historical development. Whatever it is, our trance is broken. We see that the trance was not "Reality" but simply our social conditioning or our personality development. "Reality" bursts loose in our awareness as something "larger." When this happens to us, we are having both an outward and an inward experience. The outward "world" is experienced differently. And the quiet waters of our inward world are disturbed. This inward upset might be described as dreadful or fascinating or both. And if we have the courage to experience these intensities, we are in a state of being that I have been calling "Awe." This is one of my basic definitions of "Awe": *dread and fascination and the courage to experience these intensities.* Such an understanding of "Awe" is clearly related to both "Holy Spirit" in Christian tradition and "Atman" in Hindu tradition.

When the Christian tradition spells out the meaning of "Holy Spirit," it uses a long list of subsidiary terms such as: faith, hope, love, freedom, peace, joy, and others. All these "aspects" of Holy Spirit are states of Awe. None of these terms are being understood biblically when they are reduced to finite psychological dynamics. Faith is not trusting our mother or our father. Faith is trusting that Awesome Mystery that gave us a mother and a father and that takes all mothers and fathers away. Love (in the "agape" or Spirit sense) is not a human emotion or desire or affection. Spirit Love is the courage of unqualified affirmation of every event, every friend, every enemy, every past, every future, every currently operating dynamic, every awareness we now have and every awareness we might yet have. Such love is a state of Awe. Such love is a state of relationship with the Mysterious Awesome Otherness that confronts us, that upsets our trances again and again and expands our sense of "reality."

Seeing this Awe-quality of Holy Spirit, Christians can also see how "Holy Spirit" and "Atman" point toward the same dynamics of being human. Though "Holy Spirit" and "Atman" are embedded in vastly different religious traditions, we can interpret them as parts of two different modes of symbolizing the same human experiences. Each mode of symbolizing has, or may have, strengths of awareness not possessed by the other.

For example, without speaking of merger with the Infinite, Christians also speak of Eternal Life. Properly understood, the Christian use of the term "Eternal Life" does not mean an extension beyond death of the same old finite life we are typically panicking to preserve. Eternal Life is a new quality of living, one in which detachment from the finite allurements of life is just as deep as Hindu detachment. When the Christian Bible speaks of dying with Christ, this dying means dying to finite life and thus becoming detached from its allurements and tragedies. And being "raised" does not mean being raised up to the same old enthrallments with finite living. Rather, we are raised up to a different quality of life–to life in dialogue with the Infinite Silence. In this personally experienced death and resurrection, we move from an enthrallment with the passing stuff to a dialogue with the mysterious Wholeness that acts upon us in each and every moment of passing stuff. We are aware of being encountered by and responding to this Wholeness. Christian metaphors do not emphasize timelessness, but rather being "in-but-not-of" time, being in time as a dialogue with the Infinite Thou. The Awe-dialogue takes place in the Eternal Now and is experienced as Eternal Life, yet it is moving through time as encounter and response to the Awesome Infinite Actor.

The Timeless Brahman and the Sovereign of Time

Not only do Atman and Holy Spirit overlap, but the Hindu "Brahman" also overlaps with the Christian "Almighty. I will explore the Hindu view of Brahman with the help of Ken Wilber, a Western philosopher who has adopted the Eastern metaphor of identification rather than the biblical metaphor of I-Thou dialogue. In the following quotations, Wilber describes his experience of what I understand Hindu sages are pointing to with the timeless "Brahman."

> But when I rest in simple, clear, ever present awareness, I lose face. Inside and outside completely disappear. It happens just like this:
>
> As I drop all objects–I am not this, not that–and I rest in the pure and simple Witness, all objects arise easily in my visual field, all objects arise in the space of the Witness. I am simply an opening or clearing in which all things arise. I notice that all things arise in me, arise in this opening or clearing that I am. The clouds are floating by in this vast opening that I am. The sun is shining in this vast opening that I am. The sky exists in the vast opening that I am; the sky is in me. I can taste the sky; it's closer to me than my own skin. The clouds are on the inside of me; I am seeing them from within. When all things arise in me, I am simply all things. The universe is One Taste, and I am That. [15]

And a few pages later Wilber says:

> Precisely because the ultimate reality is not anything seen but rather the Seer, it doesn't matter in the least what is seen in any moment. Whether you see peace or turmoil, whether you see equanimity or agitation, whether you see bliss or terror, whether you see

---

[15] Wilber, Ken; *The Eye of Spirit* (Shambhala, Boston, London: 1998) page 293

happiness or sadness, matters not at all: it is not those states but the
Seer of those states that is already Free.

Changing states is thus utterly beside the point; acknowledging
the ever-present Seer is the point. [16]

Now I realize that Wilber is writing poetry here, and that poetry
must not be taken literally. Wilber is describing an experience, a deep
experience that cannot be fully said in mere human language. While I
identify with Wilber's experience, I prefer to use different poetry to talk
about this experience. I prefer the poetry of dialogue rather than the
poetry of identification.

I would never say that it does not "matter in the least what is seen in
any moment." The finite contents of history matter to me because I
view these contents as the medium through which my dialogue with the
Infinite is taking place. I can affirm Wilber's sense of detachment from
peace or turmoil, equanimity or agitation, bliss or terror, happiness or
sadness. But I see such detachment as part of my trust relationship with
the Infinite Objectivity that I am confronting through every one of my
finite encounters and responses. I identify with the Seer or See-er of
which Wilber speaks. I call this See-er "the Holy Spirit." I see that the
Infinite Actor is constituting me as this See-er, but I do not assume that
I, the See-er, and Thou, the Infinite Actor, are one and the same. I see I,
the See-er, as a derived reality from that Otherness which has been and
is constituting me as this See-er.

So, in my "Christian" way of symbolizing this deepest experience of
Spirit, my Spirit Self *identifies* not with the Infinite Wholeness but with
being a *relationship* with the Infinite Wholeness. I do not see myself as
identical with the Infinite Wholeness but as being in *ongoing dialogue*
with the Infinite Wholeness. Trusting means openly entering into this
dialogue. Not trusting means despairing over the fact that the Infinite

---

[16] Ibid., page 295

Wholeness does not operate in accord with the whims, wishes, or survival cravings of my finite consciousness. The choice to trust is the choice of radical realism, the choice to be the See-er who goes on seeing what is to be seen rather than closing off from the terror of history. Trust then manifests itself as freedom, freedom from cravings and aversions. Such freedom overlaps with the freedom of which Wilber speaks. But the freedom that resides in trusting the Infinite is also the freedom to participate with the Infinite in choosing what is going to transpire next. My full picture of the I-Thou dialogue includes taking responsibility for the making of history. The Infinite Thou sends challenges to me and I respond. My responses are like requests to the Infinite Thou for specific historical outcomes. I do not control those outcomes, but my requests matter. History seldom works out exactly as I request, but having requested–having put my life on the line in free action for specific outcomes–does matter. The Infinite honors my requests. The Infinite takes me into companionship in the making of history. I am not only the See-er; I am the co-creator of what is to be created next.

This concern with history helps us grasp the importance of the I-Thou dialogue within the biblical heritage. In the biblical writings, the flow of time or history is a holy dynamic; it is the locus of dialogue with the Infinite. I realize, of course, that this "I-Thou" dialogue is metaphorical talk. The Infinite Mystery is not literally a BIG THOU–male or female or both. But since I am having a personal relationship with this ongoing Infinite Mystery, this enigmatic Otherness can feel "personal" to me. This is not the same as viewing the Mystery as a literal personal being. Literalism in any religion is bad religion. "I-Thou" symbology is still symbology even though it points to real relationship with Ultimate Reality. And "relationship" is also a symbol, a different symbol from "identification."

In both Hindu and Christian reflections, the deep interior Self and the outward Wholeness are seen as interlocking. Brahman is not being experienced unless Atman experiences it. Similarly, in Christianity there is no experience of God, the Almighty, unless Holy Spirit is operating in the human experiencer. I am convinced that the Hindu term "Brahman" and the Christian term "God, the Almighty" point toward the very same Mysterious Otherness. But this overlapping is not self-evident, since the overt symbology is so different.

The timeless Brahman can seem, at first impression, to be something quite different from the Almighty Governor of time. So we need to look at these symbols very carefully. Is the Creator of time, in being time's Creator, also timeless? Christians have sometimes spoken of their God as being changeless: the same yesterday, today, and forever. Time, not Infinity, is the realm of change. God, as the author of change, as the sovereign ruler over all change, is not seen as changing. Anything that is changing is, properly speaking, not Infinite. Anything that is changing is part of the realm of time. So the Almighty God of Christianity can be characterized as timeless. Our appropriation of the meaning of God may change. Our modes of "covenant-with" or "worship-of" God may change, but God as the Infinite Mystery, the Origin of all beings, is beyond the entire realm of what changes. So in both Hindu and Christian tradition, the Infinite Mystery is timeless. The same timeless Reality is encountered by all generations of human beings, all cultures, and all the stages of each and every human life.

The biblical heritage does, however, speak of changing "God's mind" insofar as the "mind of God" pertains to the course of historical events. But this change is not a change in the Infinite. It is a change in God's action, a change within the realm of changing things. Even though God can be said to act differently or act anew, such symbolization of God as the ruler of time does not contradict the notion that God is Infinite or timeless.

Does the Hindu emphasis on the timeless Brahman leave out awareness that Infinite Reality engages humanity in the course of temporal events? No, though Hinduism focuses on states of consciousness, this need not mean ignoring temporal events. Hindu heritage discusses how human life is lived differently when it is detached from the course of events rather than enthralled with the course of events. The detached human does not expect from life what life cannot provide. The detached human can, however, intervene in the course of events with detached freedom and thereby affect outcomes. The Hindu teacher Gandhi certainly pulled forth from Hindu heritage a passion for engagement in social change. Most modern Hindus would not wish to be caricatured as emphasizing only detachment.

Christians tend to differ from Hindus by emphasizing engagement. They emphasize obedience to God in the course of finite events. Loving God means picking up our belongings and leaving Egypt. Loving God means living 40 years in some wilderness and obeying the new rules that such living implies. Loving God means fighting for a place in the world of nations in order to preserve our gift for all the nations of the world. Loving God means returning from exile in a place of tyranny and rebuilding our heritage in a specific homeland. Loving God means going into all the world and preaching the good news that a fulfillment of clarity on loving God has finally dawned. Loving God means building Christendom. Loving God means abandoning Christendom and building a secular world of religious toleration. Loving God always means something temporal. Each generation of lovers is fated to engage the temporal in the current moment of their living. Today, one aspect of loving God means responding to the ecological crisis which humanity itself has caused by its lack of detachment from finite things. So loving God today means calling human beings to become detached from the current, thoughtless, industrialized momentum toward ecological doom. Loving God today means calling human beings to step forth in detached engagement to reconstruct a viable social-natural balance for living on this planet.

In spite of these different emphases, we find much more overlap than we do difference between lucid Christians and lucid Hindus. Both affirm being detached from time in a relationship with the Timeless.

Both affirm being engaged in time as agents of change who have been transformed by their dealings with the Timeless. Hinduism and Christianity are two very different symbol systems that nevertheless express most, if not all, of the very same experiences of Awe.

So let us, by way of summary, imagine a detached, time-transcending mystic of either Hindu or Christian origin. Then let us imagine this completely detached person walking along through the temporal world and stumbling over the I-Thou symbol system. Then let us imagine that this person has sensitive Spirit ears that can hear a chant coming forth from the I-Thou symbol system. The chant repeats over and over: "Time continues as a dialogue with the Infinite Silence."

The Return of Antiquity

16.

The Great Goddess and the Post-Patriarchal Patriarchal Religions

It is important for Jews, Christians, Muslims, Hindus, Buddhists, Taoists, Confucians, and others to admit that they are members of religions who have honored male founders, deemphasized the Spirit contributions of the women in their midst, and participated in the support and transmission of patriarchal styles of culture. All these prominent religions have come into being and accumulated their wisdom during the patriarchal era of human civilization.

Feminists in our time have been in revolt against religious conservatives in every one of these traditions. With each passing decade, it has become clearer that any religion that honors the masculine more than the feminine is out of date. We now have a basic agreement among progressive forces within all these traditions: *patriarchy must be vigorously opposed.* But in religious traditions that have been enmeshed with patriarchy for thousands of years, doing away with patriarchy is not so easy. We might ask, "Can these until-now patriarchal religions carry out a vigorous opposition to patriarchy without losing or minimizing the gifts that these religions have carried?" We might also ask, "Would it be better to simply abandon these religions and start afresh with religious expressions well rooted in feminine motifs?"

The dialogue between feminist advocates and these classical religions has been enriched by archeological explorations, which have uncovered some surprising and fascinating facts. Humanity's earliest civilizations emphasized feminine symbols, and they often established forms of religion in which goddesses or the Great Goddess formed the focal point of their worship. Such veneration of the Goddess typically corresponded with an egalitarian respect for both sexes.

Still earlier, before the dawn of any civilization, the typical tribal society also used feminine symbols and operated with an egalitarian respect for both sexes. Though tribal men did most of the hunting and protecting and tribal women did most of the gathering and domestic work, these different roles did not result in a hierarchy of values in which men dominated, owned, or degraded women. Understandably, these archeological discoveries have had a significant impact on our thinking. *Patriarchy was not always here and patriarchy need not always be here.*

The increasing interest in the Great Goddess traditions of pre-patriarchal times has had a variety of influences on current religious thinking and practice. Some feminists (both women and men) have been working to redress the language styles and moralities of the classical patriarchal religions. Other feminists (mostly women) have tended to abandon these patriarchal religions and construct alternative religious practices that draw inspiration from pre-patriarchal religious sources that honor the Great Goddess. Still others have simply added Goddess practices alongside their Buddhist meditation, their Christian worship, or some other practice.

In this essay I will first summarize the wisdom being gleaned from the Goddess recovery. Then, I will discuss how Christian theology can incorporate these wisdoms. After that, I will deal with three thorny historical questions: (1) why did patriarchy arise in the first place? (2) Did the long-standing religions that arose in the patriarchal period moderate or intensify patriarchy? And (3) can these patriarchal religions completely shed patriarchy without losing anything vitally important?

Key Motifs of the Goddess Recovery

Those of us in Western culture, after emphasizing maleness in our religious symbolism for at least 3800 years, still have a vague but persistent cultural memory of the Goddess symbolism. When we speak of "Mother Nature" or say that "the Earth is our Mother," we are carrying on an echo from some very ancient times. We still find in the undercurrents of our patriarchal culture these memory fragments of an Awe-producing heritage that tells us we were born out of the womb of nature and destined to return to that womb in our burial, that this Great Mother nurtures us and cares for us all the days of our lives. Further, we hear it said that this Great Mother is powerful and not to be fooled with.

Yet this Goddess theme is only an undercurrent in our patriarchal cultures. Even the goddesses of ancient Greece were an undercurrent, a scaling down of the motifs of the Great Goddess. The veneration of the Virgin Mary also echoes the Great Goddess, but in a much-reduced fashion. The Great Goddess with all her dreadful powers and sexual aspects has been more fully preserved in sub-Asian Hinduism; but even there male motifs and ethics predominate. So it is a challenge to recover what venerating the Great Goddess actually meant in our earliest civilizations.

This challenge has been taken up by those contemporary feminists who are sometimes called "spiritual feminists." In her book *States of Grace* Charlene Spretnak did an illuminating summary of the treasures

that contemporary "spiritual feminists" have been mining from the
Great Goddess antiquity.[17] Here is my summary of her points:

1. A thoroughgoing critique of the psyche of the male in patriarchal culture
2. An affirmation of our human connection with the Earth-body
3. The affirmation of the body of woman
4. The affirmation and ritual celebration of birth, menses, sexual
   pleasure, pregnancy, and menopause
5. The affirmation of the individual human body of men and
   women
6. The emotional completion of scientific reason

1. A thoroughgoing critique of the psyche of the male in patriarchal culture

The male within hierarchical civilization has been acculturated to
aspire to the following so-called "virtues": (1) being a firm ruler in
some contexts, (2) being a subservient servant in other contexts, and
(3) in all contexts seeking to control nature through new techniques
and social organizations. These "virtues" seemed necessary to make
civilization functional. In being composed of many diverse elements
that threatened to fly apart, a civilization differs from a tribal society.
To make a civilization many separate tribal cultures had to be amal-
gamated. So the hierarchy of a civilization was engaged in a continuing conquest of its interior peasant forces and slaves. A functional
civilization required a formidable military organization to defend the
hierarchy from within as well as to defend the whole civilization from
the expansive tendencies of adjacent civilizations. The male was

---

[17] Spretnak. Charlene; *States of Grace* (HarperSanFrancisco: 1991) pages 114-
155 I have put Spretnak's summation in my own words using her basic
overview and some of her terminology.

assigned to these tasks of defense and acculturated in the "virtues" these tasks required.

But these so-called "virtues" of the "civilized" male were in tension with the emotional and sexual ebbs and flows of the human body. In order to maintain these "civilized virtues" of the male ego, the male's inward nature had to be controlled. Being emotional and sexual might be welcome relaxation from such control, but during the "real life" of social maintenance these natural aspects of the human body were seen as weaknesses that were dangerous to the stability of male "virtue." So this virtue-acculturated male ego feared being undone by being sucked back into the womb of Mother Nature or being lost in the swamp of a sensitive relationship with a down-to-Earth woman. Therefore, women were in various ways kept at arms-length, sometimes by degrading them, sometimes by idealizing them and then requiring them to live up to these male ideals. While women could be allowed to be emotional with one another if they wished, males (that is, the fragile male ego of civilizational "virtue") had to be protected from the emotional power of women. Women had to be subservient, obedient, and careful not to undo these "virtues" of the males. These ancient patterns exist to this day. This interior acculturation of men and women is a deep and abiding part of "patriarchy."

2. An affirmation of our human connection with the Earth-body

Civilized males (including their controlled females) became controllers of nature, thus breaking vital connections with nature that had previously characterized the human species and assured its survival. So recovering the veneration of the Great Goddess is seen by spiritual feminists as recovering these vital connections with nature. We need to relearn, according to the Goddess recovery, to identify with the Earth as a whole. This living planet is our larger body. We are Earthlings in body, mind, and Spirit. We need to recover our living relations with trees, bees, animals, mountains, valleys, birth, death, generation, decay, water, desert, rock, sky, moon, sun, and stars.

3. The affirmation of the body of woman

In particular, the body of woman–the vagina, the womb, the breasts, its outward and inward movements, its emotional and sensual ebbs and flows–needs to be recovered as part of the sacred whole. Indeed, the body of woman can be symbolic of that sacred wholeness. When woman is pregnant, the Earth is pregnant with new life. When woman feels, the Earth feels itself feeling itself feeling. Therefore, there is nothing secondary about being a woman-body. The body of woman is the place of origin of both male and female bodies. The body of woman is a locus of enrichment for all embodied human life. This must be affirmed. The body of woman must be celebrated.

4. The affirmation and ritual celebration of birth, menses, sexual pleasure, pregnancy, and menopause

The recovery of Great Goddess veneration has also been a recovery of the healing power of ritual. Effective experiments in ritual have been carried out celebrating all the life passages in a woman's life story. This has proven to be an effective counteraction to the generations of shaming and hiding from view such obvious wonders as the entry into fertility, the flow of blood, pregnancy, birth, the entry into infertility. Death also can be affirmed as a wondrous natural event. And for both women and men, sexual pleasure can be embraced as a sacred rite rather than a secretive, somewhat shameful, though useful duty for repopulating civilization.

5. The affirmation of the individual human body of men and women

Males also benefit from this energetic recovery of the body. Relations between men and women, between men and men, and between women and women all take on a new tone when the human body is trusted and restored to a place of honor–when emotion, desire, and sensuality are seen as an enrichment rather than as a dangerous pit into which we might fall. Children, who naturally affirm their own bodies, are better cared for within an adult climate in which the human body is affirmed. In such a context children are not seen as bits of animal chaos to be rigorously ordered, but as new expressions of the Earth-body's flourishing creativity. Children are bits of Earth-life to be delightfully observed, encouraged, and celebrated. This is fresh air for the psyche of children and for their becoming the body-sensitive men and women a post-patriarchal society requires.

6. The emotional completion of scientific reason

The contemporary recovery of veneration of the Great Goddess, at its best, does not contradict scientific reason. Most vigorous Goddess venerators are also competent biologists, anthropologists, sociologists, physicists, or technicians. But scientific reason, as an arms-length objective discipline, can only be part of the story of our relationship with nature. The wondrous results of scientific objectivity can enrich our whole-Earth devotion, but that devotion itself is not a product of science. It is an emotional reality, a flowering of the non-rational components of our relations with nature.

I believe that "the emotional completion of scientific reason" is a step toward something even deeper–namely "the Awe completion of scientific reason." Awe cannot be understood without the emotional, yet Awe is more than the emotional even as it is more than the intellectual. Awe is Great Feels and Great Thinks that bring us to the place of courage where we can make Great Resolves to be those living relationships with the Infinite that we actually are. Therefore, the recovery of veneration of the Great Goddess is a recovery of Awe, especially the feeling aspects of Awe. And all religion, I repeat *all religion*, is enriched by this recovery, for all good religion is an expression of Awe.

What Sort of Christianity Can Repent of Patriarchy?

Many of us within the Christian tradition now see that the feminist critique of the established social order is appropriate. We see that the prophetic aspect of our own Christian heritage propels us to abolish patriarchy. The prophets, ancient and modern, have been a Spirit-based critique of the established social order. The prophetic element in Christian heritage moderated patriarchy. But the moderation of patriarchy that earlier Christians accomplished is no longer enough. Ending patriarchy completely is now possible and imperative. And this imperative is supported by the prophetic core of the Christian tradition.

Christians have been accused of believing in some far-away God who created nature as a secondary reality and then commanded us to control it, dominate it, and even to escape from nature to our more heavenly states of being. This accusation is a valid description of many Christian-identified groups and persons. But the original Christian breakthrough was not about a far-away God or about distancing ourselves from nature.

In a proper appropriation of the biblical creation myths, the object of Christian worship is a down-to-Earth Infinity walking in the garden of our everyday lives. And nature is not some secondary, unsacred material. Rather, the Infinite Oneness is met by human beings nowhere else than within the ordinary course of natural and historical events. When we see a mighty crocodile opening its jaws to attack us, we see the power of God manifested in this beast (Job 44). When we see the sun and moon and stars in their majestic circles overhead, we ask, "What is the human species anyhow, that You, the Infinite, should go to so much trouble to decorate our sky and give us warmth and light and food?" (Psalm 8) And at least a dozen Psalms tell us that there is no escape from nature–no escape from birth, no escape from finitude, no escape from death (Psalms 139, 49, 90, 104, and others). The Genesis phrase "from dust to dust" applies not only to the human body but also to the human psyche, which projects its puny sense of reality upon the landscape of mysterious nature. Awe (Spirit) dwells within us because we encounter the Awesome only through the finite dust of our natural lives. In the biblical writings, Spirit is the ongoing gift of Awesome Otherness walking with us and acting upon us through our ordinary natural lives.

From this perspective the Kingly God of Israel is actually none other than the Earth Mother Herself. We are talking about precisely the same experiences. Whether you see your origin as a Great Womb or a Great Hand in the mud or a Great Voice commanding your emergence, you are thinking about your mysterious origin with down-to-Earth images and symbols. Symbols of the Infinite are not themselves infinite. Symbols are simply fingers pointing to the moon of the Infinite.

Everything in the Goddess heritage, therefore, can be an enrichment of our experience of the God of Israel. Christianity, in the coming millennium, is called to repent of its rejection of the Goddess symbolism, of fearing and demeaning woman's magical existence, and of exalting and privileging male capabilities. Any form of Christianity that refuses to repent of these ancient practices is a perversion of the true thrust of biblical heritage. Patriarchal habits, however justifiable in ages past, are now relegated to the scrap heap of history along with sacrificing children on Yahweh's altar or owning slaves. The God of Israel is a God who does new things, and the commandment to abolish patriarchy is one of those new things.

Resurgent Christianity also has Gifts for the Goddess Recovery

Two gifts that can enrich the Goddess Recovery stand out in the contemporary resurgence of Christian practice: (1) clarity about *literalism* relative to the Divine, and (2) the *prophetic* dynamics.

With respect to *literalism*, the gifts of the Goddess heritage are lost if we misunderstand these ancient Goddess myths in a literalistic fashion. The Infinite is not literally male or female. Maleness and femaleness are finite differences that describe only the finite "end" of the Spirit relationship between our finite lives and the Infinite encounter. When we say that both males and females are capable of Spirit, we mean capable of being a relationship with the Infinite. When we are being the Spirit relationship we are, both males and females can experience the very same states of being: dread, challenge, courage, tranquility, joy, etc.

Nevertheless, the finite end of the Spirit relationship is important. When a man manifests his Spirit existence, he must manifest it as a man. And when a woman manifests her Spirit existence, she must manifest it as a woman. To manifest Spirit within the finite dynamics of maleness and femaleness are important considerations.

But when we use male or female imagery for Infinite Reality, we are not talking about the anatomy of the Infinite. We are talking about our relationships with the Infinite and about how those relationship can be expressed in the fragile symbolisms of down-to-Earth male and female analogies.

Women do not need a Big Female up in the sky to help them affirm their existence. And men do not need a Big Male up in the sky to help them affirm their existence. Both maleness and femaleness are good because they exist, not because one or the other is more divine. The renewal of the Christian heritage in our times has been effective in clarifying the deadly error of literalism. And overcoming literalism is needed for interpreting all religion, including the recovery of the Goddess heritage.

Clarity about the *prophetic dynamic* is a second contribution of the Christian heritage to the Goddess recovery. Though in its pre-Christian origins the prophetic heritage focused on justice for the poor and other social outcasts, it can also be a source of support for protest against the outcasting of women and the outcasting of nature. The prophetic heritage traditionally focused upon society rather than nature, but this focus on society was upon its transformation, not upon the moralistic perpetuation of social custom. Social transformation today includes these two priorities: (1) the liberation of women and (2) the liberation of nature from the tyranny of patriarchal, hierarchical, money-dominated, over-rational, over-controlling, moralistic rigidities.

Feminism, as it has arisen in Western cultures, has originated (at least in part) as an embodiment of prophetic heritage. Many women who led the emergence of the feminine movement were drawing from biblical sources. So let us look more closely at how an authentic recovery of the prophetic heritage supports an affirmation of nature and women. The prophet criticizes the established social order from a perspective that is wider and deeper than the assumptions of that social order. In its civilizational form human society has tended to worship itself–that is, to make the glorification of civilization and the well-being of especially its upper classes the center of value. The biblical prophet challenged this value center. The prophet asked king and peasant, ruler and commoner, rich and poor to honor "radical realism" (that is, the actions of Infinite Actuality) as the criteria for all judgments. This prophetic critique of hierarchical civilization can be expanded to include the liberation of women.

The liberation of nature is likewise consistent with the Spirit of the biblical prophet. Worshiping the Infinite does not demean nature. Rather, nature is demeaned by our enthrallment with civilization. We have sometimes called our European civilizations "Christian" or "Christendom," but there is no such thing as a Christian civilization, if by "Christian" we mean "Divine." Every civilization is a human invention; therefore, no civilization is divine. Worshiping a so-called Christian civilization is different from worshiping God. The prophetic demystification of civilization can strengthen the liberation of women and the recovery of the ancient Goddess heritage. Similarly, the Goddess heritage can provide new richness to the prophetic heritage.

The Human Invention of Patriarchy

A deeper understanding of this dialogue with the Goddess heritage can be found through exploring this question: *How did patriarchy get going in the first place?* Tribal societies were not patriarchal. Nor were the earliest civilizations. I define "the dawn of civilization" as the advent of the mode of social organization that hierarchically ordered many tribes into large agricultural arrangements. At first, these larger societies did not abandon the old tribal ties with nature. Instead, they developed the Goddess symbolism into a high art. They carved great statues, elaborated rituals, created life meanings, and established ethical practices that honored nature and adapted civilization to its natural environments. In these earliest civilizations women were given a much stronger place of honor than in the later centuries of civilizational history. In these earliest civilizations the feminine, as an aspect of the human experience, was far more prominently celebrated by both men and women. Patriarchy as we know it today had not yet been invented.

However spotty our knowledge of these early civilizations may be, this conclusion now has overwhelming historical support: *patriarchy does not represent the "always-was" in human affairs.* Furthermore, patriarchy took place not at the dawn of civilization but several hundred years later. Patriarchy was an invention that took place within the history of world civilizations.

So why did patriarchy arise? Many explanations have been proposed. Riane Eisler and others have proposed the theory that patriarchy came into being when patriarchal herders conquered and altered the more egalitarian, Goddess-honoring societies that were our earliest civilizations. But Leonard Shlain in his book *The Alphabet Versus the Goddess* argues convincingly that Eisler's explanation is simplistic. Many times in history, conquerors have adopted the cultural values of those they conquered. Why did that not happen in this case? Shlain also rejects Fredrich Engels' notion that the demise of the feminine resulted from the rise of private property. Shlain points out that private property arose much earlier than patriarchy.

After discrediting these and other such theories, Shlain proposes and documents his thesis that patriarchy came into being and has intensified from time to time because writing, especially alphabetic writing, tends to imbalance a culture in favor of the left side of the brain. Women, who have more connecting tissue between the left and right hemispheres of their brains (and thus, between linear language speaking and holistic image making), are more dependent for their empowerment on keeping this balance intact. Men, on the other hand, have less connecting tissue between the two hemispheres which enables them to more easily shut down the right side of their brains (including their emotions and holistic sensibilities) and thus focus for sustained periods of time on linear pursuits like hunting an animal or conducting a war. Shlain concludes that cultures that emphasize written language advantage the males. This is especially true of cultures that have become unbalanced by a rapid turn from oral to written media. Shlain also illustrates how rapid changes toward alphabetic literacy can make both men and women "crazy" in ways that permit acceptance not only of the oppression of women but also of violent reactions between different cultural groups who have previously lived peacefully together.

While Shlain's thesis may sound preposterous at first, he makes a convincing case. It seems to me that this thesis is at least part of the truth. But the whole truth, I believe, is even more complex.

In his examination of early civilizations, Joseph Campbell tells of nature priesthoods who maintained control of their societies by restricting each king to a five-year reign after which he was put to death. These early priesthoods apparently realized that a political realm dominated by the male military threatened the old ways of maintaining society in harmony with natural forces. Strange and cruel as royal executions may seem to us today, we can nevertheless view this ancient practice as a resistance to the rise of patriarchy.

So why did patriarchy arise? I believe that patriarchy was delayed within our earliest hierarchical civilizations because the nature priesthoods had not yet been overthrown by the kings and the increasingly important male military. Patriarchy arose when these male kings overthrew the nature priesthoods and initiated the *idolization of civilization*. The adoration of nature and the Infinite Presence within nature was replaced by an enthrallment with civilization itself and with the wonderworks that a civilization can do. This enthrallment included an enthrallment with male kingship: the king became a symbol for the civilization as a whole. The fabrics of the civilization were viewed as divine and the king was thus divine as well. As this worship of civilization got going, patriarchy got going as well.

Within this wider perspective we can include some of Shlain's insights. Perhaps written language did intensify the patriarchal trend. The political tasks of controlling and defending a civilization are left-brain tasks that are reinforced and augmented by the left-brain emphasis of written languages. Also the widespread idolization of a civilization requires a written language to promulgate this unnatural perspective. Written languages, especially phonetic alphabets, emphasize uniformity, and uniformity is one of the key characteristics that make possible a top-down, hierarchical civilization. But I believe that the self-worship of hierarchical civilization is the root cause of patri-archy, not written language. We will be able to keep and use creatively written language in a post-hierarchical, post-patriarchal, post-civiliza-tional mode of social life.

In the Semitic region of the planet, where Judaism, Christianity, and Islam emerged, patriarchy is at least 3800 years old. Around that time, we can see the dawn of patriarchy symbolized in a Babylonian myth. Marduk, a god who symbolized the male thrust of the Babylonian hierarchy, slew Tiamat, the Earth Mother, and split her body in two. With one half he formed the ground and with the other half the sky. In Marduk's deed, civilization stands apart from nature and rules over her. Marduk's cosmic deed mirrors a down-to-Earth deed by the hierarchical rulers and religious teachers of ancient Babylon. Maleness, the king, and military power were promoted to a position of dominance over the forces of nature and consequently over the symbolic power of the Goddess. The symbolic power of the Goddess had until her overthrow been yoked to our experience of nature and to our experience of the female body–the body which birthed both men and women and provided milk that fed us all.

Patriarchy and the Patriarchal Religions

If the origin of patriarchy is rooted in an enthrallment with civiliza-tion and thus a rebellion from the Infinite Presence within nature, then the classical religions of the patriarchal period, at their best, moderated patriarchy. Why? Because each of these religions focused upon a devo-tion to THAT which transcended civilization, a THAT which included the mystery of nature, a THAT which included a view of human self-hood that was greater than the self of social conditioning.

In this light, I want to explore the following generalizations about the long and complicated histories of Judaism, Christianity, Islam, Hinduism, Buddhism, Taoism, and Confucianism:

(1) None of these patriarchal religions are responsible for starting patriarchy.

(2) All of these religions carried patriarchy along and, at their worst, intensified it.

(3) At their best, all these religions moderated patriarchy.

(4) All these religions can, without loss to their essential gifts, enter the future cleansed entirely of their patriarchal thinking and styles of living.

(1) None of these patriarchal religions are responsible for starting patriarchy.

Patriarchy predated all these religions by hundreds of years. Hinduism and Judaism are the oldest. Moses left Egypt around 1300 B.C.E. Patriarchy was well underway in Babylon by 1800 B.C.E. Even Abraham, whoever this distant ancestor may have been, grew up in a patriarchal environment.

The Goddess roots in Hinduism reach back to at least 2500 B.C.E. The patriarchal qualities of Hinduism were not established until after the Aryan conquests starting around 1500 B.C.E. When the writers of the earliest Hindu texts appeared in 1000 to 700 B.C.E., society was already patriarchal. These writers did not invent patriarchy.

All the other religions we are considering are younger. So to properly evaluate their patriarchal qualities, we must keep in mind that at the time of their origin there was no historical alternative for any of these religions except to be adapted to the patriarchal times in which they had to live and grow and transmit their gifts.

(2) All of these religions carried patriarchy along and, at their worst, intensified it.

Nevertheless, all these religions bear responsibility for transmitting patriarchy through the centuries and for continuing to perpetuate patriarchy into the 21st century–a time when patriarchy is clearly dying and needs to die faster. Furthermore, at their worst, all these religions have participated in intensifying the patriarchal imbalance. Christianity, at its worst, burned at the stake innocent independent women, accusing them of being witches who were destroying the true faith. Hinduism, at its worst, burned living wives on funeral pyres with their deceased husbands. At its worst, the Taoist/Confucian culture, for the sake of a male ideal of beauty, crippled women with foot binding. And Islam, at its worst, scarred the body and psyche of young girls with the horrors of circumcision. These gross violations are but visible peaks of the mountain range of patriarchal oppression practiced by these religions.

(3) At their best, all these religions moderated patriarchy.

Yet we should not judge the future worth of a religious tradition by the worst perversions in its past. All these religious traditions also contain resources for resisting patriarchy. Taoism in its yin/yang teachings saw clearly that maleness and femaleness were two equal parts of one wholesome whole. The spunky cultural spoofing of the Taoist sages provided a force of moderation to the patriarchal cultures of the Orient. This was also true for in sensible restyling of life advanced by the Confucian teachers.

Hinduism stubbornly preserved many ancient Goddess vitalities in its mix of religious methods and artistic expressions. At its best, ancient Hinduism was like a subversive force reshaping the culture of the Aryan conquerors with Dravidian elements that reached into the deepest antiquities of the Goddess cultures. Further, the Hindu/Buddhist emphasis upon the Great Self beyond finite personality tended to make the gender of the practitioner less important. Awakened Spirit can take on both male and female embodiments. Also, the typical Western tension between reason and matter was never emphasized in sub-Asia. For the Hindu sage, reason was not a near-Divine illuminator but a passing phenomena that was just as limited as sexual desire or human emotion. Reason was seen as an illusion maker as well as a practical tool for living. In this more transrational context, both the womanly and the manly could be more easily appropriated as relevant vehicles for the embodiment of awakened Spirit.

At their best, Judaism, Christianity, and Islam functioned as prophetic criticism and correction of the oppressive practices within their hierarchical/patriarchal social environments. The One God of these traditions was, when these religions were vital, not an abstract being far away from the individual person and from the realm of nature. The One God was a head-on collision experienced by every person and every civilization. Certainly this One God, when vitally understood, was not a symbol for patriarchal civilization itself but constituted an ethical grounding that reached beyond the kings and rulers and priesthoods of the hierarchy. So when their full Spirit energies were flowing, these monotheistic faiths functioned as moderating influences upon pure patriarchy.

For example, while Jesus called God "Father" and probably organized his followers with male leadership roles, he also honored women along with all other outcasts of a culture enthralled with its own righteousness. While the Protestant Reformation continued many patriarchal customs of its immediate past, it was a significant moderation of Christendom's most extreme forms of patriarchy. Martin Luther, a celibate monk, married a nun and constructed a happy marriage and provided women with a place of respect. Mohammed, also a happily married man, initiated customs that were fresh air for women in his time. Though these themes now seem remarkably absent in the thinking of many Muslims, Jews, and Christians, the true Spirit impetus of these monotheistic religions can best be carried forward by the total release of both women and men from patriarchal oppression.

The harshest forms of patriarchy appeared in Jewish, Christian, and Islamic civilizations when these civilizations turned in upon themselves–that is, when they worshiped their religious civilizations instead of the One God that these civilizations had been invented to serve. Such turned-in-ness was a departure from the core of these religious breakthroughs. "Enthrallment with civilization" is a recurrence of the ancient social pattern from which Moses led an exodus and toward which all the prophets expressed their ire.

Though the historical elements I have cited are sketchy, perhaps I have indicated (if not proven) this important conclusion: patriarchy was moderated (though not defeated) by these many movements of Spirit enlightenment that took place within these patriarchal civilizations.

(4) All these religions can, without loss to their essence, enter the future cleansed entirely of their patriarchal thinking and styles of living.

The time for moderating patriarchy is over. Patriarchy can now be ended. Similarly, the time for moderating the maladies of hierarchical civilization is over. Both patriarchy and hierarchical civilization are already being dismantled. All the classical religions of the patriarchal period can be allies in the task of finishing this dismantlement and launching something better. One key to designing something better is contained in the essence of what made all these religions great–their devotion to Spirit rather than civilization, their devotion to a relationship with the Infinite, and their resistance to an enthrallment with the finite achievements of humanity.

When the post-patriarchal forms of these long-standing patriarchal religions join forces with (rather than oppose) the Great Goddess recovery, we might see the end of patriarchal oppression on this planet.

17.

Primordial Manyness and Biblical Oneness

Dialogue with the religions of humanity would not be complete without a dialogue with tribal religion. When we think of the religions of the world, we think first of the historical religions with sacred texts and cumulative traditions. But consider these words of Huston Smith:

> (The major historical religions) now pretty much blanket the earth, but chronologically they form only the tip of the religious iceberg, for they span a scant four thousand years as compared with the three million years or so of the religions that preceded them. During that immense time span, people lived their religion in an importantly different mode that must have shaped their sensibilities significantly. [18]

I will call these religions "tribal religions." These religions preceded the Goddess traditions of our earliest civilizations as well as the later

---

[18] Smith, Huston; *The Illustrated World's Religions* (HarperSanFrancisco: 1991) page 232

religions of the patriarchal era. I will not describe in detail the practices of any tribal group–contemporary or living thousands of years
ago. Yet these widely varying religious practices are the particulars
about which I will be making generalizations. This chapter is a dialogue with a basic religious mode that I see to be present in all these
widely varying groups.

I will discuss only the positive aspects of tribal religions. Religion of
any sort can be perverted, but I will not examine here the perversions of
tribal religions. Perversions are an important part of the wider discussion of religion, but when we are pursuing meaningful dialogue
between two religious traditions, we need to focus on what is best in
those traditions. And by "best" I mean best at expressing Spirit.

I have found, and am still finding, enrichment from my study of
tribal religions. And I have been integrating what I have learned into
revitalized forms of Christianity. This has been my focus in each chapter of this book: clarifying the resurgence of Christianity in the context
of the world of religions.

Pursuing honest dialogue with tribal humanity is complicated by the
fact that hierarchical/patriarchal civilizations have oppressed not only
women and nature but also tribal peoples. The ruthlessness and arrogance with which almost every civilization has oppressed tribal societies
is almost unbelievable. What is the root of this oppression? What madness resides in civilized people that would make this attitude understandable? What differences exist between civilized and tribal peoples
that allow civilized people to consider tribal people sub-human? And
why have many tribal people persisted in rejecting civilization in favor
of their tribal life-ways?

Civilized people demean tribal people by considering tribal life
primitive, where "primitive" means bad or less evolved. Opening ourselves fully to the humanity of tribal people requires a new attitude
toward civilization and precivilization. In common usage the word "civilized" has become a synonym for "good." Instead, let us understand

"civilization" to mean one of two primary ways that human beings have
organized their social existence. Tribal is the other. Our vision of the
future need not be tribal or civilized. Let us assume that we face the task
of creating a third primary way of organizing social existence. And let
us assume that we can learn valuable lessons on how to forge this
unprecedented future from both tribal and civilized societies. Such a
vision of future well being allows us to view tribal religion with a proper
amount of openness.

Many sensitive members of recent civilizations have become fascinated with the life of our tribal ancestors. Not only archeologists and
anthropologists but also artists, social reformers, ecologists, and others
have engaged in meaningful dialogue with tribal peoples. The paintings
of Picasso and Gauguin reflect this dialogue. The 30,000-year old cave
paintings in southern France have intrigued and mystified many of us.
A fresh wind of naturalness is blowing from this deep past into our contemporary quest for authenticity.

Many currently living peoples, the Australian Aborigine, the
Bushmen of Africa, the tribal peoples of the Americas have also drawn
intense attention. We find in these people a living enactment of the lives
that all of us lived in the deep past of our species. The Australian
Aborigines have been particularly interesting because they were, until
impacted by the British in the 18th century, a pristine extension of the
hunter-gatherer style of life. They had not been influenced by civilizations that began over 5000 years ago or by the practice of agriculture
which began over 10,000 years ago.

It was once popular to image precivilization or tribal humans as sav-
ages, people who had nothing to contribute to civilized people. They
were stereotyped as violent and uncultured animals. Yet the Australian
Aborigines (as well as other isolated tribal cultures) have amazed us
with their uncanny natural wisdom, their rich cultural heritages, their
gentleness, their communal solidarity, their mystic intensity, and their
artistic and religious creativity.

Yet religious teachers within civilized societies have typically dismissed tribal religion as "folk superstition," "unenlightened ignorance," or simply "idolatry." This dismissal of tribal religion has given encouragement to the incredible violence that civilized people have carried out toward these fellow human beings.

This violent response is more fully understood when we notice that civilized people have harbored a deep fear of the tribal way of life. When Christianized Europeans came to the Americas, they met tribal cultures that celebrated and cared for geographical places and the natural realities of human life with a passion and wholesomeness that was frightening to these emotionally and sexually reserved Europeans. Handling this cultural shock was a deep challenge to these newly arriving colonists. Some learned from these cultures, but most preferred to ignore them or destroy them.

For civilized people to openly dialogue with tribal cultures requires taking a fresh attitude toward nature. Tribal cultures seek to fit into nature. They see themselves as family members among the other living beings who make up the surrounding world. When certain Native American religious teachers speak of "all my relations," they do not mean simply grandfathers, grandmothers, aunts, and uncles. They mean all the other species of life among whom human life became possible. "All my relations" has become for me a significant expression of an attitude toward nature that I want to embody.

In his book *The Spell of the Sensuous* David Abram speaks of the tribal religious leader, the shaman, as someone who lives on the edge of society and tunes himself or herself with the surrounding nature.[19] Living in this wider connection the shaman can bring healing to members of the society who have lost their grounding in nature. The shaman can also advise the society on how to live in tune with the voices of this larger-than-human space. Abram points out that the shaman not only

---

[19] Abram, David; *The Spell of the Sensuous* (Pantheon Books: 1996) Chapter 1

sees and listens to the surrounding trees and grasses and animals, but is also aware of being listened to and seen by the surrounding trees and grasses and animals. We not only impact the larger-than-human, we are also being impacted by them.

This nature-affirming attitude was also extended to non-living realities–the mountains, the valleys, the sun, the moon, and the stars. This ancient attitude is something deeper than that of the modern tourist who escapes from the roar of the city to the peace and quiet and beauty of the countryside. Without sentimentalizing nature or avoiding its horrors, shamanically instructed societies revere nature as something Awesome, sobering, healing, entrancing, absorbing, fascinating, and crucially important. Natural beings blend into the depths of Being.

The shaman and the shaman's pupils take trips together into these unfathomable depths. Then they come back to the ordinary life of their society more in tune with one another and their own psychological phenomena and thus healthier and stronger to face their challenges. A religious life is going on here. Some anthropologists have said that these ancient cultures did not have religions; rather, their entire cultural canopy was religious.

This view is consistent with my basic definition of religion: a sociological practice of human beings that is intended to give expression to Awe. Before the dawn of the "civilization mode" of society, the entire tribal society was religious. Civilizations were the first secular societies. Within the secular canopy of a civilization religions (plural) could come into being. Before civilizations arose religious sensibilities, cultural meanings, and practical wisdoms melded together into a singular living whole.

Yet, calling civilizations "secular" can be misleading, because the so-called "secular" canopy of a typical civilization is seldom religiously neutral. In the usual case, civilization itself became a quasi-religious practice calling for people to "worship" civilization as their ultimate loyalty. It was in order to fight against this general "self-worship" of a civilization, that many specific religions separated themselves from the general society.

But in the precivilization era, religion, society, and the surrounding nature melded into one interlocking whole. This did not mean, however, that there was no sense of being a solitary Spirit person. Similarly, this interlocking wholeness did not exclude a sense of the Infinite–of a "Beyond" that is both beyond society and beyond nature as well.

The shaman's wisdom not only reaches beyond society into nature, but also includes trances that witness to a "Beyond" even more "beyond" than nature is beyond society. We in modern society tend to be enthralled with the finite scope of things. The enthrallments of the ancient shaman and his or her pupils carried them into a full experience of the Mystery of it All. The Australian Aborigine took trips to a realm of awareness they referred to as "Dreamtime." They and other shamanic-tutored cultures returned from these "trips" to their ordinary lives, enriched with practical Spirit wisdom. On their "trips" they saw animals or they took animals with them. These were strange animals; they were not simply the beings describable by modern biology. These animals were totem symbols, Awe-expressing human creations, religious beings. They were our earliest gods and goddesses, fabricated by human imagination to express Awe.

The Christian Dialogue with Tribal Religion

At first glance, the differences between Christianity and the tribal religious traditions seem almost total. While tribal religions honor many sacred beings, many sacred places, many sacred dynamics, Christianity espouses the worship of ONE GOD. Also, Christianity is explicit that nature is not God, but the creation of God. God (as nature's Creator) is beyond, INFINITELY BEYOND, nature.

So for the dialogue with tribal religion to proceed meaningfully, Christians need to look afresh at their myth of creation. I have called

"creation" a myth, because the first two chapters of the Bible are
mythic story, not scientific report. No Creator has ever been scientifically discovered. Some have attempted to make "creation" scientific by
noting the astonishing conclusions of modern cosmology that the universe had a definite beginning in what is called "the Big Bang." But Big
Bang cosmology does not demonstrate the existence of a "Creator."
The notion of "Creator" is part of a religious story–a story written to
answer these two questions of personal and ethical meaning: (1) what
is meant by the term "God"? And (2) what should be our attitude
toward natural reality?

Most Christians and Jews living today think backwards about the
story of creation. They first posit what they mean by "God" and then
move toward the notion that this God has created nature. But this was
not the order of thought in the actual writing of the creation myth.
Rather, the creation myth was written to define "God." The myth begins
with "realities" that everyone knows: light, darkness, stars, moon, sun,
plants, fish, birds, animals, and human beings. The Mysterious Source
of all these commonly known realities is the "ACTUALITY" being recommended for our worship. The writers of the opening chapters of the
Hebrew Bible are not defining "nature"; they are using taken-for-
granted descriptions of nature to define "God."

Moreover, this creation myth is saying something that is not alto-
gether obvious: namely, there is One Source for all things. We might
posit many sources. Often we posit two sources: one source for those
things we humans count "good" and another source for those things we
humans count "bad." The biblical creation myth, however, speaks of
One Source. This myth is making a radically challenging statement: all
existing things (not some existing things) are good, having the same
Source. In the second grand myth of the Bible, we are told that evil did
not enter the cosmos until we humans chose to eat the perspective that
some things are good and other things are bad, that is until we humans
made ourselves the center of value,

The holistic affirmation of all natural realities is bedrock for understanding the rest of biblical literature. This may seem strange to us, because we have experienced in the medieval and modern eras of Christianity cultures that harbored deep suspicions about nature, especially nature as a wildness that attacks our "rational" living. Sexuality, as a natural wildness within our own bodies, has been significantly suppressed in many forms of Christianity. The early stages of Western science also tended to suppress the wildness of nature. This suppression was accomplished through viewing nature is a great machine, a great clock that runs in accord with a rational order that human beings can understand through their scientific explorations. Now, in the era of post-Einsteinian science, it has become clear that "machine-like" is a gross oversimplification of nature. Amazing mathematical order can be found in nature, but nature is also a wild vitality that opens out into a mysteriousness that appears to be unfathomable no matter how much further we go with our discovery of order. It is now good scientific philosophy to state that the more we know, the more we know we don't know. Nature is a wildness that human ordering can approximate to an amazing degree, and yet that "degree" is still flimsy in comparison with what remains unknown.

This turn of events in scientific philosophy has placed us in closer contact with tribal cultures for whom the wildness (or mysteriousness) of nature was a daily experience. A completely rational ordering of nature was to them unthinkable. Fortunately for our sanity, it has also become unthinkable in the mature intellectual community of postmodern culture. We now confront in nature at least as much wildness as order, at least as much chaos as stability, at least as much mystery as rational predictability. It is this mystery-laden "nature" that the creation myth of Genesis is talking about. "Dry land" in the biblical myth is a symbol for that orderly place where humans can live. Water is a symbol for chaos. Then and now we humans are thankful for the dry land, and we humans also know that the waters of chaos surround the dry land. Chaos laps at the shores of the land–asking, it seems, to leap out and cover us. Water pours down from the skies and threatens at times to flood the entire realm of nature. But according to the biblical myth of creation, all this is good: the order and the chaos, the dry land and the water, the darkness and the light, the human and the other-than-human beings.

By "good" the creation myth does not mean that all things are pleasant or painless. The term "good" always implies a center of value. The creation myth is not talking about "good" in relation to the center of value called "human comfort" or "human desires" or "human progress." The creation myth is talking about "good" in relation to the Wholeness of Being. To "worship" this Mysterious Source as our "God" means to make this Source of all things our center of value.

But why need we believe there is such a Source? Why cannot nature be self-generating? These questions are unanswerable, because "Source" and "Self Generating" are both metaphors for the same Mysteriousness. We simply do not know why everything came to be. When the question "Why?" is asked about existence itself, it has no answer. It is natural for the human mind to play with the question "Why?" Every curious child seems to be talented in bothering his or her elders with this question. And the elders of our ancient cultures typically responded to the ever-present, child-like "Why?" with oddly playful answers they must have known were playful. Serious objectivity could not have been their concern. "One Source" is also a playful answer. But this answer has a serious meaning–namely, that all of nature, not some of it, is a generous and well-meaning gift to human beings from the One Source. And this One Source is being recommended as the proper object of devotion for the "authentic" human being. This is the meaning of the creation myth that leads off the Bible. This myth states a "primal attitude" that remains bedrock for the entire Bible: *all that is natural is also good.*

If Christians were to embrace this positive biblical attitude toward nature, then we would be on common ground with the religious

expressions of tribal peoples. Nevertheless, tribal religions differ significantly from biblical religions. The notion that there is One Source for
natural reality is rarely explicit in tribal religions. In the foreground of
these religions, we see many gods and goddesses–many sources of Awe.
Tribal religions have usually been called "polytheistic."

Polytheism

The conflict between polytheistic and monotheistic mythologies is
perhaps the greatest challenge to fruitful dialogue between Christian
and tribal religions. If we think, as we so often do, that "One God" is
describing something objective and literal, then polytheism and
monotheism are irreconcilable. Literally speaking, "One God" and
"many gods and goddesses" are opposite statements. But if we see that
both "One" and "Many" are metaphorical ways of talking about the
same Mysteriousness, then a meaningful dialogue can proceed.

The truth of polytheism is that there are many "places" where Awe is
breaking through. The Awe experience is always specific; it is always
illuminating specific aspects of living, specific geographical places, specific events in the calendar of life. A particular ancient tree is experienced as sacred. A particular landscape is experienced as holy. War and
love can each have their Awesomeness. Feminine and masculine can
each have their Sacredness.

The truth of monotheism is that all experiences of Awe are linked.
Oneness stands behind them all. One Mysterious Overallness is occasioning Awe within us through our specific encounters with the finite
events and realities of our lives. From the monotheistic perspective,
every experience of Awe (or sacredness) shows that humanity is a relationship with this One Infinite Overallness. The Source of all Awe is this
ongoing Oneness that is occasioning Awe in our lives through the specific happenings and places of human living.

Thus, if both polytheism and monotheism are defined as experiences rather than dogmas, we can say that most polytheistic religions include expression of monotheism. The legends and stories of a polytheistic culture typically link together various points of Awe. Various gods and goddesses appear in the same story. Perhaps a pantheon of ordered relationships between the gods and goddesses is conceived. Perhaps some concept like "mana" links all Awe experiences. Perhaps some Chief God or Great Spirit appears in the mythological story-scape. These factors point to oneness within the pluralness of tribal religious cultures. This oneness may not be emphasized, but it may be present like a common light that shines through the manyness of Awe experiences.

Similarly, biblical monotheism is not without expressions of polytheism, if by polytheism we mean that Awe is experienced in many specific ways. Specific events are seen as holy encounters. Specific lands and places take on sacred meanings. "Angels" is a device used in the Bible to express the manyness with which the Oneness moves towards us.

In the eighteenth chapter of Genesis, three figures walk up to Abraham as he sits by his tent door in the heat of the day. They turn out to be messengers of the Oneness. In one verse **these three figures** are speaking to Abraham; then, in the very next verse, **GOD** is speaking to him. Then the three figures walk on down the road. These verses might be used to forge our basic definition of a biblical angel: an angel is a bit of the created manyness that serves as a messenger of the Overall Oneness.

When Isaiah "sees" God in the temple (Isaiah 6), he describes an Infinite King hidden behind the wings of many "super-angels." These angels cry out their message of Awe: "Holy, Holy, Holy." In the New Testament angels appear in dreams warning wise men. Angels appear in the sky singing to shepherds. When Jesus, driven by the Spirit to a lonely place, rejects the three false directions for his life, angels come and minister to him. In the book of Revelation, even cities have their angels. If such angels are not literal beings, what are they? They are mythic ways of talking about the specific occurrences of Awe in our lives. Since each angel is sent by the Oneness, the biblical metaphor of angels is not in conflict with biblical monotheism. We can understand "angels" as an expression of "pluralness" within the experience of "Oneness" being affirmed by biblical monotheism.

Christian-identified persons could improve their dialogue with tribal religions by simply viewing tribal gods and goddesses as angels of the One God. Members of tribal heritages might thereby be enabled to see that the One Source is a Unity with which they are also familiar. If practitioners of tribal religion see this Oneness in the midst of their manyness, and if practitioners of biblical religion see the manyness within their Oneness, then a meaningful dialogue can take place. Irreconcilable conflict would be replaced by mutual enrichment.

The Gifts of Christianity to the Ongoing Dialogue with Tribal Religion

A down-to-Earth form of Christianity can bring to the dialogue with tribal people the awareness that all perceptions of sacredness are experiences of Awe and that all Awe is good for us. Sacredness is not something dangerous or spooky that adheres to a particular place or tree or animal. All Awe is good Awe. There are no devilish Awe-bringers. All Awe-bringers are angels representing the One Source that loves us dearly. All Awe is good Awe. Evil enters the story of human life through the human agency of rejecting the Awe that the angels bring. This rejection creates the so-called "evil spirits." An evil spirit is a fallen angel who is fallen because a human rejection of the Awe is mingling with the Awe that the angel is bringing.

The Gifts of Tribal Religion to the Ongoing Dialogue with Christianity

Tribal religious persons bring to the dialogue with Christians many millennia of practical wisdom and experience in discerning and celebrating the sacredness of nature. This gift is a deep gift, not something we members of "civilized" heritages can quickly master. Christians need to move beyond the view that the wisdom of ancient cultures is crass and immature. Rather, tribal people have had a dreadful and fascinating communion with the Awe of the natural world. Christians in dialoguing with tribal people will be embarking upon a trek, a vision quest, a long journey into a strange "land of mystery"–a vast land of deep dreads and overwhelming joys.

Tribal religious expressions connect us not only to the deeps of nature but also to the deep past of our own humanity. They teach us that being human has always been about being a religious being. In every millennium the religious expression of Spirit has been central in human uniqueness. What makes us vitally human is more than our rational minds or our technological prowess or our capacity for social organization. Our essential humanity is expressed in our ability to discern Awe in a tree, a star, a sun, a piece of ground, a river, a mountain, a birth, a death, an era of time, a cycle of seasons. Awe connects us to the Wholeness of our surroundings and to one another. Awe releases us to our deepest joy and compassion. Awe heals us from numbness and boredom and moves us beyond naiveté and wickedness. The other amazing capabilities of the human species are only practical developments which have been derived from this central hub of being Awe-perceiving beings.

Dialogue with tribal religious expressions can give us a deeper awareness and appreciation for the "childhood" of our species. Recovering the gifts of that long precivilization period of our humanity will enrich our future. Mentally, technologically, and organizationally, civilized humanity cannot go back to some idealized primitivism. Once we are aware of new potentialities, we cannot easily become unaware of them. Yet, whatever be the gifts of modern culture, in the arena of experiencing Awe in surrounding nature, it is the civilized who are the novices. We, the civilized, have too often forgotten what we, as tribal humanity, once knew.

Ancient humanity was not as clear as some modern humans are about the metaphorical nature of all religious expression. But this does not mean that the religion of ancient humanity was only "foolish magic" that we have now "progressed" beyond. Seeing the foolishness of taking any religious expression literally is a great modern achievement, but this achievement does not make us more proficient than our tribal ancestry in actually using religious metaphors to express our experiences of living Awe. Our tribal ancestry had the advantage of living before the modern exaggeration of the mental aspects of human life. Our tribal ancestry came naturally and intuitively to the task of giving metaphorical expression to their experiences of the Infinite Mystery. We modern people who have learned to talk so lucidly are still novices in actually doing what tribal humanity courageously did. Whatever the failures of tribal peoples, they succeeded in preserving our Awe-experiencing humanity through thousands of centuries. It is not yet clear that we, their contemporary descendants, will preserve Awe-experiencing humanity for another seven generations.

Building a viable future for the human species hinges on our ability to courageously express and boldly live the Awe streaming towards us through the natural world. In this arena our tribal ancestors are our teachers. Contemporary tribal peoples are our teachers as well. Contemporary tribal peoples possess connections with our ancestors that most of us have lost. The dialogue that we Christians pursue with our contemporary tribal companions can assist us to deepen our awareness of the roots in our humanity. This dialogue can help us understand that the mania within "civilized" cultures to reject tribal people is also a rejection of the roots of our own humanity. Furthermore, our thoughtless desecration of the natural world is also a result of this same loss of humanity that allows us to harbor our anti-tribal attitudes.

So we Christians need to keep in mind that we have nothing to fear from a dialogue with tribal humanity. As our own heritage teaches us, all Awe is good Awe.

An End Note on Pantheism

Finally, I want to note how various monotheistic thinkers have used a theological abstraction to clog up the dialogue with tribal people. These monotheistic thinkers believe that they must oppose what they have called "pantheism." They distinguish the worship of the Infinite God from the worship of finite nature. This is an important distinction if nature is viewed as an objective, Awe-less sort of stuff. Since the time of Sir Isaac Newton, "nature" has been seen by many people as a rational machine. But when "nature" is seen as an interconnected wholeness that is penetrated at every point by a mysteriousness no human scientist can fathom, then the distinction between monotheism and pantheism blurs.

Christian theology (when it gives up its commitment to a literal supernatural realm and embraces the metaphorical nature of all religious thinking) can see that the Mysterious Infinite Oneness is encountered by human beings only through our encounters with the many, finite, natural events. It is misleading to view nature is an outward experience and the Infinite Oneness an inward experience. There is no outward experience without its inward component. And there is no inward experience without its outward component. The following two phrases express the same experience: (1) a Mysterious Oneness operating in and through the always present natural manyness and (2) nature as a vast diversity of sacred beings which breathe the Awe of a Mysterious Interconnectedness.

Christians who see their monotheism in this transparent manner, and thus bring to the dialogue their actual experience of the Infinite Oneness, can join with their lucid tribal companions in rejecting the widespread and misleading versions of Christian monotheism. Christians and tribal people can be allies in affirming the sacredness of the human body and the natural world. Both heritages can learn how both have gifts for expressing that sacredness.

18.

Some Non-Concluding Remarks on Interreligious Dialogue

Each interreligious dialogue in this book provides only a taste (at most a full swallow) of the other-than-Christian tradition selected. No chapter provides what we might call the "full diet of dialogue" which might be appropriate sometime in our lives.

I view this book as only an introduction to a particular type of interreligious dialogue. *Ongoing* is the very nature of dialogue. There can be no end to the possibilities for creative dialogue among these vast religious traditions.

But why should such dialogue proceed for anyone? And why for Christians in particular? If interreligious dialogue needs to be an ongoing part of Christian nurture, what place does it have within a religious practice rooted in Christian language, myths, rites, icons, and communal forms? We only have 24 hours in each of our days. We can allot only a part of our time to religious practice. So why should Christian-identified people devote a significant amount of time to interreligious dialogue? Obviously, each of us could devote all of the time we are setting aside for religious practice to the Christian tradition alone.

1. Why is interreligious dialogue timely?

We now live in a world in which many religions exist in close proximity. We no longer live in a small village or urban neighborhood informed by a general culture that basically practices one religion (or one family of religions). In earlier times creative religious innovators, such as Augustine or Luther, could focus their attention on one religious tradition and on the shaping of that tradition to be taught in a widespread fashion throughout one cultural area. For those times, that strategy was appropriate. But we no longer live in those times.

Every urban center and most rural places contain a mix of people practicing a variety of religious traditions. When awakenment happens in any one of these heritages, it affects us all. Similarly, any awakenment within Christian heritage will impact all people, not just Christian people. However unprecedented and confusing these times may be, these are the times in which we live.

Christian religion, at its best, has always been a creative response to its times. "The God of history," we sometimes say, "is acting in a new fashion and is requiring of us a new response." Good Christian religion is never timeless; rather it is timely. Today, Christian-identified persons are confronted with the historical actuality that interreligious dialogue is timely.

Much Christian theology in the last century has been an impassioned dialogue with the scientific movements of secular enlightenment in the Christianized Western world. Paul Tillich understood his theology as such a dialogue, forging Christian answers to secular questions. Rudolf Bultmann's project of demythologizing the New Testament was likewise aimed at rehearing the New Testament message within the context of secular, scientific and existential philosophies. Christian dialogue with secular thought continues, but this well-established dialogue is now moving into a wider context. This new context is a lively dialogue among all the profound religious heritages of the human species.

Good religion of whatever variety is confronting a secular worldview that not only criticizes bad religion but also tends to dismiss all religion as an out-of-date aberration. "Religion," say some of these secular viewpoints, "characterized earlier periods of human cultures but no longer needs to characterize post-modern culture." So every resurgence of genuine religion finds itself an ally with every other such resurgence in challenging this formidable secular foe. We who treasure any religious tradition are now challenged to join in the common task of showing secular culture that relationship with the Infinite is real and unavoidable and good for us.

2. So what is good religion?

Effective religious dialogue cannot avoid noticing that every long-standing religious tradition is beset with thoroughly out-of-date forms that have become defensive perversions of the greatness of that religion. These defensive religious practitioners typically refuse to take the modern scientific age seriously. Religion that opposes the scientific worldview in a superficial manner deserves to be dismissed as superstition. Religious superstition of an almost unending variety is rampant. Religion as a whole is being discredited in the minds of secularly competent persons by the widespread practice of bad religion. People gathering for "the return of Christ" or for committing corporate suicide to join other souls on a passing comet are only the tip of an iceberg of illusions. A supermall of old and new religious superstitions offers our naive and bored populations ever new possibilities of escape from reality, escape from sanity, and escape from ordinary truthfulness.

This groundless flurry of religious froth is not being adequately criticized. Some religious leaders imply that there is no religious truth–that there are only religious opinions and that every religious opinion is as good as any other. We who know that such thoroughgoing relativism is foolishness need to clearly define "good religion." And we need to define "good religion" in a context large enough to include every good religion on earth. It is bigotry to define "good religion" as the religion authorized by my particular religious community or by my chosen group of religious teachers. "Good religion" needs to be defined as clearly as we define "good science." Without such clarity, well-meaning members of these secular times will dismiss all religion along with the superstitious froth.

Good religion is any religion that is not an escape from reality but is rather an expression of reality, especially of the reality of Awe before the Awesome Mysteriousness streaming through actual, ordinary, human existence. This common-sense definition, while profound, is difficult to apply to the many forms of religious expression. It is, nevertheless, an effective guideline for all interreligious dialogue and for the dialogue between good religion and good secular science.

This understanding of good religion has important implications for "prophetic" Christianity: *Being an expression of prophetic Christianity means forging a critique not only of bad Christian religion but also of every other form of bad religion.* This is a daunting expansion of the Christian theological task. How can we perform a critique of all religion without falling back into Christian bigotry? An unbigoted critique entails remaining clear that all religions are finite efforts to express the Infinite. Thus our criteria of judgment cannot be our own finite religious heritage. Our criticism of any religion has to be rooted in our own actual, living relationship with the Infinite Presence.

3. Is interreligious dialogue only a matter of thought, or does it also entail practice?

The dialogue we need cannot take place by merely thinking interreligiously in an arms-length fashion. We must also, to some extent, participate in religious practices other than our own. For example, we cannot fully understand the wisdom of Buddhism without actually doing some meditation. Similarly, the deepest gifts of Native American religions are inaccessible through mere book reading. So we need to participate in sweat lodges, attend pipe ceremonies, or at least go to an Indian dance (pow wow) and watch with an open heart. The paintings of primitive tribal peoples or the sculpture of medieval Hinduism can at least be viewed in published books, and perhaps in person. These are some of the ways in which a full dialogue can proceed.

Religion is not merely ideas; it is symbolic practices. Opening ourselves to full interreligious dialogue will entail risking ourselves in unfamiliar symbolic practices no matter how fearful we may be. We must have the courage to venture into religions not our own, keeping our critical mind alive and yet having the courage to say both yeses and noes to what we experience.

4. Will participating in interreligious dialogue mean that Christians will tend to lose their Christian identification?

"No!" is my one word answer. Quite the contrary, losing our Christian identification will most likely happen if we wall ourselves off into obsolete Christian expressions. Sooner or later we will discover the futility of attempting to preserve Christianity in this fashion. Then we will probably abandon Christianity entirely.

It is a huge challenge, of course, to reconstruct our Christian identity within the context of worldwide interreligious dialogue. Some

Christian-identified persons do not offer Christian heritage the sympathetic hearing they offer other religious heritages. My intention in this book has been to show the possibility of being open to other religions and, at the same time, recovering some fresh understanding of what is essential in Christian awareness and practice.

Further, if we Christians truly want to maintain our Christian identification, we must not only *understand* our heritage better; we must also *practice* a resurgent form of Christianity. We must practice it daily, weekly, and yearly. We must practice in solitary disciplines and in communal meetings. This means reforming and/or replacing the typical practices now taking place in the existing Christian congregations. These typical practices are out of sync with the times in which we live and with the living Truth of the biblical witness. So great is the discontinuity of the new Christian forms required that we may feel we are starting an entirely new religion, but this is not the case. Christian heritage is like a vast but locked treasure chest that can be opened and adapted to nurture our lives today.

Those of us who have been scarred or traumatized by obsolete Christian forms may dread risking ourselves in the practice of new Christian forms that, of course, are also capable of perversion. Nevertheless, the call of the Awe to awakening Christian-identified persons is just this: to take on the messy, dreadful, and unclear task of religious reconstruction. For those of us embedded in Christian memory, constructing a new Christianity may be the core of our proper service to the future of religion on this planet. Rebuilding Christianity may be the cross we need to bear, the trauma we are called to endure, the tomb through which we have to pass to heal our lives and many others. Unless some of us who love the Christian heritage take this journey on behalf of this planet, the deep gifts of the Christian heritage may not be contributed to the life of the coming centuries.

The community of Awed humans, who embrace the Awe and revere the Awesome, will not pass away. These dynamics are built into the structure of Reality. No "hell" is strong enough to prevail against these Eternal dynamics. But Christianity, as a religion, is a finite and fragile thing. Like any other religion, it can pass away and with its passing might go considerable human awareness of the non-passing, "cosmic" dynamics of Awe. But we do not need to suffer the loss of a relevant Christian religion. The future of Christianity depends upon those of us who can enter into this era of vibrant interreligious dialogue and still remain, in a very meaningful sense, Christian. In the past, Christianity, in spite of its soured forms, "saved" many of us, but now it is up to us who have been so "saved" to save Christianity as a viable community of nurture for the future.

Afterword:
The Never-Ending Dialogue

Dialogue is a fundamental dynamic in human life. Language itself is dialogue. Human personality might be described as a nest of dialogues. While most of our dialogues are with finite realities about our finite concerns, increasingly many of us find ourselves in dialogue with the Infinite. And as this Infinite dialogue gains prominence in our lives, we become aware of the extent to which humanity in all places and times has been in dialogue with the Infinite. Most of these dialogues use religious language very different from our own, so we are challenged, when we dialogue with these alien groups, to dialogue with the Infinite in some fresh ways.

To inspire you to dialogue with the Infinite in some fresh ways has been my purpose in writing this book. I want to underline that none of these dialogues with any of these religions are over for me, or for you. Dialogues among the religious communities of humankind are never-ending. The human dialogue with the Infinite is also never-ending.

Some of the stars we see in the heavens have long since burned out, but the light produced when these stars were alive is still reaching us. So it is with our dialogue with the Infinite. The dialogue lives on after our time-bound living burns out. When I reflect on the person of Abraham in the Old Testament, I realize that the factual details we have of his life are meager. Most of what we have left of Abraham is stories of his dialogues with the Infinite. Nevertheless, these mostly fictitious stories transmit to us what is valuable to us about Abraham: his exemplary dialogues with the Infinite. So it is of Isaac and Jacob, Sarah, Rachel, and

Rebecca. So it is of Buddha and Lao Tzu. So it is of Jesus. The extent to which Jesus in the New Testament is a poem rather than a historical figure has shocked many contemporary Christians. That poem, however, is about Jesus as an exemplary dialogue with the Infinite. This dialogue was the deep aliveness of Jesus, and this dialogue has indeed lived on.

So if this book has drawn you into participating in the some fresh dialogues with the Infinite, you have joined the never-ending dialogue with the Never-Ending. All our endings and all our beginnings take on a new aliveness when we see them as ingredients in this never-ending dialogue.

Dialogue is also a wonder-filled reality because it is so unpredictable. We are free to respond in a multitude of ways. And the response to us by the Infinite is likewise sure to take us by surprise. Therefore, let us cultivate our capacity for surprise. Let us become a surprise ourselves. Let us rise each morning and prepare to surprise the planet with our responses and prepare to be surprised by the responses that the Infinite Actor makes to our surprising lives.

Postscript:
My Life as a Writer

It occurs to me that those reading my writing for the first time might be interested in a survey of the years of reflection that have led to this book. Since 1983 I have been writing on these four interlocking topics: (1) Christian Resurgence, (2) Interreligious Dialogue, (3) Social Transformation, and (4) Science and Religion.

The first book I ever wrote was on interreligious dialogue and to some extent science and religion. It was called *The Future of Religion*. It wasn't a very good book. It is now out of print. Everything in it I have now written about better. I don't recommend that anyone read it. But in 1983 it was the beginning of a serious writing career, and its topics are still interesting to me.

In 1985 I published a second book entitled *A Primer on Radical Christianity*. This book focused on Christian Resurgence and was my first attempt to put down in one volume what I felt were the basics of Christian theology, community, and ethics. Though I have written further and perhaps more clearly on every topic in this book, this *Primer* still seems to me a basic text.

In 1987 I published *The Reign of Reality: A Fresh Start for the Earth*. My wife Joyce co-authored this book with me; she wrote the chapter on "Post-Patriarchal Women and Men" and assisted mightily with the rest of the book as she has with all my books. The first 34 pages are on Christian theology, but the rest of this book is a pull together of our best thinking at that time on vision and strategy for social transformation. The theological part was about translating the biblical phrase, The

Kingdom of God. "The Reign of Reality" is a secular rendering of that phrase. The book is about how the New Testament teachings on this topic provide a context for embracing the challenge to embark on thoroughgoing social transformation in our world today.

In 1994 I published *To Be or Not to Be a Christian: Meditations and Essays on Authentic Christian Community*. This book is a collection of essays, sermons, and other short pieces I had been writing for seven years or more. The book came together around questions I found many people asking: why be a Christian at all? Why is this heritage important and what might it mean to have an effective religious practice of a resurgent form of Christianity? The metaphorical translation of Christian heritage was thoroughly explored in this book.

In 1996 I decided to stop self-publishing large quantities of perfect-bound volumes and to publish instead a series of short-run study books of 34 to 65 pages in length. The first of these was on interreligious dialogue and social transformation with very little direct mention of Christianity. I gave it a long humorous title *The Birth & Rebirth & Rebirth & Rebirth…of Spirit: some reflections upon the origins and survival possibilities of the last remaining upright-walking primates.*

This book was followed the same year by a book on the philosophy of religion entitled Great *Thinks, Great Feels, and Great Resolves: some reflections on the essence of religious experience.* This book established Awe and the dynamics of Awe as a permanent theme in all my writing.

Later in 1996 I returned to the theme of Christian Resurgence, putting into a brief 65 pages a rethinking of this entire topic. I titled this book *Good Christian Religion as a Social Project: how to view the Jesus Christ happening as the central illumination of my life without becoming a bigot.* While this book does not now contain my latest thinking on some topics, it remains an accessible introduction to Christian resurgence and one of the best short study books in this collection.

In 1997 and 1998 I published three 55 to 65-page study books on the Bible. I had become convinced that no lasting Christian Resurgence was possible without a recovery of the Bible. I had also become convinced that people were ready to hear the poetry of the Bible provided that it was well translated into contemporary metaphors. So these three books were written and published to encourage this recovery:

The Infinite Silence Speaks: poetic discourses on the book of Genesis

Speaking Back to the Infinite Silence: rediscovering the Psalms as oral poetry

The Infinite Silence Walks Among Us: dialogues with the Gospel of John

In 1999 I published another book on Christian Resurgence, *Fresh Wineskins for the Christian Breakthrough: fragments of visionary brooding on the sociological future of Christianity.* This book set the context for launching a research group that we have called "The Symposium on Christian Resurgence for Century Twenty One." The book focuses on basic overviews and practical themes needed for organizing what we came to call "Christian Resurgence Circles." The last chapter of this book was another attempt to pull together a vision of planet-wide social transformation and how these circles of Christian resurgence might contribute to that wider transformation.

In 2000 I published a 37-page study book on the life passage from adolescence to adulthood. I called it *Pets, Children, and Spirit Maturity: reflections on the inner journey.* It was written with adolescents and parents of adolescents in mind, but it is actually a short philosophical treatise on the journey of consciousness from mammalian beginnings into human childhood and then into maturity as a Spirit-filled adult.

Later that year I published another study book on the Bible in which I used a rather imaginative approach to helping people overcome the widespread misunderstandings that surrounds the first Christian theologian, Paul. I imagined Paul coming back to life today and talking with us in modern terms. I called this book *The Reincarnation of Paul: a fictitious dialogue with the New Testament letter writer.*

I also finished in 2000 a book on science and religion, a book dealing with the secular context of our times and how religion is a necessary and vital part of human life. This book is entitled *Stages of Consciousness and the Experience of Spirit: clarifying discourses for the Spirit explorer of the 21st century.* This book might also be described as a philosophy of religion. At the present time it has only been published as e-matter. It can be downloaded from:
http://www.RealisticLiving.org/PDF/stages/

In 2001 I electronically published another book on Christian Resurgence: *Christianity in Change: an invitation to deeper dialogue.* This book explores in greater depth some of the more thorny topics that plague the contemporary churches and prevent Christians and non-Christians alike from giving resurgent Christianity a full hearing. This book can be downloaded from:
http://www.RealisticLiving.org/PDF/change/

I also published electronically in 2001 another book on the Bible: *Meditations upon the Metaphorical Translation of the Gospel of Mark.* This is a commentary on each passage of the Gospel of Mark with discussion questions for group or individual use. The book was written with small groups in mind. For recovering the New Testament, this may be the most helpful and accessible book of this collection. It can be downloaded from:
http://www.RealisticLiving.org/PDF/Mark/

In 2001 I also put up on the web a collection of poems *Teaching Poems: a collection of poems for the communication of Spirit.* These poems, written over many years and sometimes published in other volumes, have been pulled together to use for both teaching and personal inspiration. It can be downloaded from:
http://www.RealisticLiving.org/PDF/TeachingPoems.pdf

Also in 2001, I finished a short four-chapter book on Science and Religion *Space/Time and the Living Here/Now: a philosophical inquiry into scientific knowledge and personal experience.* This may be my most thorough and illuminating presentation on this topic. I have tried to make edge scientific and philosophical issues understandable to the general reader. This book is also published on the web: http://www.RealisticLiving.org/PDF/SpaceTime/

In 2002, I and the Symposium on Christian Resurgence completed a construct for teaching social transformation in a one-day course we entitled *Earth, Democracy, and You*. The course is subtitled *Creative Responses for the Twenty First Century*. This course outline contains a set of scripts that reflect much of my latest thinking on social transformation. This course outline can be downloaded from: http://www.RealisticLiving.org/PDF/DEY/

Finally as a follow up to this book I am writing a book entitled *When Awed Ones Gather: An Inquiry into Redemptive Christian Community*, which will provide historical and contemporary context for organizing Christian Resurgence Circles. For information on its publication you can contact me by e-mail at: books@RealisticLiving.org

In some ways I lean toward being a systematic thinker; but as I look back over what I have actually written, it seems to me that I have not been doing systematic thought but rather some open-ended dialogue into an ever-changing field of awareness. All these writings, including *The Call of the Awe*, are time-specific expressions along an ever-changing path. Tomorrow, if the time of my life permits, I may deal with many of these topics more clearly than I have done in this book. Nevertheless, I offer up this collection of fragmentary communication as a witness that there is no final formulation of Christian theology or of any other religious lineage. We are always on the move in never-ending dialogue with an ever-surprising Infinite Dialogue Partner.

0-595-26353-4